My Brother Slaves

MY
BROTHER
SLAVES

Friendship, Masculinity, and Resistance in the Antebellum South

Sergio A. Lussana

UNIVERSITY PRESS OF KENTUCKY

Scholarly publisher for the Commonwealth,
serving Bellarmine University, Berea College, Centre College of Kentucky,
Eastern Kentucky University, The Filson Historical Society, Georgetown
College, Kentucky Historical Society, Kentucky State University, Morehead
State University, Murray State University, Northern Kentucky University,
Transylvania University, University of Kentucky, University of Louisville, and
Western Kentucky University.
All rights reserved.

Editorial and Sales Offices: The University Press of Kentucky
663 South Limestone Street, Lexington, Kentucky 40508-4008
www.kentuckypress.com

Library of Congress Cataloging-in-Publication Data

Names: Lussana, Sergio, author.
Title: My brother slaves : friendship, masculinity, and resistance in the
    antebellum south / Sergio A. Lussana.
Description: Lexington, Kentucky : University Press of Kentucky, 2016. |
    Series: New directions in Southern history | Includes bibliographical
    references and index.
Identifiers: LCCN 2015048920| ISBN 9780813166940 (hardcover : alk. paper) |
    ISBN 9780813166964 (pdf) | ISBN 9780813166957 (epub)
Subjects: LCSH: Slaves—Southern States—Social conditions—19th century. |
    Male friendship—Southern States—History—19th century. |
    Masculinity—Southern States—History—19th century. | Southern
    States—Social conditions—19th century. | Slavery—Southern States.
Classification: LCC E185.18 .L87 2016 | DDC 306.3/62097509034—dc23
LC record available at http://lccn.loc.gov/2015048920

Member of the Association of
American University Presses

For my grandmother,
Yvonne Frances Runtz.

Contents

Introduction

"For much of the happiness, or absence of misery, with which I passed this year, I am indebted to the genial temper and ardent friendship of my brother slaves. They were every one of them manly, generous, and brave; yes, I say they were brave, and I will add fine looking. It is seldom the lot of any to have truer and better friends than were the slaves on this farm. It was not uncommon to charge slaves with great treachery toward each other, but I must say I never loved, esteemed, or confided in men more than I did in these. They were as true as steel, and no band of brothers could be more loving. There were no mean advantages taken of each other, no tattling, no giving each other bad names to Mr. Freeland, and no elevating one at the expense of the other. We never undertook anything of any importance which was likely to affect each other, without mutual consultation. We were generally a unit, and moved together."[1] With these words, Frederick Douglass, one of the most celebrated black men in American history, described the men he had lived and worked with while enslaved in Maryland in 1835. Trapped in a world of brutal physical punishment, unremitting back-breaking labor, and forced separation from loved ones, Douglass testified that the friendship he shared with other enslaved men carried him through his dark days of enslavement. These men were central to Douglass; their friendship eased the pain of slavery. It was to this circle of men that he turned for emotional comfort. He affirmed the masculinity of his friends and pronounced that their lives were interdependent. They were a "unit" and "moved together." They were a "band of brothers."

Douglass's musings are insightful because they shed light on an intimate area of enslaved life: enslaved men and their relationships with other men. Yet, in contrast to studies of enslaved women and gender, works on enslaved men and issues of masculinity have proved less forthcoming because historians have generally failed to employ the techniques of gender history to analyze the lives of enslaved men. Only recently have scholarly articles begun to examine how enslaved men negotiated masculine identities under slavery.[2] The lack of focus on enslaved men and masculinity contrasts markedly with the plethora of monographs recently published on white masculinity in the antebellum South. By exploring the lives of men and using masculinity as a category of analysis, these works have considerably deepened our knowledge of the unique social and cultural worlds of the antebellum American South.[3] However, our knowledge of African American men and issues of masculinity in the antebellum South remains considerably underdeveloped. Fundamental questions persist: How did enslaved men construct masculine identities while living under an emasculating institution? How did they relate to one another? Who were their friends? How significant were these relationships in their lives? These are just some of the questions addressed in *My Brother Slaves: Friendship, Masculinity, and Resistance in the Antebellum South.*

Provider/Protector Masculinity

When the issue of slave masculinity has been discussed in studies of American slavery, it has usually been considered as part of a wider discussion of the slave family. In 1939, sociologist E. Franklin Frazier argued that the slave family was "matrifocal." Enslaved fathers and husbands were deprived of their masculine authority as a result of the sexual exploitation of enslaved women, the sale and separation of families, the illegality of marriage for slaves, and the overarching power of the master. Furthermore, because in the American South the legal status of children followed that of their mothers, men's authority was further undermined.[4] Frazier's thesis was supported in the 1950s by historians Kenneth Stampp and Stanley Elkins, who both contended that, unable to provide and protect their families, enslaved men were emasculated. Stampp emphasized the victimization of enslaved people, arguing that the enslaved were condemned to live "in a kind of cultural chaos." For enslaved men, he argued, the family did not have the same social importance that it had in the life of a white man. The husband "was not the head of the family, the holder of property, the provider, or the protector." In a patriarchal age, the enslaved male's only vital function was producing children; accordingly, the slave family was matriarchal.[5] Elkins, too, asserted that the slave father was "virtually without authority over his child, since discipline, parental responsibility, and control of rewards and punishments all rested in other hands." He continued:

The slave father could not even protect the mother of his children except by appealing directly to the master. Indeed, the mother's role loomed far larger for the slave child than did that of the father. She controlled those few activities—household care, preparation of food, and rearing of children—that were left to the slave family. For that matter, the very etiquette of plantation life removed even the honorific attributes of fatherhood from the Negro male, who was addressed as "boy"—until, when the vigorous years of his prime were past, he was allowed to assume the title of "uncle."[6]

The publication, in 1965, of Daniel Moynihan's government-funded report, *The Negro Family: The Case for National Action,* developed the findings of Frazier, Stampp, and Elkins. In his report, Moynihan traced the origins of African American family breakdown back to slavery. The contemporary African American family, he argued, was trapped in a "tangle of pathology" because it had been "forced into a matriarchal structure," which imposed a "crushing burden on the Negro male." African American men felt insufficient performing the roles of husband and father and deserted families accordingly. In Moynihan's view, the emasculating slave-rooted matriarchal family arrangement continued to persist after slavery.[7]

    In response to the Moynihan report and the likes of Stampp and Elkins, historians of the 1970s vehemently attacked the matriarchy thesis. Shaped by the civil rights movement and the "new social history," which set out to write history "from the bottom up," historians writing during this period, such as Herbert Gutman, Eugene Genovese, and John Blassingame, maintained that slavery did not necessarily destroy the family life of enslaved people. Indeed, the slave family, they claimed, served as an important buffer protecting enslaved people from the worst abuses of the slave system. Most slave children, argued Herbert Gutman, lived with two parents, and most adults enjoyed long-lasting marriages.[8] Gutman reassessed the role of the male in the slave family and identified patrilineal slave-naming practices, which, in his view, indicated the importance of the father and strengthened family ties.[9] Genovese concurred with Gutman that the enslaved, despite considerable constraints, valued a "two-parent, male-centered household." He opened his chapter entitled "The Myth of the Absent Family" by attacking the "conventional wisdom according to which slavery had emasculated black men, created a matriarchy, and prevented the emergence of a strong sense of family." Many enslaved men, argued Genovese, despite the emasculating effects of slavery, acted as providers and protectors.[10] Similarly for Blassingame, although his authority was curtailed, the enslaved father and husband still played pivotal roles in family life, providing extra food, building furnishings, and bringing up children.[11]

Nonetheless, by the early 1980s, some historians voiced concerns that these revisionist historians, by emphasizing the vitality of a slave community and the strength of the slave family, were in danger of creating a "utopian slave community."[12] Deborah Gray White maintained that slave families were matrifocal. Enslaved women, she argued, could not depend on their husbands' protection against punishments, such as whipping or sexual exploitation. Additionally, enslaved men were generally unable to provide women with food, clothing, and shelter and were thus denied "this exercise of authority."[13] A decade later, sociologist Orlando Patterson published a scathing critique of the revisionist historians, claiming that slavery was "most virulent in its devastation of the roles of father and husband."[14] Echoing Moynihan, he argued that the contemporary African American community was facing a crisis in gender relations, with 60 percent of African American children raised without the material or emotional support of a father. Patterson traced these problems back to slavery and posed the following questions:

> Could he monopolize his partner's sexual services and guarantee that her progeny were in fact his own? Could he protect her from the sexual predation of other men? Could he at least partly provide for her materially? Could he prevent her from being brutalized and physically punished by other men? Could he prevent her from being torn from the place where she was brought up, bundled like cargo, and sold away from him, her children, her kinsmen, and her friends? If the answer to any of these questions is "No," the role of the husband did not exist. If the slave could do none of these things, then the role of the husband had been devastated.[15]

More recently, Wilma Dunaway criticized the likes of Gutman and Genovese, whose generalizations about the stability of the slave family, she claimed, "sound more like a Disney script than scholarly research."[16] Dunaway's research contended that the majority of slave holdings in the Appalachian region were small plantations (Gutman's and Genovese's studies had focused on large plantations of the Deep South). In Dunaway's view, slave families on small plantations were more prone to slave sales, received more manipulation from the owner, and were more likely to be headed by one parent. Other regional studies, similarly, have emphasized that slave families were devastated and, therefore, the familial role and masculine authority of enslaved men were severely undermined.[17]

Recently, however, Emily West has refuted the counter-revisionist argument that slave families and the masculine role of enslaved men were significantly weakened. Even when enslaved couples were separated, many maintained cross-plantation marriages, which, in West's opinion, were "far from weak and nominal relationships." In South Carolina, the region of West's study, cross-plantation marriages accounted for 33.5 percent of all slave marriages, alongside nuclear marriages, calculated at 46.2 percent.[18] In cross-plantation marriages, "it was men, not women, who saw it as their duty to undertake visits, and this role-adoption suggests wider conclusions—that male slaves, despite living under oppression, saw themselves as initiators, protectors, and providers."[19] Similarly, Rebecca Fraser has contended that pursing courtships off the plantation enabled enslaved men to "enhance their own sense of masculine identity and resist the negative gender characteristics that had been imposed upon them in the context of slavery."[20] The enslaved men of Fraser's study performed extra labor in return for cash, worked garden patches, and hunted to provide resources for their families. Her work also demonstrated that while women could not rely on their male partners for protection against punishment, there were occasions when enslaved men took whippings for their wives or girlfriends and for women they wished to court, with whom they had no established familial or affectionate ties. These men, accordingly, enhanced their own sense of masculine identity, adopting the role of "protector" while also defending the femininity of enslaved women—something these women would have been further stripped of had they received whippings.[21]

The Homosocial World of Enslaved Men

In these historiographical debates, when historians have discussed notions of enslaved masculinity, they have almost always framed their analyses within the context of courtship, marriage, and family life. Masculinity, in these works, is equated with the ability to provide and protect—establishing familial authority and responsibility. For men in antebellum America, these were certainly hallmarks of masculinity.[22] Indeed, anthropologists, sociologists, and historians agree that in most societies, establishing and heading a family is the vital purpose of masculinity.[23] However, as scholar Michael Kimmel has noted, "in large part, it's other men who are important to American men; American men define their masculinity, not as much in relation to women, but in relation to each other." Indeed, he stated that "masculinity is largely a homosocial enactment." It is performed for and judged by other men.[24] David D. Gilmore, in his cross-cultural anthropological study of masculinity, contended that for most males, manhood is a "critical threshold" that must be passed through "testing." Gilmore found that as well as protecting and providing for their families, various exploits—such as boyhood rituals, feats of risk-taking, and heavy drinking—were key ways men crafted masculine identities in all-male environments. In this way, masculinity is a test—something that has to be proved in the company of one's peers.[25] Anthropologist and feminist scholar Michelle Rosaldo similarly argued that for a boy to become a man, "he must prove himself—his masculinity—among his peers."[26]

This was particularly the case in the antebellum South, where masculinity was a social designation that required testing and confirmation in public in the presence of other men. Among elite southern whites, for example, a boy became a man when he proved to his community that he was one.[27] Bertram Wyatt-Brown's groundbreaking work on southern honor demonstrated that a white man's identity in the Old South was decided among "the *deme* or larger 'family' of peers and superiors called community." Southern men were governed by a code of honor, a set of ethical rules by which "judgements of behavior are ratified by community consensus."[28] A southern man was not regarded as manly unless he was honorable, but this required demonstrating, and the judgment could only be bestowed upon him by his fellow peers. Men demonstrated and validated their masculinity through family and work but also through recreational pursuits. Southern men prized activities such as drinking, gambling, hunting, and fighting. They enjoyed these exploits in homosocial spaces. Here, they displayed physical prowess, daring, and a capacity to drink. They competed for recognition, honor, and respect and affirmed social ties accordingly; they dramatized their masculinity in the presence of other men and, in the process, created an all-male subculture.[29]

Enslaved men, too, created an all-male subculture in the antebellum South. *My Brother Slaves:* reveals that, similar to southern whites, enslaved men engaged in homosocial recreational pursuits such as drinking, gambling, wrestling, and hunting. These activities were extremely important for enslaved men, yet historians have failed to analyze their gendered implications. In slave communities, men claimed these activities as masculine preserves. It was here, in an all-male world, they constructed markers of status, identity, and masculinity and forged lasting friendships. It was here, together, that they fought the humiliating, degrading, and emasculating features of their enslavement. In this homosocial world, they became men.

The arguments presented here owe much to the immense advances made in the past three decades by historians researching gender and the lives of enslaved women.[30] Deborah G. White pioneered this approach in slave studies, placing the lifecycle, family, labor, and social life of enslaved women at the center of analysis. The impact of White's work is still being felt today, with many historians using gender as a category of analysis to examine the lives of enslaved women to great effect and, in the process, emphasizing the many important nuances of slave life. These studies continue to teach historians of slavery that gender was central to defining the experiences of enslaved men and women and that gender rarely operated independently of race and class. Rather, it was constitutive of the class and racial hierarchies that shaped the system of slavery in the American South and thus served as "a primary way of signifying relationships of power."[31]

One of the key tenets of Deborah G. White's thesis was that enslaved women functioned in groups; cooperation and interdependence characterized adult female life. For much of the day, enslaved women were in each other's company: on large plantations they worked in sex-segregated gangs together, socialized together, supported one another during childbirth, shared childcare responsibilities, and passed skills down from one generation to the next. White termed this interdependence the "female slave network." She claimed it was perhaps easier for enslaved women to maintain significant emotional relationships with other enslaved women than with enslaved men. Male-female relationships were not unfulfilling, or of no consequence, but they faced considerable uncertainty as a result of cross-plantation marriages, and the daily threat of sale—both of which added to the independence of women from their spouses. When men were not readily present to rely on, women turned to one another for daily emotional and practical support. The female network was always there, between a husband's weekly visits from another plantation and when a husband or son was sold off or ran away. As a result, female solidarity increased and women forged strong friendships. The female slave network was integral to enslaved women's understanding of femininity: through each other, White claimed, enslaved women could "forge their own independent definition of womanhood." The company of other women "sustained" female slaves during their enslavement. "Few women . . . survived without friends, without female company."[32]

White's insights can certainly help shed light on the homosocial world of enslaved men. Indeed, as White reflected, if enslaved women cooperated with one another and functioned in groups, "odds are that the same can be said of men."[33] The current volume develops White's framework to explore the homosocial world and friendships of enslaved men. The experiences of enslaved men and women were in many ways distinct from each other. Like those of the female slaves of White's study, the lives of enslaved men were interconnected. Across the antebellum South, male group cooperation and interdependence characterized everyday life for many enslaved men. This book's central objective is the examination of a male homosocial network. On large plantations, men labored together in sex-segregated work gangs; those employed in industry lived and worked in a distinct homosocial world cut off from regular plantation life. The book explores how enslaved men, in such environments, fashioned their own unique masculine work culture. It pays attention, too, to the social spaces occupied by enslaved men. Many men drank, gambled, and wrestled in all-male settings. At night, during the week, and at weekends, they teamed up to evade the white patrol gangs who policed their plantations' boundaries in order to visit loved ones on different plantations. The book underscores the centrality and importance of such activities in the lives of many enslaved men. Through these pursuits, they negotiated distinct masculine identities; they performed, witnessed, and assessed masculine behavior and affirmed social ties. In these spaces, they formed lifelong, meaningful friendships. Borrowing White's terminology, enslaved men created their own male slave network.

Resistance is a second theme of this book; resistance to slavery was not always direct and overt, and it manifested itself in nuanced ways. Historians have paid a great deal attention to slave revolts, quite rare in the American South, which were mostly organized by men. In 1829, free black abolitionist David Walker, in his *Appeal to the Colored Citizens of the World,* urged enslaved men to rise up and rebel against their white oppressors. The masculine implications of his message were explicit: "You have to prove to the Americans and the world, that we are MEN, and not brutes." "When

shall we arise from this death-like apathy?—And be men!!"[34] He equated
manhood with heroic rebellion and freedom. A number of African American writers of the nineteenth century, as well as subsequent scholars, have
equated slave rebellion with masculinity. In this way, only those who defi-
antly and violently challenged their enslavement proved their masculinity.
This approach, however, is unhelpful, for it implies that those men who
did not violently rebel somehow lacked masculinity.[35] *My Brother Slaves*
reconceptualizes male resistance to slavery by shifting attention from the
visible, organized, collective world of slave rebellion to the intimate, hidden, and private world of enslaved men.[36] It was in their everyday spaces
that enslaved men developed their male subculture and negotiated their
masculinity. Denied the opportunity of open, organized political and public expression, they turned to everyday forms of resistance, "hidden transcripts," in order to contest the public transcript of power relations.[37] Every
day, men fought over their personal lives and gendered identity, often in
defiance of the spatial and temporal regulations that governed their lives.
Covertly, against their masters' will, they left the plantations at night to
meet up with one another to share a drink, gamble, and organize wrestling
matches. Enslaved men risked their lives, too, evading and sometimes fighting the patrol gangs when they left the plantation without permission and
traversed into these forbidden spaces. Men also regularly used their contacts with other men to spread subversive news, gossip, and rumors from
plantation to plantation. Moreover, they used their links with one another
to harbor and assist runaways. The book probes the intimate friendships
established by enslaved men. Friendship framed, shaped, and gave meaning
to the homosocial relationships of enslaved men. Moreover, it served as a
vital coping mechanism to endure the brutalizing characteristics of slavery;
few men could survive slavery without friends.

The third focus of this study is a response to recent calls from historians to link the everyday world of enslaved people to the overt, collective,
rebellious struggles waged by the likes of Gabriel Prosser, Denmark Vesey,
and Nat Turner. As Walter Johnson has declared in studies of slavery, the
terms "everyday" and "revolutionary" have "been allowed for too long to
stand in unproductive opposition to one another rather than being thought
of as dialectically inter-related." He posed a series of questions for historians: "How, we might ask, did enslaved people set about forming social solidarities and political movements at the scale of everyday life? How did they
talk to one another about slavery, resistance, and revolution? How did they

sort through which of their fellows they could trust and which they could not?"[38] *My Brother Slaves* addresses Johnson's questions. Through friendship, enslaved men met, grumbled to one another, plotted rebellion, and ran away. In the private, everyday world of friendship, enslaved men formulated their politics. These friendships grew out of the solidarities affirmed among men on a day-to-day basis. The routine mobility of these enslaved men and the cross-plantation contacts they maintained with one another through the course of their social activities facilitated the collective coordination of resistance across plantations. The book dissolves dichotomies, such as personal/political and everyday resistance/organized rebellion, and argues that we cannot fully explore the complexity of slavery in an either/or framework.[39]

One area of enslaved life that this book does not cover is homosexuality. Formerly enslaved people did not discuss the subject in their recollections of slavery; indeed, one of the problems confronting historians studying homosexuality in western society is that until fairly recently, most homosexual people in history did not speak openly about their sexuality because in doing so they risked social ruin. Often, the law, religion, and medicine stigmatized homosexuality; accordingly, people concealed their sexual identities, leaving few sources behind for historians.[40] We can only speculate that such relationships existed among enslaved men, as they have done in all human societies. Certainly, some of the friendships shared among enslaved men were intense; however, without evidence, it is simply impossible to shed light on the lives of gay male slaves.

Sources

This project utilizes a variety of different source materials to examine the world of enslaved men—in particular, the testimony of enslaved people. Between 1936 and 1938, the Federal Writers Project of the Works Progress Administration (WPA) collected thousands of interviews from former slaves across seventeen states. These were first made available in 1972, as publication of George Rawick's eventual forty-one-volume work *The American Slave* began. There has been considerable debate concerning the use of the WPA narratives in studies of slavery. Some scholars have drawn attention to the power relations between white southern interviewers and former slaves, which allegedly influenced the latter's responses. John Blassingame has stressed that African American vulnerability to white oppression was "painfully evident" in the Depression South, where more than seventy lynchings occurred between 1931 and 1935. Additionally, it was not uncommon for formerly enslaved people to remain resident in the same areas as their masters' descendants. These former slaves were dependent on whites in order to claim their pensions, and, consequently, they sometimes responded to questions with flattery and embellishment to gain the approval of their interviewers. In such a climate, interviewers adopted racist and paternalistic lines of questioning, transcribing the records of their meetings accordingly. Some interviewers also heavily edited their narratives, altering, or censoring their accounts. Blassingame argues that the former slaves who talked to black interviewers in the Fisk University interviews, conducted a few years earlier, revealed a different picture of slavery than those interviewed by the all-white team of the South Carolina WPA project.[41] Age is another factor to consider. Ex-slaves were interviewed seventy or eighty years after their experiences of slavery; two-thirds of the respondents were more than eighty years old. Some scholars, therefore, have questioned the accuracy of such recollections, claiming that the interviewees' long-term memories were suspect.[42] Moreover, because the interviews were conducted in the 1930s, many of the informants only experienced enslavement as children or adolescents.

Nevertheless, evidence from the narratives clearly shows that former slaves were willing to discuss stories that were hardly flattering to white interviewers. As Edward E. Baptist has noted, "some ex-slaves were directly confrontational." Indeed, as many of these elderly former slaves neared the ends of their lives, there was little left to lose, and, for some, those years "became the peak of moral courage." According to Baptist, the interviewer's race did not necessarily change the responses from former slaves—the narratives of Virginia, where most interviewers were black, resembled those from Texas, where most were white.[43] If former slaves were reluctant to discuss certain things, these were sensitive subjects such as sexual abuse and other personal matters, particularly when women were interviewed by men.[44] Furthermore, evidence shows that certain lines of questioning were not necessarily affected by the race of the interviewer.[45] Regarding editing, it is worth mentioning that in 1977 and 1979, Rawick, with Jan Hillegas and Ken Lawrence, published twenty-two narratives in two supplementary series to *The American Slave*.[46] These had been collected as part of the WPA project but were not sent to Washington, DC, and instead remained in various state archives and depositories. In these archives, Rawick and his team of researchers also found unedited versions of narratives that had been sent to the Writers' Project. Rawick explained their withholding, claiming that, for example, the Mississippi collection, was most likely "too hot to handle." Indeed, according to some historians, the Mississippi interviews sent to Washington offer a more "consensual" portrayal of slavery than those that remained in the Mississippi archives.[47] Many of the sources used in this book draw on Rawick's supplementary series. Finally, on the subject of age, historian Paul Escott has emphasized that recent studies "have shown that aging does not impair the recollection of the elderly, despite society's common assumption that it does." In fact, argues Escott, intellect actually improves with age. People are more likely to recall events at critical junctures in their lives, such as wedding days, graduation, and birth and deaths in modern America; for former slaves, then, events such as their day of emancipation or the sale of a relative would almost certainly remain vivid in their minds.[48] Moreover, although many narratives are childhood memories and concern stories that had been told and retold by family and friends, it is important to remember the strong oral tradition that existed among African American communities in the aftermath of emancipation. Forbidden to learn to read or write, members of these communities placed much more importance on the spoken word and the ability to recount a story with purpose and depth.[49]

For historians, the WPA narratives are an immensely rich source. Indeed, they have revolutionized slavery studies. Before the publication of the narratives, studies relied mostly on travel accounts from northerners and European whites and on slaveholder plantation records. Accordingly, historians, relying on these white sources, cast enslaved people in submissive and passive roles—perhaps best embodied by the humble and docile "Sambo" stereotype.[50] In contrast, historians in the 1970s, using these narratives for the first time, were able to view slaves as active subjects in their own right. The WPA narratives provide historians with firsthand accounts from exslaves on a range of personal subjects, including courtship, family, religion, culture, punishment, and resistance. They allow historians to enter the private world of enslaved people. They give enslaved people agency. This book, therefore, makes extensive use of these invaluable sources.

My Brother Slaves also uses autobiographies penned by formerly enslaved people who chronicled their experiences of slavery. Between 1760 and 1947, more than two hundred American slave autobiographies were published. These can generally be divided into three kinds. Those published from the 1770s to the 1820s are usually narrated as spiritual journeys by authors who considered themselves Africans, not slaves. From the 1820s through to the Civil War period, the slave narrative evolved into a distinct autobiographical genre highlighting the horrors of slavery to further the abolitionist cause. These narratives usually describe slave auctions, slave sales, the separation of family members, brutal punishments, and eventual escape to the North; they were characteristically sensationalist, and many were promoted, edited, and distributed by abolitionists. After the Civil War, the narratives changed tone. Losing their urgency, they became less devoted to depicting the horrors of slavery, with many becoming nostalgic and written as a sentimental reaffirmation of plantation life. These usually end with the author's adjustment to freedom.[51]

The slave autobiographies are not without their problems. Many of the antebellum ones were narrated by literate mulattos and house slaves, and the vast majority of these fugitive slaves were enslaved near the Mason-Dixon Line, as opposed to the Deep South. This inevitably raises the issue of how representative these accounts were of typical rank-and-file slaves. These slaves, who had managed to escape slavery, comprised a tiny minority of the slave population; they were extraordinary people who were usually skilled, resourceful, and possessed a significant degree of knowledge.[52] Exaggeration is another problem in autobiographies—to portray themselves more heroically, people are prone to exaggerate the difficulties they faced.[53] Moreover, critics have argued that accounts published in the antebellum period were edited by abolitionists who did not hesitate to exclude or exaggerate certain information in order to further the abolitionist cause.

However, the autobiographies of formerly enslaved people are invaluable sources for historians of slavery because, like the WPA narratives, they provide rich firsthand accounts of slavery from the perspective of enslaved people. The slave autobiographies permit us access into the private world of enslaved people, taking the reader to conversations that took place within the slave cabin.[54] Indeed, because the slave autobiographies are subjective and there is extensive ego involvement throughout the accounts, they are invaluable for studies of slave self-perception. These works reveal how enslaved people felt about slavery—their anxieties, aspirations, loves, dreams, and frustrations.[55] John Blassingame has defended the slave autobiographies from accusations that they are rife with exaggeration from interfering abolitionists. Normally, he asserts, the editors of antebellum narratives were "an impressive group of people noted for their integrity."[56]

Most of the editors included professionals, such as lawyers, teachers, and scientists, who were apt at applying rules of evidence, and separating fact from fiction. In fact, most of these editors, according to Blassingame, had little to do with abolitionism.[57] The slave autobiographies also provide the reader with important information documenting the everyday life of common field slaves. Charles Ball's account, the longest published slave narrative, describes, in rich detail, the daily routines of typical field slaves—what they ate, their work patterns, and what crops they grew. Ball's account also provides detailed knowledge of the landscape and buildings that existed on the plantation where he was enslaved in South Carolina. In fact, Ball's descriptions have been corroborated by scholars.[58] Used in this way, the narratives are not wholly restricted to egotistical accounts of exceptional, literate, "unrepresentative" slaves.

This book also utilizes slave folklore. Folklorist William R. Bascom argued that there are four main functions of folklore, all of them serving to maintain the stability of culture: to entertain and allow one to escape in fantasy, validate culture, educate, and ensure conformity to the accepted cultural norms.[59] Accordingly, for the historian of slavery, folklore is an excellent source from which to examine the values, morals, and attitudes of the enslaved. Indeed, folklore has been employed as a historical source in studies of slavery ever since the revisionist historians of the 1970s pioneered the use of African American sources, such as the WPA narratives and slave autobiographies.[60] Through their folklore, enslaved people created a "sacred world" free from the control of their masters.[61] Here, they resisted the owners' attempts to dehumanize them, affirming their own culture. Their folklore articulated how to survive slavery, resist, conduct courtships, and generally behave. As Sterling Stuckey has argued, through folklore enslaved people "affirmed their humanity" and fashioned a "life style and set of values—an ethos" that contradicted the white racist discourses which sought to define them.[62]

Interviewees for the WPA narratives fondly recalled slavery-era folktales. "The tales told in slavery time are unequaled. They told tales of animals and dey doings," commented former slave Henry Warfield before he proceeded to relay a tale about Brer Guinea and Brer Rabbit.[63] Former slave Sabe Rutledge stated that his mother spun cotton in the evenings and told Brer Rabbit tales to him and his siblings as they crouched down by the fire picking seeds out of cotton. Rutledge recalled, "I 'member all them Buh Rabbit story! Mudder tell 'em and we laugh." Rutledge then told from memory a tale involving "Buh Rabbit and Buh Patridge."[64] Like Rutledge, many other former slaves mentioned that folktales were passed down to each generation by fathers, mothers, and "de ole plantation mammies."[65] *My Brother Slaves* examines a variety of folklore collections, particularly those gathered by Charles Colcock Jones Jr. and published as *Negro Myths of the Georgia Coast* in 1888. Jones was born in 1831, in Savannah, Georgia, where he eventually served as mayor. His family had owned more than a hundred slaves who worked rice and Sea Island cotton along the Newport River in Liberty County. Although trained as a lawyer, Jones had an academic interest in preserving folklore, and his interest in Native American relics led to his election as the first president of the American Anthropological Association, publishing *Antiquities of the Southern Indians, Particularly of the Georgia Tribes* in 1873. Concerned that African American folklore was in danger of vanishing, Jones spent five years collecting it along the Georgia coast, where his family members had their plantations. Unlike Joel Chandler Harris, who invented the Uncle Remus character to serve as a mouthpiece through which to narrate the Brer Rabbit tales, Jones provided the barest of introductions, instead choosing to let African Americans tell their own stories.[66] Although Jones's tales are relayed in Gullah dialect, which at times can be extremely challenging to read, they are immensely rewarding and authentic historical sources of African American folklore, offering the historian an indispensable insight into slave culture.[67] Because reliable and systematic collection of African American folklore commenced only after the Civil War, some historians, such as Kenneth Stampp, have doubted whether these collections were "true expressions" of the enslaved.[68] However, since the 1970s, when revisionist historians used such collections in their works and broke new ground, attitudes have changed. Scholars maintain that postbellum African American animal stories, as well as dancing and music, can be extended "well back into slavery-time" showing "no significant change."[69] For example, historian Gilbert Osofsky concluded that much of the tone of the late-nineteenth- and twentieth-century collections of African American folklore repeated the wit of the antebellum slave narratives. For him, these collections seemed to supplement, rather than call into question, the authenticity of the slave narrative material, continuing a centuries-old African American oral tradition.[70]

My Brother Slaves makes extensive use of these rich African American sources—slave autobiographies, oral narratives, and folklore—to probe the emotional and secret lives of enslaved men. It also draws on a wide vari-

ety of white sources. Plantation records—accounts, diaries, and letters—
are essential sources for historians of slavery. These document the rhythms
of plantation operation and management; they detail daily labor routines,
as well as instances of punishment and resistance; and furthermore, they
chronicle the racial attitudes of antebellum white southerners, master-slave
relationships, and the worldview of slave owners. Petitions are similarly
revealing. A significant number of southerners (both black and white) sub-
mitted petitions to their legislatures for redress of grievances during the
antebellum period; many of these concern issues of race and slavery, dealing
with topics such as manumission, laws governing slavery, and miscegena-
tion. They reveal the fears and preoccupations of antebellum white society,
the grim realities of slavery, and the desires of enslaved people to gain their
freedom.[71] Newspapers and trial records of enslaved people are equally useful. Together, these sources reveal much about the social, economic, and
cultural world of the antebellum South.

My Brother Slaves draws on works by a range of sociologists and anthropologists to interpret the behavior and actions of enslaved men. These are
valuable because they often help decode the rituals of masculinity across
time and space, such as rites of passage, risk-taking behavior, and fighting. Anthropological studies of traditional West African communities, for
example, are particularly useful for understanding the community-forming rituals of plantation wrestling among enslaved men in the antebellum
South. These matches were, in many cases, African-derived cultural activities inherently connected to masculinity.

This book examines the lives of enslaved men throughout the antebellum South—from the slaveholding border states, down to the Lowcountry
and Deep South, and across to the southwestern slaveholding states such
as Texas. Although the rhythms of enslaved life varied according to region,
crop, and size of plantation, many enslaved men throughout the antebellum South responded to their enslavement in markedly similar ways. Issues
of masculinity, friendship, and resistance were generally uniform across the
South; many men, whether enslaved in Maryland or Texas, drank, gambled, wrestled, hunted, evaded the patrol gangs, stole, forged friendships,
and resisted their enslavement. As Stephanie Camp has argued, "for all of
the important variations attributed to crop, region, and local demographics,
American slavery was, above all, a system of economic exploitation, racial
formation, and racial domination that, when studied in a broad geographic
range, reveals strong continuities as well as differences."[72] The years covered

by this study mostly fall in the late antebellum period—between approximately 1830 and the outbreak of the Civil War.

Overview of Chapters

My Brother Slaves is arranged thematically. Chapter 1 analyzes the work of enslaved men. Throughout the South, on large plantations, in industry, and in skilled work, enslaved men often worked in distinctly homosocial spaces. Owners of large plantations tended to divide their enslaved workforces into sex-segregated gangs; male workers ran the labor-intensive industries of the South—the coal mines, ironworks, and lumber industries—and enslaved men occupied most skilled positions. The chapter argues that enslaved men fashioned their own masculine work culture and, where evidence permits, suggests that a strong sense of solidarity characterized their everyday working relationships.

Chapter 2 explores the leisure time of enslaved men. Men not only spent this time with their families and loved ones, they socialized with other men by drinking, gambling, and wrestling. In these spaces, men reinforced certain gender, age, and status roles and fostered homosocial solidarity and reaffirmed friendships. Slaveholding mastery in the antebellum South depended on the domination and control of the slave body. By drinking and wrestling, enslaved men challenged the hegemony of the slave owner. In the process, they reclaimed their bodies from the exigencies of slavery. The chapter emphasizes how the male slave body served as a profoundly personal and political site of resistance. Chapter 3 examines how enslaved men challenged and transgressed the spatial and temporal constraints imposed by slaveholders. Enslaved men left the plantation behind when they hunted, evaded the patrol gangs, and engaged in cross-plantation theft. Crossing into illicit territory was extremely dangerous, and enslaved men often took part in these activities in the presence of other men. In these hazardous spaces, they tested one another, proved themselves to their peers, and established distinct male roles.

Chapter 4 investigates one of the most intimate areas of life for enslaved men: male friendship. These relationships played central roles in men's everyday lives; friendship offered vital emotional and practical support to resist the dehumanizing features of slavery. The chapter exposes how the private world of friendship instigated and nurtured a culture oppositional to enslavement. Narratives demonstrate how male friendship was pivotal in effecting successful escapes to freedom in the North. Trusted friends plotted with one another, exchanged illicit information, and supported each other materially and emotionally before and during an escape. Many men risked their lives for their friends. Slaveholders tightly regulated enslaved people's access to the outside world; however, as chapter 5 demonstrates, despite their best efforts, owners failed to prevent the operation of an illicit "grapevine telegraph"—a network that spread news and correspondence between enslaved communities maintained by mobile bondpeople. Enslaved men were key players in this illicit network; their mobility presented them with more opportunities than their female counterparts to acquire geographical knowledge and make contact with abolitionist sources. This chapter unravels the secret operations of this network: through this system of communication, enslaved men exchanged subversive ideas as well as daily news. Indeed, evidence shows that men used the grapevine telegraph to forge an inter-plantation network with other men and hold conspiratorial meetings.

My Brother Slaves studies the relationships shared between enslaved men and emphasizes that their lives were intertwined. On plantations across the South, they created an all-male subculture through which they constructed their own independent notions of masculinity, friendship, and resistance. Homosocial company was integral to the gendered identity and self-esteem of enslaved men. The emotional landscape they created together offered them a vital mutual support network through which to resist the horrors of slavery. Through each other, enslaved men created a secret world that defied and subverted the slaveholder's authority.

1

Enslaved Men and Work

This chapter examines the everyday work spaces of enslaved men across the antebellum South. Enslaved men spent most of their day in the field, laboring in backbreaking conditions from sunup to sundown. Many—particularly those on large plantations—worked alongside other men in sex-segregated gangs, in which men usually plowed while women hoed. Together, these men lived intensive lives: they performed demanding labor for the owner and shared meals, commiserated together, and sang work songs. This chapter explores how the slaveholder organized gang labor and how the system shaped the lives of enslaved men across the antebellum South. It surveys the practices employed by planters on the sugar plantations of Louisiana; the tobacco, corn, and wheat fields of Virginia and North Carolina; the cotton plantations of the Southwest and Deep South; and the rice plantations of the Lowcountry. Enslaved men also toiled together in the homosocial spaces of southern industry. The involvement of enslaved people in southern industry is a subject generally neglected by historians, which is unfortunate because, typically, it was predominantly men who worked in this sector. In difficult conditions, enslaved men worked in factories, ironworks, mining, as well as the lumber and naval stores industries. They constructed the South's infrastructure. Life was particularly hard: many were separated from their families and members of the opposite sex for most of the year as they labored in dangerous conditions. To survive, these men relied on and trusted one another; the bonds between them were strong. The chapter also analyzes the skilled work performed by enslaved men. Across the South, men undertook most of the skilled work available to enslaved people. Together, they took pride in their work and passed on their prized skills to younger men, creating an intergenerational male network. Working in homosocial spaces—whether on plantations, in industry, or in skilled work—enslaved men developed their own masculine work culture:

"a way of doing things and a way of assigning values that flowed from the perspective that they had on Southern plantation life."[1] The homosocial world of enslaved men, for many, was born in the workplace. It was here, performing labor for their owners, that many enslaved men learned to co-operate and trust and depend on one another.

Plantation Work

Plantation slavery flourished throughout the South. Slaves labored on the lucrative cotton plantations of the Black Belt, which stretched from Georgia through Alabama and Mississippi to Louisiana and by the 1850s extended to Texas. In the swampy coastal regions of South Carolina and Georgia, large rice and indigo plantations prospered. Sugar production dominated the parishes of southern Louisiana, while tobacco plantations covered Virginia's central and southern Piedmont and parts of North Carolina. Other staples—corn and wheat—grew throughout the South, the latter becoming an important cash crop in parts of Virginia and North Carolina. Some parts of the South, however—the great Appalachian heartland that stretched from western Virginia down to northeastern Alabama—were generally inhospitable to large plantation–scale slavery.

Slaves comprised 33 percent of the total southern population. Slave populations were high in the lower South. In 1860, black majorities in South Carolina and Mississippi comprised 57.2 percent and 55.2 percent of the respective state populations. Slave populations were 43.7 percent in Georgia, 44 percent in Florida, 45.1 percent in Alabama, and 46.9 percent in Louisiana. In contrast, the states of the upper South had considerably lower slave populations. About one third of Virginia and North Carolina's population were enslaved, and a quarter in Tennessee and a fifth in Kentucky. Slaves accounted for 12.7 percent of the population in Maryland and a tiny 1.6 percent of inhabitants in Delaware. According to the 1850 census, the total slave population for the antebellum South was 3,204,313. Although many slaves worked in mixed farming, most of the enslaved labor force cultivated the great staple crops of the antebellum South. The census of 1850 estimates that out of the 2.5 million slaves working in agriculture, 1.815 million were engaged in cotton production, 350,000 in tobacco, 150,000 in sugar, 125,000 in rice, and 60,000 in hemp.[2]

Slaveholders employed two distinct labor practices in the antebellum South: the task system and the gang system. Under the task system, each slave was assigned a specific job for the day or week. After completing their assigned work, slaves were "free" to do as they pleased; usually, they returned home and tended small garden plots, performed housework, or went hunting. The task system was utilized extensively in the Lowcountry rice and Sea Island cotton regions of South Carolina and Georgia.[3] Planters usually allotted tasks based on age and physical ability; they categorized individual men and women as quarter-, half-, three-quarter-, or full-task hands. On a visit to a large Lowcountry rice plantation, Frederick Law Olmsted observed the system firsthand:

> The field-hands are all divided into four classes, according to their physical capacities. The children beginning as "quarter-hands," advancing to "half-hands," and then to "three-quarter-hands;" and, finally, when mature, and able-bodied, healthy, and strong, to "full hands." As they decline in strength, from age, sickness, or other cause, they retrograde in the scale, and proportionally less labor is required of them. Many, of naturally weak frame, never are put among the full hands. Finally, the aged are left out at the annual classification, and no more regular field-work is required of them, although they are generally provided with some light, sedentary occupation.[4]

Although under the task system the enslaved were treated as individuals and assigned individual work tasks, many continued to work in groups; the stronger and faster slaves helped the slower and weaker ones with work, allowing them to keep up with the group. As slave owner James Sparkman remarked in an 1858 letter, "it is customary (*and never objected to*) for the more active and industrious hand to assist those who are slower and more tardy in finishing their daily tasks."[5]

Under the gang system, slaveholders divided their workforce into groups under the supervision of a driver or leader and compelled them to work the entire day. Thus, the enslaved were not afforded the measure of independence available to those working under the task system. The gang system was commonly used on the tobacco plantations of the upper South, on most cotton plantations, and on the sugar plantations of southern Louisiana. As with the task system, planters rated the enslaved workforce as quarter hands, half hands, three-quarter hands, and full hands.[6]

Under both systems, owners of large plantations divided their workforces into sex-segregated gangs. On small holdings, however, there were simply not enough workers to permit planters to divide their workforce in this way. One WPA respondent, formerly enslaved on a small farm holding eight slaves in White County, Tennessee, claimed that "the women would plow, hoe corn, just like the men would."[7] Phoebe Lyons, enslaved in Lincoln County, Georgia, recalled that on her plantation "dey wuz'nt many slaves." Accordingly, her mother "had to wuk en de fiel' en plow jus' like er man, en de res' us chilluns big nuff ter pull weeds er swing er hoe, wuz out en er fiel' wukin,' fum daylight till too dark ter see."[8] Enslaved in a small community in Buena Vista, Alabama, Adaline Montgomery remarked her mother's master had only two slaves: one manservant and her mother. As a result, her mother "had to go out an' work jes' like a man, cut logs an' split rails."[9] Another former slave who worked on a small holding in West Virginia claimed her master "worked men or women slaves just alike."[10]

Historians estimate slaveholders needed upward of fourteen working hands before gangs could be organized.[11] In 1860, planters possessing more than twenty slaves owned 48 percent of all enslaved people.[12] Thus, almost half the slave population lived on plantations where it was possible to assign work by gender; the larger the plantation, the more likely that work was divided into sex-segregated gangs. In 1860, a quarter of the enslaved population lived on large plantations holding more than fifty slaves. The sugar plantations located along the banks of the lower Mississippi River and the coastal Lowcountry rice plantations of South Carolina and Georgia were the largest slaveholdings in the South.[13] In gangs, men undertook the more physically challenging task of plowing while women hoed.[14] Slave owners were, of course, interested foremost in making a return on their investment. Accordingly, they did not hesitate to dissolve these sex-segregated gangs in response to specific labor requirements. For instance, during the busy harvesttime in the cotton fields, every hand was needed; hence it was not unusual for men and women to labor side by side picking cotton. Nevertheless, owners maintained that separating their workforce was advantageous: it prevented enslaved people from interacting and flirting and thus disrupting the work routine. Furthermore, men were prevented from helping women with quotas or protecting them from punishments.[15]

Large sugar plantations dominated the landscape of southern Louisiana. In Ascension Parish, half of all the enslaved population lived on plantations holding 175 or more slaves.[16] Unlike planters who grew cotton, tobacco, or rice, sugar planters imported far more male than female slaves in the domestic slave trade; 85 percent of all slaves who were sold to sugar plantations were male. Working on a sugar plantation was extremely physical; therefore, owners preferred a male workforce. Women were relatively scarce, and on some plantations, the ratio of enslaved men to women stood at almost three to one. According to historian Richard Follett, "the region mirrored the slave gulags of the Caribbean, where nineteenth-century sugar planters demonstrated a similar preference for males as agricultural workers." As a result, Louisiana's slave population suffered a natural decrease of about 13 percent per decade.[17]

Given the gender ratio in Louisiana, many enslaved men would have faced difficulties in finding female partners; it is plausible that they attached more significance to homosocial relationships. Men, after all, worked from sunup to sundown in sex-segregated gangs on the large sugar plantations of Louisiana. The plow gang was distinctly male—comprising the strongest men. The hoe gangs included both men and women; however, men and women frequently worked in separate hoe gangs.[18] After a trip to the sugar plantations of Louisiana, William Russell Howard commented: "Three gangs of negroes were at work: one gang of men, with twenty mules and ploughs, was engaged in running through the furrows between the canes, cutting up the weeds, and clearing away the grass. . . . Another gang consisted of forty men, who were hoeing out the grass in Indian corn. The third gang, of thirty-six women, were engaged in hoeing out cane."[19] Owners of large sugar plantations in Louisiana frequently organized their workforces according to gender for a variety of tasks. Franklin A. Hudson, owner of the Blythewood Plantation on Bayou Goula, Iberville Parish, often detailed the division of labor in his plantation diary. The following entries were typical: "7 men ditching in Road ditch x Women cutting hay"; "Men cutting down trees on Congress land—women cutting corn stalks"; and "women gang taking grass from plant cane, men cutting wood."[20] Hudson commonly ordered gangs of enslaved men to undertake the more physically demanding work: digging ditches, cutting down and hauling wood. Work gangs of women cut sugar cane, hay, corn stalks, and cleaned the ditches and drains.[21] Sixty miles north of New Orleans, situated on the banks of the Mississippi, was the St. James Sugar Refinery, owned by one of the antebellum South's wealthiest planters: Valcour Aime. As on Hudson's plantation, the enslaved workforce was divided: male gangs dug ditches and chopped and hauled wood, while female gangs cut weeds, gathered corn, repaired roads, and cleaned ditches.[22] Enslaved men and women on the

On large plantations, many enslaved men and women worked in sex-segregated work gangs. In this scene, men work in the background, while women work together gathering the sugar cane. *Gathering the Cane,* in T. B. Thorpe, "Sugar and the Sugar Region of Louisiana," *Harper's New Monthly Magazine* 7, no. 42 (November 1853): 760.

large sugar plantations of Louisiana worked in homosocial spaces throughout the working day.

As in Louisiana, on the large tobacco, wheat, and corn plantations of the Upper South, slaveholders divided their workforces by gender. Initially, in the seventeenth-century Chesapeake, enslaved workers in the tobacco fields toiled together at the same tasks in mixed-sex work groups; however, as planters increasingly diversified their plantations from the middle

of the eighteenth century—growing wheat and corn alongside tobacco—
they organized sex-segregated work gangs. Slaveholders assigned a variety
of tasks to enslaved men: sowing and mowing grain, plowing, harrowing, carting, ditching, lumbering, and fishing. Enslaved women worked in
all-female gangs hoeing and weeding, building fences, grubbing swamps,
cleaning winnowed grain, breaking up new ground, cleaning stables,
and loading and spreading manure.[23] Such trends continued into the
antebellum period. On White Hill Plantation, located in Prince George
County, Virginia, the enslaved harvested wheat, corn, and tobacco. The
owner, Charles Friend, organized his workforce according to gender; in
January 1846, he listed in his plantation diary the names of thirty-four
male and twenty-nine female slaves. Friend frequently tasked the gangs
of men to chop and haul wood and plow, and the women and children
usually grubbed.[24] In some diary entries, Friend records that the women
were occasionally joined by elderly enslaved men Jack and Dick, who as of
January 1846 were sixty and sixty-five years old.[25] On other occasions, a
slave named Billy worked with the women. Records document two slaves
named William on the plantation, aged thirty-five and twenty-two as of
January 1846. Additionally, a slave named Ned who was forty-five years
old worked with the women on a few instances. As these men were not
elderly, it plausible that they had been assigned places in the women's work
gangs as a result of injury or health.[26]

In Burke and McDowell counties, North Carolina, James Hervey
Greenlee raised a variety of crops—wheat, corn, cotton, and oats—as well
as livestock such as hogs and cattle. According to the U.S. census, in 1850
Greenlee owned twenty-six slaves and approximately $16,000 of property.
On his plantation, women gangs cut and cleaned up briars, dug potatoes,
cut sprouts, and hoed and spun cotton, while male gangs plowed, hauled
wood, and dug ditches.[27] On another North Carolina plantation, located in
Franklin County, which produced tobacco, cotton and grain, owner Nicholas Bryor Massenburg also preferred to divide his labor force by gender.
Children worked with the women, while men plowed and undertook the
heavy work: chopping and hauling wood, and digging ditches. According
to plantation records, no woman was instructed to dig ditches, work on the
roads, or cut and collect timber.[28] On the large plantations of the upper
South, enslaved men and women would have spent the majority—if not
all—of the working day in same-sex gangs performing tasks assigned on
the basis of gender.

Owners of large cotton plantations in the Southwest and the Lowcountry often divided their workforces by gender. Although they forced men and women to work side by side during the busy harvest season, for the rest of the year they tasked sex-segregated gangs to plant and cultivate the cotton plant.[29] As elsewhere, men usually plowed and women hoed. In Mississippi, women and children beat down the old plants in order to prepare the cotton crop. Male gangs then plowed the field to break up the soil and create furrows for cultivation. Women sowed the seeds and, afterwards, the men plowed light harrows to cover them. Hoe gangs then "scraped" the fields to prevent weeds and grass growing on the ridges while the seedlings sprouted. They also thinned the crop. Without delay, plow gangs then ran plows through the rows with a mould board, which threw dirt onto the plants. Hoe gangs followed chopping cotton. The hoe gangs performed occasional scraping until the crop was ready for harvest. During his visit to Mississippi, Frederick Law Olmsted observed that workers on a plantation of 135 slaves were divided into two gangs: male and female: "We found in the field thirty plows, moving together, turning the earth from the cotton plants, and from thirty to forty hoers, the latter mainly women." Sometimes, both sexes worked together pulling stalks, and erecting fences; on other occasions women worked in their own gangs fencing. As well as plowing, male gangs worked together chopping and hauling wood.[30] Indoor tasks assigned to enslaved men and women differed. Women spun, wove, knitted, and mended clothes; they sometimes ground corn into meal or hominy. Men shelled corn, thrashed peas, cut potatoes for planting, platted shucks, and cleaned the corn crib. If required, skilled men repaired plantation equipment.[31]

Although plowing was men's work on many plantations, Olmsted observed women plowing in large gangs on a cotton plantation in Mississippi. He admitted that he "watched with some interest for any indication that their sex unfitted them for the occupation": "Twenty of them were plowing together with double teams and heavy plows. They were superintended by a male negro driver, who carried a whip, which he frequently cracked at them, permitting no dawdling or delay at the turning; and they twitched their plows around on the head-land, jerking their reins, and yelling to their mules, with apparent ease, energy, and rapidity."[32] But, in this case, although women undertook "men's work," the workers still worked in sex-segregated gangs; they remained in the company of their own sex throughout the working day.

Planters in the cotton-growing regions of Georgia and South Carolina similarly divided their workforces by sex. Historian Susan O'Donovan has claimed that in southwest Georgia, "although the boundaries and categories were never absolute, more often than not the distinctions between men's work and women's work held steady." Men performed the most physical tasks: they chopped down trees, hauled and mauled wood, prepared fertilizer, cut oats and wheat, wrestled cattle to the ground for branding and castration, packed cotton, and moved gin and milling machinery. In contrast, women chopped cotton, hoed weeds, spread manure on the fields, knocked down cotton stalks, burned brush, pulled fodder, dug potatoes, harvested vegetables, shucked grain, and strewed seed. As in Mississippi, women occasionally plowed in gangs. However, the plowing experiences of women in Georgia differed considerably from those of men. Unlike the heavy, iron, V-shaped plows used by teams of enslaved men, if called to plow in the late spring and summer, enslaved women used smaller, lighter contraptions called "scooters," designed to only scratch the surface of the ground to uproot weeds and grass from between the growing crops.[33]

John Edwin Fripp, owner of a large South Carolina Sea Island cotton plantation, sent only men to work in the swamps to chop and haul wood. On his plantation, the men plowed and dug ditches, while the women dug slips, burnt grass, listed, raked, and hoed. After the cotton was picked, the women assorted and moated the produce, and the men weighed it.[34] Depending on the equipment available, ginning tended to be reserved for enslaved women.[35] On most large cotton plantations throughout the South, planters divided their workforces by gender. Men and women labored in sex-segregated spaces throughout the long working day.

Owners of large rice plantations in the Lowcountry often divided their enslaved workforces by gender; Olmsted remarked that "the field hands, are nearly always worked in gangs, the strength of a gang varying according to the work that engages it; usually it numbers twenty or more, and is directed by a driver."[36] Gangs of women prepared the rice field by burning the stubble of the preceding crop. Duncan Clinch Heyward, member of one of the largest rice planting families of the Lowcountry, recalled:

Burning stubble was usually done by women, who dragged the fire with their hoes. When the stubble was thoroughly dry and a stiff breeze blowing, they sometimes had to jump across the quarter ditches to avoid the advancing fire. There was considerable excitement in this work, and the women seemed to enjoy it. Their dresses were tied up to their knees and did not hinder them from jumping the ditches when they were caught in a close place by the fire. "Look out, Sister!" they would often call to each other. "Don't let dat fire ketch 'ona. Jump across de ditch."[37]

After the burning and plowing, women hoed to level and prepare the soil; they pulled up weeds and spread manure to fertilize the land. Elizabeth Pringle, who grew up on one of the largest slave plantations in South Carolina, commented that the male laborers associated the hoe with female work: "The hoe they consider purely a feminine implement."[38] Planting the rice seed—the next stage—was also customarily regarded as women's work. According to Heyward, women always planted the rice seeds. He commented, "Women always did this work, for the men used to say that this was 'woman's wuck,' and I do not recall seeing one of the men attempt it."[39] Men and women, however, did work together on some tasks—processing rice, for example. Enslaved men and women also cleaned ditches together. But, almost always, only male gangs dug ditches.[40] Slaveholder James R. Sparkman described the practice on his plantation: "In the preparation of the Rice Lands, as ditching, embanking etc. the *men* alone are engaged with the spade."[41] As on other large plantations throughout the antebellum South, men chopped and hauled wood.[42]

Even when men and women labored together—cleaning ditches and processing rice—they worked in separate spaces.[43] In fact, throughout the long working day, most men and women on large Lowcountry rice plantations worked in different spaces. When Olmsted visited one of these, he noted that it was divided by embankments into fields of about twenty acres each. In one field, he observed a gang of twenty to thirty women raking and burning stubble. In the next, twenty young men and boys plowed. Olmsted presumed that the men had half an hour for breakfast, which was taken together "in a social company about a fire." He observed that in one upland field a gang comprised "entirely of men" ditched; in another field, a female gang hoed a corn field. Each gang "had a fire burning on the ground, near where they were at work, to light their pipes and warm their breakfast by."[44] Each sex-segregated gang spent all day together working and sharing precious little breaks.

From the sugar plantations of Louisiana; to the Virginia and North Carolina tobacco, wheat, and corn fields; to the cotton belts of the Southwest and Deep South; and to the rice fields of the Lowcountry, slaveholders of large plantations routinely divided their workforce into sex-segregated gangs. Usually, men plowed and women hoed. Even if assigned similar jobs, enslaved men and women still found themselves in sex-segregated gangs. Although women plowed on occasion, enslaved men were able to claim a distinct gendered identity in the field because their owners generally regarded male labor as "superior," typically assigning men the most physically arduous tasks.[45] Indeed, telling are the responses of many former slaves who regarded plowing, ditching, or working wood as man's work.[46] Working all day together would have strengthened masculine camaraderie. In the field, these men suffered together, took breaks and ate their food together, and, most likely, commiserated with one another.

Industrial Work

Although the South's economy was predominantly agricultural, by the beginning of the nineteenth century certain industries—such as crop processing, manufacturing, and transportation enterprises—had begun to develop. Industrialization accelerated in towns such as Richmond, and industrial output increased accordingly. By 1860, about 15 percent of America's industrial capacity was centered in the South. Slave labor was extensively employed; in the 1850s about 5 percent of the total slave population, between 160,000 and 200,000, worked in various kinds of industry. Slaves worked in southern textile, sugar, grist, and rice mills; iron and salt works; tobacco and hemp factories; coal, gold, lead, and iron mines; fisheries; and the lumber and turpentine industries. They built the South's infrastructure—railroads, roads, and canals. They worked in construction and on steamboats as deck hands, firemen, engineers, and even pilots. Although some industrial slaves were women and children, the vast majority were men.[47] Industry was a mostly masculine world. Indeed, enslaved men who worked in the naval stores or lumber industries or on the railroads and canals lived in isolated areas, cut off from their families for most of the year. Living, socializing, and working together under particularly dangerous conditions, these men forged strong bonds of solidarity and developed an interdependent masculine work culture.

Slaves comprised the majority of the workforce in the upper South ironworks. In Maryland and Virginia, eighty ironworks employed slave labor by the nineteenth century. Collectively, the ironworks of the Upper

South utilized seven thousand workers between 1800 and 1860.[48] Some of the well-known establishments, such as the Oxford Iron Works of Virginia, owned 220 slaves. On the eve of the Civil War, the Tredegar Iron Company of Richmond employed a total of 900 workers, half of whom were enslaved.[49] The manufacture of iron was labor-intensive, and therefore many slaves who worked in iron production were men.[50] Together, these men chopped wood, manned charcoal pits, hauled charcoal long distances, mined iron ore, and extracted limestone. Day and night, in dirty, sweaty, noisy conditions, the teams fed the blast furnaces with iron ore, charcoal, and limestone into blast furnaces. At the forge, gangs of slave heaters and hammermen turned pig iron into merchant bars (refined iron that had been hammered into standard-sized bars).[51] Women and children worked in a variety of operations: William Weaver's Buffalo Forge near Lexington, Virginia; David Ross's Oxford Iron Works; and the Tredegar Iron Works. In these large-scale operations, they labored separately from men as plantation hands and assistants in the charcoal-making process. They raked leaves, which were used with dirt to cover smoldering wood and convert it to charcoal. Women also cleaned and picked over the ore to free it from impurities before it went to the furnace. Although records suggest that women did work at the furnace and forge, no records exist through which to ascertain their precise roles.[52]

Enslaved men worked in distinctly homosocial spaces in mines. In 1820, the United States was rated sixth in the world for coal production, and three-quarters of the nation's exports came from the mines of southwestern Virginia, western Maryland, and West Virginia. By 1860, two-thirds of the 3,579 Appalachian coal miners in 1860 were enslaved workers.[53] In contrast to the iron industry, whereby many slaves were owned by the various iron manufacturing enterprises, coal mines tended to hire their hands. In an almost exclusively male enterprise, "coal miners never had the female component frequently found at ironworks. . . . If the men had families, they resided elsewhere."[54] The census of 1860 showed that no females worked at the Midlothian mines in Virginia. Only one female slave was listed as a worker among a workforce of sixty-six at the Clover Hill Coal Mining Company, near Petersburg.[55] If employed at the coal mines, female slaves most likely cooked and cleaned for the pitmen.[56] As with the iron industry, coal companies implemented overwork systems whereby enslaved men could earn extra money for themselves and their families, thus enabling them to fill economic provider roles for their families. The money paid for overtime varied among the different coal companies. One newspaper article reported that in the Midlothian mines "many of the slaves lay up $50 per annum for work done out of the regular hours."[57]

Coal mining in the antebellum South was exceedingly dangerous. Enslaved miners faced the daily horrors of collapsing tunnels, explosions, fires, flooding, and suffocation. In March 1855, for example, an explosion at the Midlothian mines "broke down a partition wall between the pit in which the miners were at work," resulting in the deaths of "five white men, two white boys, and thirty colored men."[58] More than likely, a strong camaraderie united these male workers. Studies have shown that camaraderie "appears to be a universal element found in all mining communities throughout history." For miners, the strong sense of fellowship serves as a vital support system in their everyday working lives and also as a means of survival in the event of an accident or disaster. Working in dangerous conditions, miners have to take responsibility for each other's safety. The unwritten code dictates that miners always watch out for each other; in the case of an accident, they know they are able to rely on their fellow workers to do everything possible to make sure they all get out safely. As one twentieth-century miner from Kentucky remarked, "Miners is about the closest people to each other that you'll ever find . . . they know what each other has been through."[59]

Mines were, and mostly still are, resolutely masculine spaces. Like most miners around the world, Appalachians were superstitious: they believed a woman's presence in a mine brought bad luck. In fact, as the United States industrialized, such superstition led seventeen states to pass laws forbidding women from working underground in the mines.[60] Cornish miners, who worked alongside the enslaved in the Gold Hill gold mine of antebellum North Carolina, shared this superstition.[61] In Gold Hill, men drilled, mined, and hauled lumps of rock; women worked aboveground and operated the log rockers that rewashed ore waste from the mills—they also washed and sewed.[62] Collectively, the gold mines of North Carolina produced tens of millions of dollars of America's wealth. Many utilized slave labor.[63] As with most extractive industries, it was a labor-intensive enterprise involving mostly men. Fraternity and friendship flourished among the North Carolina miners: one white miner wrote in a letter, "When I left [Asheboro] and went to Gold hill I soon contracted friendships as pure and strong and lasting as in earlier life and never have I experienced greater pleasure . . . than in getting back to Gold Hill." At Gold Hill "there is a set of such brotherly, warm-hearted, wholesouled fellows . . . , that any one would become attached to." Whatever ties of friendship and fraternity that existed among the miners, it most likely found expression within the boundaries of different ethnic groups. Whether or not these ties extended across racial and ethnic boundaries, it is likely that the same camaraderie existed among the enslaved African American male gold miners. By 1850, half of the miners and laborers at Gold hill were single men who lived in boardinghouses.[64] They slept and worked together, and at the end of the working day, they most likely shared a drink, a joke, and a laugh.

Enslaved men worked extensively in the naval stores industry, producing tar, turpentine, and their derivatives (turpentine spirits, rosin, and pitch). North Carolina led the way in production and by 1840 produced 95.9 percent of the naval stores in America. According to one report, in 1847 the state produced 800,000 barrels of turpentine, which had an estimated market value of $1.7 million to $2 million. Originally dominated by small farmers, by the late antebellum period the naval stores industry's labor force consisted chiefly of slaves.[65] Most of the work, such as boxing, chipping, and cornering, required considerable strength, and hence enslaved men dominated the work force. If enslaved women and children were employed in the industry, they carried out the lighter task of "dipping."[66] The task system structured work in the turpentine industry deep in the pine forests of southeastern North Carolina. Taking advantage of transportation improvements in the mid-nineteenth century, producers moved their operations, equipment, and labor force into isolated work camps. Here, enslaved men lived cut off from agricultural plantation life, denied regular contact with their families.[67] Some scholars have speculated that the uneven sex ratio left workers "lonely and miserable." Accordingly, it is highly likely that the men turned to one another for support and friendship to survive life in the forests of North Carolina.[68]

The southern lumber industry, based in the forests, was an exclusively masculine enterprise. Workers cut and sawed timber, shingles, and barrel staves. Lumbering was so widespread in the Carolinas that by 1845 Wilmington alone supported at least nine steam sawmills. Slave labor was used to log the pine, cypress, and oak trees in the swamps and forests of the South. By 1860, the southern lumber industry employed about 16,000 workers, most of whom were enslaved.[69] When Frederick Law Olmsted visited the Great Dismal Swamp, he reported that the work in the swamp was "entirely done by slaves," who were usually hired by the lumber compa-

STATE OF NORTH CAROLINA,

GATES COUNTY.

COUNTY COURT CLERK'S OFFICE, *August* 3/ 185*7* .

Robert the property of *James S. Seguine*
Norfolk County, *Virginia*, and by him registered as one of his hands employed to work in the Great Dismal Swamp in the County of Gates aforesaid, *Robert* is about *Seventeen* years of age is *very Black, has a small scar on his upper lip, and another on his left knee just above the knee pan + has lost his little toe on the left foot* and stands without shoes *four* feet *two & 1/2* inches high.

4 feet 3 inch high

September 3rd,

IN TESTIMONY OF WHICH, I HENRY L. EURE, Clerk of the Court of Pleas and Quarter Sessions in and for the County of Gates, at Office in Gatesville, do hereunto affix my name and seal of Office the day and date first before written

Henry L. Eure CLERK.

Slaveholders selected enslaved men to work as lumbermen in the Great Dismal Swamp. Although the work was extremely physical, lumbermen enjoyed a degree of relative autonomy far from plantation supervision. Long-term passes, such as this one, were issued to men to allow them to work in the swamp. These recorded in detail the particulars of each enslaved man. Available in Gates County Criminal Actions Concerning Slaves Records. (Courtesy of the North Carolina Office of Archives and History, Raleigh, North Carolina.)

nies for an average of $100 a year. Apart from one or two months in winter spent at their masters' residences, these workers labored throughout the year deep in the swamp. Olmsted noted that when the swamp was dry, typically in early February, the enslaved entered it in gangs: each worker was "examined and registered at the Court-house, and 'passes,' good for a year, are given them, in which their features and the marks upon their persons are minutely described."[70] Fortunately, records such as those mentioned by Olmsted still exist today. They offer the historian valuable insights into who exactly worked in gangs cutting and hauling lumber deep in the forest and swamps of the antebellum South. In the North Carolina State Archives, a registration book of slaves exists that lists and describes hundreds of slaves who worked in the Dismal Swamp from 1847 to 1861. All of the legible

Author and illustrator David Hunter Strother (known by his pseudonym, Porte Crayon) visited the Great Dismal Swamp and in 1856 published sketches made during his trip, of enslaved men working and living together. He observed young boys transporting shingles in carts, like this one. Porte Crayon, *Carting Shingles,* in "The Dismal Swamp," *Harper's Monthly Magazine* 13, no. 76 (September 1856): 450.

entries in the book describe enslaved men. Unsurprisingly, given the labor-intensive nature of lumbering, most were strong, young men in their twenties and thirties.[71] As Moses Roper recalled when his owner sent him to cut trees in a swamp, it was "the heaviest work which men of twenty-five or thirty years of age have to do."[72] Not all of the men listed in the registration book, however, were in their twenties and thirties; a young boy of only twelve and an older man of sixty were both sent to the swamp to work. One can only speculate what their precise roles were. Perhaps the young boy carried water to the workers and the elderly man cooked, cleaned, and looked after the camp while the rest were at work. It is, however, possible to observe

During his visit to the Great Dismal Swamp, David Hunter Strother stopped at the headquarters of the swamp's shingle-makers. He remarked: "Although of the rudest character, there seemed to be every material for physical comfort in abundance. There was bacon, salt fish, meal, molasses, whisky, and sweet potatoes." Porte Crayon, *Horse Camp*, in "The Dismal Swamp," *Harper's Monthly Magazine* 13, no. 76 (September 1856): 449, 451 (quotation).

that the hundreds of male workers in the swamp were part of an intergenerational interdependent network. Performing highly dangerous labor, they relied on one another for their lives, while others—too young or too old— served the community in other ways. Older men, for example, most likely served as father figures and role models for young boys, performing the roles of surrogate father and brother.[73]

Enslaved lumbermen worked under the task system without a driver and were required to provide a certain quantity of shingles at the end of their service in the swamps. They led independent lives in a distinctly masculine world. As Olmsted remarked, "the slave lumberman . . . lives measurably as a free man; hunts, fishes, eats, drinks, smokes and sleeps, plays and works, each when and as much as he pleases."[74] Workers lived in very close proximity to each other. One observer described their living arrangements: "Their houses, or shanties, are barely wide enough for five or six men to lie in, closely packed side by side—their heads to the back wall, and their feet stretched to the open front, close by a fire kept up through the night. The roof is sloping to shed the rain, and where highest, not above four feet from the floor. Of the shavings made in smoothing the shingles, the thinnest make a bed for the laborers, and the balance form the only dry and solid foundation for their house, and their homestead, or working yard."[75]

Enslaved men labored together to build the South's infrastructure. During the antebellum period, thousands of workers were needed to construct the rail network throughout the South. The scale of the projects was huge, and southern railroads relied upon enslaved labor. By 1861, 76 percent of the 118 antebellum southern railroads employed enslaved labor. Most railroads purchased their own slaves, hired them, or contracted companies who hired them out. Although some historians have cited cases of women working on the railroads, the enslaved laborers were overwhelmingly male.[76] With little mechanical help available, railroad building in the antebellum period was especially labor-intensive. Workers hauled earth, gravel, timber, and stone in carts and wagons; animals dragged plows and scrapers to grade the earth. Men with picks hacked at embankments, hills, and rocks. Men with axes swung at trees, chopped them, and made crossties. Hand-driven spikes fastened the iron rails into position.[77] In this intense environment, a distinct masculine work culture developed. According to former slave Fannie Berry, enslaved men arrived for work at daybreak with axes on their shoulders to clear trees for the rail tracks in Appomattox County, Virginia. They sung this song:

> A col' frosty mo'nin,'
> De niggers mighty good,
> Take yo' ax upon yo' shoulder,
> Nigger, TALK to de wood.

Berry remembered how the woods echoed as hundreds of workers sang and swung their axes in unison: "Dey be lined up to a tree, an' dey sing dis song to mark de blows. Fust de one chop, den his pardner, an' when dey sing TALK dey all chop together; an' perty soon dey git de tree ready to fall an' dey yell 'Hi' an' de niggers all scramble out de way quick 'cause you can't never tell what way a pine tree gonna fall." Occasionally, she remarked, the workers sung a different song:

Dis time tomorrow night,
Where will I be?
I'll be gone, gone, gone,
Down to Tennessee.[78]

Cut off from regular plantation life, enslaved workers lived in makeshift shanty camps along the railroad, near their work. One observer described the cramped conditions of enslaved men who worked on the Manchester & Wilmington line and commented that they rarely saw women and were separated from their families:

> The railroad hands sleep in miserable shanties along the line. Their bed is an inclined pine board—nothing better, softer, or warmer. . . . The temperature of the cabin, at this season of the year (November), is bitterly cold and uncomfortable. I frequently awoke, at all hours, shivering with cold, and found shivering slaves huddled up near the fire. . . . Poor fellows! in that God-forsaken section of the earth they seldom see a woman from Christmas to Christmas. If they are married men, they are tantalized by the thought that their wives are performing for rich women of another race those services that would brighten their own gloomy life-pathway. They may, perhaps—who knows?—have still sadder reflections.[79]

Canal workers faced similar conditions. Digging canals was backbreaking physical work requiring strong men. As historian David Cecelski has remarked, it was "the cruelest, most dangerous, unhealthy, and exhausting labor in the American South."[80] Unsurprisingly, most southern canals—the Brunswick and Altamaha, the Muscle Shoals, and the Dismal Swamp, for example—were dug by enslaved men.[81] Many canal companies owned their enslaved workforce. Those that sought to hire them placed advertisements in local newspapers. In 1848, an advertisement required "150 ABLE BODIED NEGRO MEN" to work on the James River and Kanawha Canal. The notice attempted to alleviate slaveholders' fears of the notorious working conditions of canal workers: "We will feed and house the hands well, and will also pay the Doctors' bill, if any. We believe our work and location is as healthy as any portion so the state . . . and have not had a solitary case of fever. . . . Our work is unusually light and dry, and but little risk to encounter; and our Shanties are of the best kind."[82] This was not the experience of Moses Grandy, who commented on the working conditions for enslaved men on the Dismal Swamp Canal: "The labor there is very severe. The ground is often very boggy: the negroes are up to the middle or much deeper in mud and water, cutting away roots and baling out mud: if they can keep their heads above water, they work on." Grandy also remarked on the living conditions of the enslaved workforce: "They lodge in huts, or as they are called camps, made of shingles or boards. They lie down in the mud which has adhered to them, making a great fire to dry themselves, and keep off the cold. No bedding whatever is allowed them; it is only by work done over his task, that any of them can get a blanket."[83] As in the railroad, turpentine and lumber industry, these men lived in separate, all-male work camps, cut off from the opposite sex and their families.[84] Usually, they were permitted only very limited visiting rights to see their wives and families. Particularly revealing is the correspondence of a slave owner, Iverson L. Twyman of Virginia, who regularly hired out his slaves to work on the canals and railroads. At the beginning of 1851, he arranged for one of his slaves, Gilbert, to visit his wife only "three times in a year, with an allowance of nine days at each time." This was apparently a generous arrangement—Twyman believed he was doing the couple a favor so "they may be better satisfied."[85] Separated from their loved ones, canal workers soon learned to depend on one another as they dug day after day in boggy, dangerous, disease-ridden conditions. Sometimes they exhibited exceptional displays of solidarity in the most miserable circumstances. At Juniper Bay, North Carolina, the overseer spent an entire day whipping every single canal worker because none would identity the slave who had stolen his fowl. None confessed or informed on their workmates.[86]

Enslaved men worked together as fishermen. In 1835, around 8,000 slaves worked for the Potomac River fisheries. In 1850, approximately 5,000 enslaved and free African Americans worked along the Albemarle Sound. The Albemarle commercial shad, rockfish, and herring seine fisheries relied heavily on enslaved labor. Gangs of enslaved men fished, while women and children gutted and cleaned the fish on the shore.[87] The lack of large commercial fisheries meant that most enslaved fishermen worked after their masters' cotton was hoed or tobacco was cut. These men usually fished for themselves, their masters' families, and for local barter, rather than commercial purposes. Fishermen worked in small gangs or alone—often in remote places. Life was dangerous, and little profit was made. However, enslaved fishermen enjoyed the independence of their job.[88] Former slave

Charles Ball recalled the autonomy and camaraderie enjoyed by fishermen while they operated a shad fishery for their master during spring. Initially supervised by a white fisherman, Ball and three other enslaved fishermen were left to their own devices while seining at night. Separated from the rest of the enslaved on his master's cotton plantation, Ball and his team worked, slept, and ate together. Ball recalled, "We all lived well, and did not perform more work than we were able to bear." He also traded some of the shad they caught for a supply of bacon, enabling him and his companions to live "sumptuously . . . unmolested by our master." Ball revealed the bond he felt to one of his fellow fisherman: "He was a good natured, kind hearted man, and did many acts of benevolence for me, such as one slave is able to perform for another, and I felt a real affection for him."[89]

Enslaved men worked together in factories across the South, processing plantation crops. Hired male slaves comprised the majority of the workforce in the tobacco factories of Virginia and North Carolina. By 1860, 12,843 slaves worked in this industry. In 1850, 90 percent of the enslaved workforce was male. The few women who worked in tobacco factories were stemmers (they removed the midribs from the tobacco leaves) or cooks, while the men performed the arduous task of pressing.[90] As in the ironworks and coal mines, companies paid slaves for overtime. Enslaved men took advantage of this arrangement and provided extra food and clothing for their loved ones.[91] In the rice mills and sugar refineries, tasks were often assigned on a gendered basis: men performed heavy tasks; women and children placed sugar cane on conveyor belts, fed the cars, carted trash, washed, and boiled juice.[92] Salt firms utilized a predominantly male workforce. Of the workers who labored in the salt industries of Kanawha, Virginia, 75 percent were men. Women often worked as cooks.[93] Hemp production was dirty and laborious and almost entirely performed by slaves. Men undertook most of the work in the fields because, in the words of one observer, "None but our strong, able negro men can handle it to advantage." Indeed, one commentator asserted, "Negro women cannot labor at hemp at all and are scarcely worth anything." Most of the factory workforce was male; women cooked and performed housekeeping duties for enslaved people who were housed and fed on the premises.[94] Perhaps the only industry that utilized predominantly women in its enslaved workforce—for reasons of cost and control—was the textile industry.[95]

Many enslaved men who worked in city factories lived in distinct male homosocial spaces. It was common for slaves working in the city to live with their masters or agents or to find their own accommodation, which prevented the concentration of slaves free from white supervision. However, some slaves who worked in the large tobacco and iron enterprises were housed in large, men-only dormitories and barracks that contained anywhere from ten to a hundred slaves. According to historian Richard Wade, this arrangement was not uncommon in cities such as Richmond and Charleston. Wade suggests that the greater instability of slavery in the towns meant that relationships between the sexes were weak and rarely permanent. As one observer commented, "husbands and wives most commonly belong to different families. Laboring apart, and having their meals apart, the domestic bonds of domestic life are few and weak." In the absence of such ties, it is conceivable that enslaved urban men turned to each other for practical and emotional support, thus strengthening male solidarity.[96]

Enslaved men who worked in southern industries labored in markedly homosocial masculine spaces and developed their own masculine work culture. These men lived interdependent lives—living, sleeping, and working in close proximity to one another. In many cases, they were forced to live and work disconnected from their families and regular plantation life.

Skilled Work

Apart from household work, midwifery, nursing, and seamstress roles, skilled occupations were almost exclusively held by enslaved men, who worked as carpenters, blacksmiths, bricklayers, coopers, cobblers, ironsmiths, masons, tanners, and wheelwrights. Men used these jobs to rank and order themselves in the homosocial sphere and wider community. Using the words of Deborah Gray White, these skilled jobs "created a yardstick" through which enslaved men could "measure their achievements."[97] Men took pride in these roles and enjoyed benefits that were simply unavailable to field slaves. Skilled slaves created their own masculine work culture; they served as important mentors and masculine role models to younger boys.

On most farms and plantations throughout the South, the enslaved workforce was too small to assign permanent skilled roles. On small and medium plantations, skilled slaves usually performed specialized tasks when required and then returned to the field. To permanently allocate formal labor divisions between house and field slaves, planters needed well over fifty slaves.[98] But even on large plantations, during the busy planting and harvesting seasons, owners did not hesitate to send skilled and semiskilled slaves into the fields.[99] Historians calculate that approximately 25 percent of slaves were skilled—the remainder worked as field laborers. Skilled work included household, artisanal, mechanical, and transportation work; working with livestock; and midwifery and nursing roles.[100] The very concept of "skill," however, has been debated by historians. For example, Charles Joyner has asserted, "One could plausibly argue that virtually all the field hands on a rice plantation should be classified as skilled laborers, in view of the level of competence required in rice culture."[101] Recently, Daina Berry has emphasized that "agricultural workers (male and female alike) acquired skills crucial to the production of staple crops; therefore, in some instances, the connection between field and unskilled labor is inappropriate."[102] For the purposes of this discussion, though, "skilled labor" refers to the non-agricultural skilled tasks, chiefly artisanal work, performed by enslaved men away from the field. In spite of some variations, on large plantations throughout the South, the experiences of skilled slaves were generally the same: planters selected enslaved men to work as artisans, mechanics, animal minders, drivers, and transporters and women as midwives, nurses, and domestic servants.[103]

"Dey had special mens on de plantation for all de special wuk," recalled former slave Bill Heard.[104] On large plantations, enslaved men worked in a variety of skilled roles: carpenters, blacksmiths, bricklayers, coopers, cobblers, ironsmiths, masons, tanners, and wheelwrights. Skilled slaves were valuable assets for slaveholders; as one former slave recalled, a carpenter or blacksmith "always was worth more money dan a field hand."[105] Accordingly, masters knew that if slaves learned trades, it would increase their values.[106] Slave owners were profit-motivated individuals; when they were not employing the services of these men on their own plantations, they hired them out for money to other plantations in the neighborhood. James Henry Stith recalled that his enslaved father was a carpenter "of the first class" and was constantly in demand. When he wasn't working for his master, W. W. Simpson, "he was working for the next big farmer, and then the next one, and then the next one . . . sometimes he worked a contract." In this way, the master received wages for Stith's father's work. According to Stith, his father's time "was valuable."[107] Skilled men gained respect from both the black and white community. Duncan Heyward recollected that the blacksmith Caesar Pencile, who worked on his family's rice plantation, was "respected by master and overseer alike."[108] Likewise, Elizabeth W. Allston Pringle, daughter of Robert F. W. Allston, owner of one of the largest plantations in South Carolina, recalled that on Chicora Wood plantation the head carpenter "was a great person . . . so dignified."[109] Margaret Devereux, the young mistress of a North Carolina plantation, fondly described the work of one of the enslaved plantation carpenters as "beautiful." According to her, the head carpenter, Jim, who was also a preacher, was "highly thought of by both white and back."[110]

Within slave communities, social status was not dependent on what enslaved laborers could do for the white slaveholding class. Rather, as John W. Blassingame has argued, "slaves reserved the top rungs of the social ladder for those blacks who performed services for other slaves rather than for whites." In Blassingame's classification system, conjurors, physicians, midwives, preachers, teachers, and entertainers were placed at the top. The "middle class" chiefly consisted of self-employed slaves, mobile slaves, and artisans, while the "lower class" was made up of ordinary field hands and short-term live-in house servants. Exploitative drivers, live-in house servants with a long tenure, voluntary concubines, and informants were regarded as the lowest of the low.[111] WPA testimony indicates that enslaved male artisans employed their skills for the benefit of their families and others and were, accordingly, afforded a great deal of respect from both enslaved men and women. Mark Oliver recalled the "pretty smart one among the slaves" who was the plantation carpenter. He marveled at the "beautiful" beds the carpenter made for the enslaved community: "Every one of them had a tester, like a canopy over it."[112] Luke Wilson recalled that his uncle, the carpenter on his plantation, "kept the houses in good shape," ensuring that slaves "had good comfortable quarters."[113] Enslaved artisans directly employed their skills for the benefit of their own families. George Washington Browning, whose father was a shoemaker, recalled, "many a night I have held the light for my father to see by to make shoes for us. He often give me a dime."[114] Former slaves fondly recollected the occasions their fathers made furniture for their family.[115] Zach Herndon declared, "All us had, was a table, benches and beds. And my paw made dem."[116] Another boasted, "My pappy made all de furniture dat went in our house an' it were might' good furniture too."[117]

Many enslaved artisans provided for their families from the proceeds of hiring-out arrangements. Some planters presented these men with gifts for their services, such as food, cloth, and other items, which could be used for their families, bartered, or sold for cash within slave communities.[118] It was not unusual for slaveholders to give male artisans small portions of the money they made for their owners as a result of their hire. J. H. Curry described his father as a "fine carpenter." "Sometimes he went off and worked and would bring the money back to his master, and his master would give him some for himself."[119] Men used this money to provide for their families. Harriet Jacobs disclosed, at the start of her slave narrative, that she felt "shielded growing up in a comfortable home" where her father was an "intelligent and skilful" carpenter who brought home wages for his family.[120] Such accounts confirm that skilled slaves performed the masculine role of provider for their families and gained respect accordingly.

What is particularly striking in the WPA narratives, however, is the relationship shared between father and son. Skilled work enabled them to spend time with one another, teaching and learning skills. Carey Davenport, for instance, proudly proclaimed that his father was a blacksmith, a carpenter, and a wheelwright—a "valuable man" on the plantation. Davenport boasted, "He make the bes' Carey plows in that part of the country." "He uster be specially good at makin' the mould board (turning shear). The mould board was made out of hardwood. It had a iron point what my pa make." Davenport listed many other examples of his father's skills: "He make horseshoes, nails and anything make out of iron, and he shod the horses and the mules. He uster make spinnin' wheels and parts of looms . . . he make wheels, make the hub and put the spokes in and set up the whole wagon wheel." Davenport's father also made oxen yokes: "He shape up the beam and make the bows. He holler out a place in a log and put the wood he goin' to make the bow outer in it. There was two pieces of wood standin' up about the middle of the bow. They put a lever on it and ben' up one end and put a clevis on it. Den he put the lever on the other end and put the clevis on that and that kep' it bent. Then he let it season and git the shape. I help him make many a one."[121] The detail of knowledge Davenport evinces is significant: it demonstrates that he spent many occasions with his father and picked up extensive knowledge of his father's skills. Indeed, rather than learning their trade from whites, by the mid-eighteenth century, the majority of enslaved artisans acquired their skills from other slaves.[122] In the antebellum South, these skills were passed down from one generation to the next, typically from father to son. Many WPA interviewees revealed that they learned skills from their fathers; Morris Hillyer, for example, learned carpentry from his father.[123] Likewise, James Henry Stith followed his father's occupation of carpentry and made a living out of it for fifty-four years.[124] Learning a trade enabled men to forge closer father-son ties. If skilled artisans were separated from their sons, they may have "adopted" other youngsters to teach their skills to. In this sense, apprenticeships between older and younger men could have operated similarly to kin ties. By passing skills down, enslaved men affirmed intergenerational masculine bonds in the slave community. Elders served as role models for boys and young men. Learning trades also took place in masculine spaces; with women working in the field, or as domestic servants, the workshops located on large plantations were exclusively masculine worlds. Margaret Devereux, for instance, recalled that on her plantation in North Carolina, four men—Jim, Austin, Bill, and Frank—worked together in the "carpenter's shop."[125]

On large plantations, in industry, and in skilled work, enslaved men often labored together in markedly homosocial spaces, where they created their own distinctive masculine work culture and identity. On large plantations, in sex-segregated gangs, enslaved men usually undertook the most physically arduous tasks—plowing; ditch-digging; and chopping, mauling, and hauling wood—while women grubbed and hoed. Although enslaved women sometimes plowed and chopped wood in separate work gangs, enslaved men considered these jobs masculine.[126] Enslaved men who worked in certain southern industries—naval stores or lumber—or those working on the railroads and canals, lived, slept, and worked together in male camps, separated from their families for long durations. These men performed particularly dangerous jobs. They relied on each other for support and friendship; cooperation and interdependence characterized their everyday lives. Both the free and enslaved communities highly respected artisanal work. Enslaved artisans took pride in their work; it was an avenue through which they could forge their own unique work culture.

2

Enslaved Men and Leisure

After their day was done, enslaved men returned home to begin their own domestic chores and, if possible, spend time with their families. They also spent their precious free time socializing with other men. As in the all-male world of the work gang, men created homosocial spaces in their leisure time. Many drank, gambled, and wrestled; for enslaved men, these were welcome moments of pleasure. Here, they could escape the grueling demands of work and affirm their own humanity. As former slave Frank Williams recalled, "de mos' fun we had in dem days was stealin' whiskey, drinkin' it and fightin.'"[1] This chapter analyzes the leisure activities of enslaved men. It argues that these were not safety valves working to the advantage of the owner, but rather, through these activities, enslaved men resisted their enslavement. Drinking, gambling, and wrestling together, enslaved men contested the emasculating effects of slavery and constructed their own notions of masculinity. Together, in homosocial spaces, enslaved men exercised agency, fostered camaraderie, and raised their self-esteem. To understand male resistance to slavery, it is crucial to study the everyday battles these men fought for control over their lives. Like most subordinate classes, enslaved men were denied access to "formal, organized political activity," and so, as historians, we must look to everyday hidden spaces to examine the conflicts between masters and slaves.[2] This chapter, therefore, shifts attention from the visible, organized world of slave rebellion—of which much has been written—to the hidden and private world of enslaved men.[3] Indeed, to understand slave rebellion, we must first examine the personal and private spaces of enslaved men; for here, in defiance of their owners, they created a homosocial culture of opposition that shaped the fraternal world of conspiracy and rebellion.

The task system in the Lowcountry afforded slaves a relative degree of autonomy after their daily tasks were completed for their owners. But most were compelled to spend the remainder of the day working their own gardens, performing domestic chores, fishing, or hunting. As former South Carolina slave Sam Polite recalled, "You haf for wuk 'til tas' t'ru . . . W'en you knock off wuk, you kin wuk on your land."[4] In the Upcountry, where the gang labor system was employed, enslaved people usually labored from sunup to sundown. Returning home in the dark, they tended garden patches and hunted in the moonlight and completed domestic chores by candlelight.[5] Little leisure time, therefore, was available; however, many enslaved people managed to carve out time for recreation. Most slaves in the Upcountry and Lowcountry were granted Saturday nights and Sundays off; some had Saturday afternoons off as well. Matthew Hume recalled that his fellow slaves in Kentucky were "free from Saturday noon until Monday morning," during which time the majority would "drink, gamble and fight."[6] Holidays, such as Christmas and the Fourth of July, were special days when no work was undertaken. Depending on the owner, the Christmas holidays could last from a few days to two weeks.[7] Corn shuckings were also occasions for much celebration and festivity: these intense periods of work culminated in organized parties, barbecues, games, dancing, and wrestling for the enslaved. Although masters staged these events, formerly enslaved people fondly recalled them: "Dat am de time dat weuns all looks fo'ward to," recalled former slave Charley Hurt.[8] In addition to these authorized days off, many slaves defied the temporal restrictions imposed by their owners and pursued their own leisure activities at night, away from the eyes of the slaveholders.[9]

Drinking

Alcohol was produced on numerous plantations of the antebellum South.[10] Respondents to the WPA interviews recalled in detail how the enslaved workforce produced cider, brandy, and corn liquor from fruit such as apples and peaches. Abraham Coker commented, "Dey'd put it in lahge barrels and let it sour, den dey'd drain it through copper pipes." Coker's master had a large orchard, and so he permitted his slaves to gather all the fruit they wanted: "Mawster Johnson would ob felt insulted if yo' come up and ast to buy fruit."[11] George Patterson recalled that when the plantation owners in the Enoree River section had a surplus of fruit, they made apple and peach brandy and stored the alcohol in kegs until they were either sold for forty cents a gallon or consumed by the owners themselves.[12] Although various laws restricted drinking among enslaved people, masters often distributed alcohol to them to keep warm during the cold winter months, for medicinal purposes, and during harvesttime and the Christmas period.[13]

"All the slaves got their whiskey with their 'weekly rashins,' 'cording to the size of the fam'ly," Luke Wilson reported. "Everybody had to have a drink—or 'toddy'—before they went to work in the mawning—during the Fall and Winter—to 'keep off the chills.'"[14] Children were given some "toddy" when the weather proved particularly cold. As Joseph Holmes testified, "mah daddy wud git de brandy out an' mah maw wud put a li'l water an' sugar wid hit an' gib tuh us chillun. An' den she'd take sum in her mouf' an' put hit in de baby's mouf'."[15] Slaveholders distributed whiskey to enslaved people to treat all kinds of ailments: measles, snakebites, and cramps; it was also given to women after childbirth. Enslaved in Georgia, Andrew Moss remembered his master gave the slaves a glass of whiskey every night, believing it would keep them free from disease.[16]

Slave owners distributed large quantities of alcohol to their slaves during corn shuckings—periods when the workforce had to work especially hard to gather in the harvest from the fields. First, a "general," who led the singing, was elected among the workers. The faster the general sung, the faster the "shucks flew." Enslaved people from neighboring plantations assisted, and "plenty of corn liquor was passed 'round" to make the workers "hustle."[17] Owners usually distributed alcohol to men during the shuckings. Former slave William Henry commented that whiskey was given to the men in order to "revive em," while Millie Smith stated that the master would "come round now and then and give the men a drink."[18] Indeed, slaveholder Richard Eppes recorded in his plantation diary that while harvesting the wheat from one of his plantations on the James River, he distributed whiskey only to the male workforce—the women, along with three men, "drew no whiskey."[19] Some men brought their own whiskey to the field, and "dey'd take a drink after comin' out of each row."[20] Big crowds sung while they worked, and anyone who found a red ear of corn could expect a prize such as "kissin' a gal, or de drink ob brandy."[21] Although it was hard work, enslaved men clearly looked forward to corn shuckings; as Jim Allen reported, "the men didn't care if dey worked all night, for we had the 'Heavenly Banner's' (women and whiskey) by us."[22] But the most fun was reserved for after the corn shuckings, whereby big barbecues, frolics, and dances were organized and enjoyed by the enslaved. James Bolton described how the slaves tried to finish the shucking by sundown so that they could frolic, drink liquor, and dance from sundown to sunup.[23]

Likewise, on holidays, such as the Fourth of July and Christmas, masters staged festivals of drinking, barbecues, singing, and dancing for the enslaved, inviting slaves from neighboring plantations to gather. Similar to the corn shuckings, during these holiday periods slaveholders distributed alcohol to the men. Cato Carter recollected, it was a time of "presents for every body," when both young and old were glad, "'specially the Nigger mens 'count of plenty good whiskey."[24] Harriet Jones recalled, her owners would give the men "a keg of cider or wine on de back porch, so dey all have a li'l Christmas Spirit."[25] If faced with a less than generous owner, one former slave indicated, "the men would save enough out of the crops to buy their Christmas whiskey."[26]

Men dominated the underground trade in alcohol. To enjoy the pleasures of drink during the week and on weekends, they stole alcohol from stores, farms, and slave owners. Formerly enslaved people remembered the theft fondly; they sometimes recounted it in almost folkloric fashion, replete with the wit and trickery of a Brer Rabbit tale. Ephriam Lawrence, for example, relayed how his master had to keep a lot of liquor on the plantation because the master's friend, Mr. Binyard, drank a lot when he visited—as did the slaves secretly. Lawrence admired how "slick" one slave, John Fraser, was when the master called for him to fetch some liquor from the cellar. Fraser returned from the cellar empty-handed and claimed that Binyard had drunk all the liquor while a guest at supper the previous night. He exclaimed, "You know how Mr. Binyard drink. Sometime he drink when your back t'un. How you 'speck um to last?" The master was not satisfied but could not prove that Fraser or the other slaves were helping themselves to the liquor.[27] Enslaved men sometimes bored holes in whiskey barrels in order to siphon the alcohol out with straws. "I always slip all I want," recounted Jerry Boykins, who admitted that one day he was caught in the act because he couldn't resist a drink: "Ole Master caught me on the floor one day too drunk to git away, he whupped me 'til I got sober."[28]

When no alcohol was available to steal on the plantation, some enslaved men stole valuable goods from the plantation and traded them with neighboring poor whites or free blacks for alcohol. Ben Horry's father regularly stole rice from his master and traded it for whiskey in town: "My father love he liquor. That take money. He ain't have money but he have the rice barn key and *rice* been money!" Horry commented on his father's cunning and shrewdness: "he have a head, my father"; he described how his father smuggled the rice into the woods and placed it in a hollow stump, where, to prepare it for sale, he ground it under torchlight with two pestles he had hidden. While accompanying his master to town on Saturday to acquire the weekly provisions, Horry's father would sell the stolen rice and buy liquor.[29] Leaving the plantation on business was usually reserved for enslaved men who transported goods to town, retrieved purchases, and ran errands. As Horry's testimony demonstrates, some men took advantage of these arrangements and stole, purchased, and traded to supply enslaved communities with alcohol.

In addition to the authorized social occasions of corn shuckings, Christmas, and the Fourth of July, enslaved men enjoyed drinking the alcohol they illicitly acquired throughout the year at parties on Saturday nights or at occasional secretly organized parties on weekday nights. The WPA narratives are replete with descriptions of these dances and parties, enjoyed by both enslaved men and women and filled with music, dance, and entertainment. "Saturday night . . . the slaves had moonlight dance," reported former slave Mary Gaffney; "that was the happiest time of the slaves because the rest of the time it was just about like being a convict, we had to do just like Maser told us." "Out there in the woods" Gaffney's master "would not be there to holler instructions." Not having to work on Sunday, they danced "all night long" to the sound of a "negro banjo picker" and the sound of "beating on tin pans."[30] One prominent feature of these social gatherings recalled by those interviewed for the WPA narratives was the drinking of alcohol by men. Albert Oxner remembered how "nearly every man would get drunk."[31] Indeed, one former enslaved man admitted that he "uster live mighty bad sometimes," dancing and drinking all night long; he was able to "drink a pint of whiskey at a time."[32] "Some uf dem men folks wud git a lit'l too much to drink," recalled Rina Brown, "but dey never done no mischief."[33]

Through the conspicuous consumption of alcohol at social gatherings, enslaved men affirmed their masculinity. Many cross-cultural studies emphasize the gendered implications of drinking; they argue that gendered differences are universal and have remained remarkably consistent over time: "Men's drinking predominates for virtually all ages, ethnic groups, geographic regions, religions, education levels, incomes, and categories of marital status," claim Russell Lemle and Marc Mishkind.[34] Mary Douglas has argued that drinking is a "social act": it allows people to reaffirm their social world and acts as "markers of personal identity" and of "boundaries of inclusion and exclusion."[35] Men drink to underscore specific gendered demarcations and, in the process, emphasize their masculinity. Drinking was a highly gendered activity in the African cultural background of many enslaved people. In precolonial Ghana, male elders and chiefs—those who held the highest ranks in rural communities—tightly controlled alcohol and excluded women and young men from drinking. It was, therefore, an important means of reinforcing gender, age, and status roles.[36] Similarly, in the United States, enslaved men reinforced gendered roles through drinking. Speaking in the mid-1930s, formerly enslaved people noted the cultural differences between slavery and contemporary times. Frankie Goole was angry that women of the current generation were drinking and declared that he was "disgusted" at his "own color." He admitted, "I tries ter shame deze 'omen, dey drink (I call hit ole bust haid whiskey), en do such mean things."[37] Recalling his enslavement, W. M. Green stated, "Nobody ever heard of a girl drinking and smoking den."[38] This is not to deny that enslaved women drank alcohol—evidence shows they sometimes did.[39] Rather, Green's comment demonstrates how men identified the "social act" of drinking as a masculine preserve; it was a way enslaved men affirmed their masculinity. As well as commenting on the gendered differences of drinking, those interviewed for the WPA narratives noted that drinking was a preserve of elders and that "the older ones would get drunk."[40] Gus Bradshaw described growing up in slavery: "Chil'ren was raised right then" compared to the youngsters of the contemporary period. He expressed his disgust at the younger generation who drank in front of their elders: "I wouldn't dare do that when I was coming up."[41] Former slave Neal Upson recalled a failed attempt to be masculine like his father: as a young boy he stole his father's liquor and drank it until he passed out. His father gave him a "tannin'," but Upson drank the alcohol because he did "love to follow" his father.[42] The drinking of alcohol by enslaved men, therefore, acted as a social marker signifying manhood and enforced age and status roles.

Homosocial Drinking and Gambling Spaces

Enslaved men regularly met with other men to drink and gamble—usually at night or on the Sabbath; they held these homosocial gatherings in secret, sometimes beyond the boundaries of the plantations in woods, swamps, or outhouses. Here, far from the eyes of their owners, they created an autonomous masculine world. For example, during the antebellum period, all the groups of slaves brought before the Court of Magistrates and Freeholders in upcountry South Carolina charged with drunkenness, disorderly conduct, and drinking on the Sabbath shared a common characteristic: they were all men.[43] Gambling—especially cards and craps—was a popular activity enjoyed by groups of enslaved men.[44] Former slave Midge Burnett recalled a scene from his days of bondage in North Carolina: "On moonlight nights yo' could hear a heap of voices an' when yo' peep ober de dike dar am a gang of niggers a-shootin' craps an' bettin' eber'thing dey has stold frum de plantation. Sometimes a pretty yaller gal er a fat black gal would be dar, but mostly hit would be jist men."[45] In upcountry South Carolina, groups of enslaved men were brought before the courts and charged with illicit assembly, gaming, and gambling.[46] In Kershaw District, trial testimony describes how a patrol stumbled upon a group of enslaved men playing cards gathered between the hours of 1:00 and 2:00 a.m. under the dwelling of one Mr. H. R. Cook. On discovery, "the party blew out the candle & Ran & Escaped by jumping through the windows and doors."[47] In Laurens District, Silas, a slave of Robert and Mary McClintock, was convicted of gaming with cards on July 6, 1861, and sentenced to 105 lashes. During the trial, one slave testified that he had played cards and gambled money with Silas and that "they played five up . . . in his masters negro house until nearly day light."[48] As the testimony of Midge Burnett indicates, many enslaved men gambled with items stolen from the plantation. Silas, for example, apparently stole his stake money from a Captain B. J. Jones, who had fallen off his horse. While the captain lay there dazed, Silas took $37 from his pocket.[49] Similarly, in Anderson District, two enslaved men, George and Manuel, were found guilty of gambling and stealing $39 in bank notes from Daniel Mattison's plantation. Witnesses at the trial claimed they "had seen Manuel and George playing cards several times and betting money."[50]

Sociologists and anthropologists have studied the social characteristics of gambling—as well as the psychological motivations of individuals. Monetary gain, they have argued, is not necessarily the most important motivation. For example, Irving Zola's study of gambling among men in a 1960s New England working-class neighborhood drew attention, rather, to the friendships and group solidarity that developed, arguing that gambling "creates a bond between the men—a bond which defines insiders and outsiders."[51] Similarly, on the subject of gambling in the white antebellum South, Wyatt-Brown purports that the rationale for gambling was the "camaraderie" it afforded.[52] The "insiders and outsiders" that Zola mentions are comparable to the boundaries of "inclusion and exclusion" that Douglas proposed exists through the act of drinking. By slipping off to the woods together to gamble, slave men defied the spatial regulations imposed by the slaveholder and erected physical boundaries and symbolic borders to reinforce the division of gender and simultaneously foster homosocial group solidarity. Moreover, as trial records demonstrate, these gatherings had the potential to develop cross-plantation contacts, friendships, and solidarity. Certainly, all of the cases of gaming and gambling brought before the courts in Anderson District, South Carolina, shared three common features: they were composed exclusively of enslaved men, who were always in groups, and with cross-plantation company. On occasions, however, gambling threatened to dissolve friendships and cross-plantation alliances. As Primous Magee disclosed in his testimony, "I'se gone deep in de woods many a time wid a bunch o' niggers an' build a big fire and shot craps all night. Some times hit would go off alright an' again dier would be a disagreement wid a few fights."[53] According to trial testimony from Anderson District, South Carolina, one Sunday evening, four enslaved men who were gambling with playing cards got into an argument over a coat. One of the witnesses at the trial, Aleck, the slave of E. Norris, heard a "considerable noise out in the woods." When Aleck approached the scene to see what was going on, he saw Joe and Berry "in a quarrel about a coat, saw a scuffle & Clement's boys took the coat of Berry."[54]

Although "crap shootin' wuz de style den," Charlie Crump recollected that most of the time "dey can't find nothin ter bet."[55] Given how precious the meager property of the enslaved was, gambling was not as widespread as drinking. The few accounts of gambling pursuits relayed by the enslaved in the WPA narratives are dwarfed by the many stories of drinking—the main leisure pursuit for male homosocial groups.

Sociologists and anthropologists agree that drinking is primarily a social pursuit and a vital expression of sociability. In diverse cultures throughout the world, people drink to socialize, make friends, and affirm their friendships. To offer someone a drink is a sign of hospitality. Rituals such as the toast endorse the acceptance of an individual in a group.[56] In traditional rural West Africa—the cultural background of enslaved people—drink functions as a powerful unifying network fostering solidarity and affection. Presenting beer among equals is a mark of affection; close friends save drinks for one another. Named drinking societies facilitate institutionalized male friendships.[57] Similarly, in the American South, enslaved men drank together to enhance sociability, foster camaraderie, and validate friendship. Former slave Andrew Jackson Jarnagin recounted his enslavement in Noxubee County, Mississippi:

> Us "niggers" used to git together some nights, and we would clink our whiskey glasses together (dat meant friendship) and recite a toast:
>
> Come all of you Virginia boys
> And listen to my song
> And let us concern the young man that made no corn.
> July's corn was knee high,
> September laid it by.
> And the weeds and grass growed so high,
> It caused the young man to cry.[58]

In this way—inviting men to share a drink, toasting, and singing in groups—male solidarity was reaffirmed. As Jarnagin states, by "clinking" their glasses together, these enslaved men symbolically expressed and confirmed their friendship. Friendship also extended beyond the plantation: groups of enslaved men brought before the courts in Anderson District, South Carolina, charged with drinking and drunkenness often hailed from different plantations.[59] In these cases, male drinkers networked with other men from different plantations, fostering cross-plantation ties and friendships.

Enslaved male drinkers reinforced social order among themselves: getting too drunk and losing control of oneself was taboo.[60] According to slave testimony, drinkers in peer groups monitored one another. Although, as Wash Wilson remarked, "mos' eberyboddy could carry dey likker purty well," some individuals drank excessively and were subsequently reproached for their behavior.[61] Calvin Moye recalled, "If any man gits drunk some men would takes him off and keeps him away till he sobers up." "If he was tryin ter be tough," he continued, "some men would goes to him and tells him plainly, 'Now you sobers up and behaves yourself or we is goin to gives you a good lesson.' And pretty soon you would see him sober up."[62] Moye's use of language is especially telling: if a man became too drunk, the other men physically removed him from the group and kept him away until he sobered up. Here, then, the boundaries of inclusion and exclusion operated:

the man had disrupted the drinking group by his intoxicated state and was therefore ostracized until he was deemed fit enough to be welcomed back. In this instance, masculinity seems to be equated with not how much a man drank but how well he could take his drink. Furthermore, Moye's description of the incident reveals the egalitarian nature of the drinking group: drinkers considered it unacceptable for one individual to try to be "tough" at the expense of the other men. Punishment in the form of exclusion ensued. The assertiveness of an individual was subordinate to the egalitarian group.

On occasions, the drinking group could not contain the egos, and fighting broke out. Anderson Furr remembered that if they got "too rowdy-lak, drinkin' liquor and fightin'," the white folks "slapped 'em in de gyardhouse, widout a bite to eat."[63] Cases brought before the Court of Magistrates and Freeholders in Anderson District, South Carolina, demonstrate the destructive effects of alcohol. In one case, two enslaved men were charged with drunkenness and the attempted murder of each other. Whiskey was found in their possession, and one witness claimed, "Charles said that he would knock Moses head off."[64] Indeed, rivalry between two men fuelled by drink also spilled out into work, as Mandy Jones recalled: "I 'members two men's gettin' drunk once and got to fightin'.' Overseer he made 'em quit an' shake hands and git back to work."[65] Drink, therefore, in addition to fostering solidarity, occasionally exacerbated antagonisms between individuals.

Psychologists have argued that men drink to attain or regain "a feeling of strength," making them seem "big, strong, and important."[66] Indeed, male respondents for the WPA interviews described the empowering effects of alcohol on individuals: "When dey gits likker in dem, dey thinks dey is important as de president," claimed Ballam Lyles.[67] Likewise, Will Parker admitted that drinking altered his disposition: it "makes me think I owns de world."[68] These feelings are especially important when considered within the context of slavery. By drinking, enslaved men had the potential to feel powerful and significant and hence temporarily renegotiate the power their owners held. To illustrate this idea, it is helpful to consider the "three bodies" theory Stephanie Camp employed in her research of enslaved women: "Enslaved people . . . possessed at least three bodies. The first served as a site of domination." This was the body that was "acted upon" by the slave owner, the "bio-text" upon which the owner "inscribed" his authority. "The second body was the subjective experience of this process," Camp writes. This was the "colonized body," where "sexual and nonsexual violence, disease, and exploitative labor" were experienced. The third was the "reclaimed body." In the struggle for mastery over bodies, enslaved women could reclaim this body from the view and control of the master by seeking pleasure in activities such as dancing, drinking, and attending illicit parties. As enslaved women sought pleasure in their bodies in this way, the third body potentially acted as a vital political site and source of resistance in opposition to the economic and symbolic imperatives of slavery.[69] One can draw on this idea to analyze enslaved men as well: men who intoxicated themselves exercised mastery over their bodies, temporarily alleviating feelings of humiliation, degradation, and emasculation. The drinker's "reclaimed body" therefore served as a site of resistance to slavery.

Southern whites feared intoxicated slaves: they equated slave drunkenness with agency, reduced productivity, and social disorder. In a report detailing the "moral and religious condition of the slave negro population," Presbyterian minister and slaveholder Charles Colcock Jones claimed shops selling alcohol to slaves "injure the pecuniary interests of the country . . . corrupt the morals, injure the health and destroy the lives of many of the Negroes; and are the greatest nuisances and sources of evil tolerated in the country."[70] Similarly, a petition presented to the Virginia Assembly in 1860 claimed one of "the great and most operative causes of the corrupting of the habits and morals of slaves, and of infusing into their minds discontent and the spirit of insubordination, and consequently of producing discomfort and unhappiness to themselves" and causing "injury to their masters" was the "unlicensed selling of intoxicating liquors to slaves."[71] Frederick Law Olmsted's travel narrative recorded the grievances of authorities in New Orleans who complained that "hundreds" of slaves "spend their nights drinking, carousing, gambling, and contracting the worst of habits, which not only make them useless to their owners but dangerous pests to society."[72] Indeed, petitions presented to southern legislatures pleaded for the introduction of legislation in order to prevent "any slave to be drunk, or engaged in any riotous, clamorous or disorderly conduct in any public place, store, shop, street or public road."[73] Slaveholders dreaded the ultimate form of social disorder: violent slave rebellion. They were aware that unruly, intoxicated slaves could become violent and resist their enslavement. Former slave Minnie Davis recalled that owners "couldn't risk giving slaves much whiskey because it made them mean, and then they would fight the white folks." Masters, she added, "had to be mighty careful about things like that in order to keep down uprisings."[74] Indeed, after the Nat Turner revolt and the

Denmark Vesey conspiracy, white authorities placed restrictions on African American drinking. For example, in South Carolina in 1831, authorities banned free African Americans from owning or operating stills.[75]

Political scientist James C. Scott has observed that in European culture authorities saw the social spaces of drinking—the pub, the tavern, the inn, and the beer cellar—as "places of subversion." In these spaces, subordinate classes gathered "off-stage and off-duty in an atmosphere of freedom encouraged by alcohol." Drinking in these establishments was "the main point of unauthorized assembly for lower-class neighbors and workers"; it was "the closest thing to a neighborhood meeting of subordinates." For subordinate groups who are precluded from open political activity, the drinking establishment *is* political life, and it constitutes part of the everyday, low-profile forms of resistance that Scott terms "the infrapolitics of the powerless."[76] The evidence from the antebellum South supports Scott's thesis. White authorities recognized the subversive potential of drinking congregations. Indeed, Nat Turner's rebellion was organized and initiated by a gang of enslaved men who met up to secretly drink the night before their rampage.[77] For these men, denied the "luxury of relatively safe, open political opposition," the informal organization of the drinking group functioned as a political discourse. Far from the authority and control of the slaveholder, they could drink and freely converse, complain, and scheme together to address their grievances.[78]

Organized Fighting Activities

Throughout the South, most enslaved men enjoyed the illicit pleasures of drinking and gambling; but one activity was prized above all: organized fighting. Both slaveholders and slaves arranged fighting matches between enslaved men. These were exclusively male spaces—only men engaged in these activities. Fighting was central to the homosocial culture of enslaved men. In the ring, they could stand tall. Momentarily, in front of their male peers, they could prove themselves men: tough, resilient and strong. They could rank themselves and bond with other men. Moreover, fighters could exercise mastery over their bodies.

Although as small boys enslaved men played mostly noncombative games—ring games, wolf-over-the-river, and hide-and-seek—some also wrestled.[79] Too young to enter the field and commence serious labor, slave boys typically ran errands and performed light chores; thus, they had more time for recreation than enslaved adults did. It was not unusual for slave children, while at play, to be joined by the master's children; as Gabriel Gilbert added, "De li'l white folks and nigger chillen uster jis' play 'roun' like brudder and sister." On these occasions, Gilbert added that the slave boys "hab fights and us fight de white boys and niggers jis' de same."[80] Other narratives document the reciprocal nature of this play. G. W. Offley explained his interaction with his master's son: "I learned him the art of wrestling, boxing and fighting, and he learned me to read."[81] Nonetheless, serious wrestling and other fighting activities tended to be reserved for the older boys and men. Furthermore, as slave boys came of age, they soon learned that fighting with the progeny of their white masters was unacceptable. Unlike those of small children, the fighting activities of older boys and young men were limited to the periods when they were not laboring in the field.

Often, fighting activities for enslaved men were controlled and monitored by the slaveholder. Isaac Wilson relayed that whereas the master provided a "play-ground fer de slave chillum ter play in," he had the older ones "run foot races, wrestle an' box." Wilson commented that some said these exercises were designed "to make de slaves develope an' long winded," but he nevertheless reported that he "had many a gran' time in deir."[82] Others reported that the masters had slaves "wrestling and knocking each other about" every Saturday night.[83] Henry Bibb gave perhaps the most descriptive account of such fights:

> Those who make no profession of religion, resort to the woods in large numbers on that day to gamble, fight, get drunk, and break the Sabbath. This is often encouraged by slaveholders. When they wish to have a little sport of that kind, they go among the slaves and give them whiskey, to see them dance, "pat juber," sing and play on the banjo. Then get them to wrestling, fighting, jumping, running foot races, and butting each other like sheep. This is urged on by giving them whiskey; making bets on them; laying chips on one slave's head, and daring another to tip it off with his hand; and if he tipped it off, it be called an insult, and cause a fight. Before fighting, the parties choose their seconds to stand by them while fighting; a ring or a circle is formed to fight in, and no one is allowed to enter the ring while they are fighting, but their seconds, and the white gentlemen. They are not allowed to fight a duel, nor to use weapons any kind. The blows are

Henry Bibb reported that large numbers of enslaved men drank, gambled, and fought one another on the Sabbath. This illustration, from Bibb's slave narrative, depicts plantation merriments on the Sabbath. On the right, two enslaved men, egged on by the slaveholder, wrestle. In the middle, two enslaved men knock their heads together—an African-derived fighting technique. *The Sabbath among Slaves*, in *Narrative of the Life and Adventures of Henry Bibb, an American Slave, Written by Himself* (New York: Author, 1849), 22.

made by kicking, knocking, and butting with their heads; they grab each other by their ears, and jam their heads together like sheep. If they are likely to hurt each other very bad, their masters would rap them with their walking canes, and make them stop. After fighting, they make friends, shake hands, and take a dram together, and there is no more of it.[84]

In this instance, the fighters seem to have been at the mercy of their owners. As Kenneth Greenberg points out, "They were like marionettes whose reaction to insult was determined by their masters." In terms of honor, Greenberg claims that the fighting replicated the form of the duel "without its substance."[85] One could hence argue that the impotence of enslaved men in this context served to validate the mastery of their owners. However, Bibb's narrative mentions two important points: this was not a fight to the death, and after the contest the two fighters shook hands and shared a drink, with there being "no more of it." Recently, in his analysis of African martial arts tradition in the Atlantic World, historian T. J. Desch-Obi has emphasized that these types of matches—intraplantation contests—"while serious," were not "life threatening" and thus were "not necessarily damaging to the contestants or in conflict with the bondsmen's honor code."[86]

The most common accounts of organized slave fights record those held at corn shuckings. As mentioned above, these were grand occasions affectionately remembered by the formerly enslaved as a time when they could indulge in various types of amusement. One such amusement was the "rastlin' match after de corn wus shucked."[87] Carter J. Jackson recalled how they had some "good fights" between men on the plantation at corn shuckings, but "no one was killed." Slaveholders, he recounted, staged and supervised organized cross-plantation bouts: "They matched fights between the Niggers from the different plantations. The Masters of the two fighting managed the fight to see it was fair."[88] Another ex-slave described how big these events were, involving large numbers of fighters from two plantations: "a crowd from Big Harper" and "a crowd from Little Harper." After the shucking, contestants were given whiskey, and "there'd be plenty of fighting," whereby "Little Harper white folks would take up for their darkies and the Big Harper white folks would do the same."[89] Many enslaved people relished the opportunity; they classed the matches as "amusements" where "everybody made the most of it."[90] One former slave commented: "I used to think them was the best times."[91]

Sometimes, masters raised some of their enslaved men as prizefighters and arranged fights with other slaves from different plantations for money. Oscar Felix Junell related how as soon as his father was "large enough to go to walkin' about," his master's son would "carry him about and make him rassle." Junell remarked that his father was "a good rassler," and, as a result, "as far as work was concerned, he didn't do nothing much of that. He just followed his young master all around rasslin."[92] Indicating the potentially rich rewards a good prizefighter could fetch for his owner, Josh Miles recalled a scene from the auction block that depicted prizefighting ability as a unique selling point: "De ole auctioneer start de biddin' off. He say, 'Dis nigger is eighteen years ole, he soun' as a dollar, an' he kin pick three hundred pounds ob cotton a day, good disposition, easy ter manage, come up an' examine him, look at his shoulders, regular prize-fighter; good cotton picker.'"[93]

An extraordinary account survives from John Finnely, a former slave who described in detail one of these inter-plantation prizefights. Finnely was enslaved with about seventy-five others on a cotton plantation in Jackson County, Alabama. For "'joyments," he remembered, "weuns have de co'n huskin' an' de nigger fights." Finnely delighted in his recollection of the slave fights he witnessed growing up in antebellum Alabama, noting that although they were arranged for the enjoyment of whites, enslaved people were allowed to see them. The masters of different plantations matched their slaves by size and then bet on them. Finnely's master owned an undefeated fighter named Tom, who weighed 150 pounds. Tom was quick and powerful and possessed a love for fighting. Finnely recalled witnessing a fight staged between him and a new challenger. The account is worth quoting at length because of its remarkable attention to every aspect of the fight, including descriptions of the rules, the fighting techniques, and the crowd:

De fight am held at night by de pine torch light. A ring am made by de fo'ks standin' 'roun' in de circle an' de niggers git in dat circle. Deys fight widout a rest 'til one give up or can't git up. Deys 'lowed to do anything wid dey hands, head and teeth. Sho, dat's it. Nothin' barred 'cept de knife an' clubs. Well sar, dem two niggers gits into de ring. Tom, dat am de Marster's nigger, him stahts quick lak him always do but de udder nigger stahts jus' as quick an' dat 'sprise Tom. It am de fust time a niggers jus' as quick as him. W'en deys come togedder, it am lak two bulls. Kersmash!, it sounds w'en deys hits. Den it am hit, kick, bite, an' butt anywhar, anyplace, anyway fo' to best de udder. Fust one down an' de udder on top apoundin', den 'tis de udder one on top. De one on de bottom, bites knees or anything dat him can do. Dat's de way it goes fo' ha'f an houah. Both am awful tired an' gittin' slow but am still fightin.' 'Taint much 'vantage fo' either one. Finally dat udder nigger gits Tom in de stomach wid his knee an' a lick 'side de jaw at de same time. Down goes Tom an' de udder nigger jumps on him wid both feet, den straddles him an' hits wid right, left, right, left, right, side Tom's head. Dere Tom layed makin' no 'sistence. Ever'body am saysin,' "Tom have met his match, him am done." Both am bleedin' an' am awful sight. Well, dat nigger relaxes fo 'to git his wind or something an' den Tom, quick lak a flash, flips him off an' jumps to his feet. Befo' dat nigger could git to his feet, Tom kicks him in de stomach, 'gain an' 'gain. Dat nigger's body stahts to quiver an' his Marster says, "'nough." Dat am de clostest dat Tom ever came to gittin' whupped dat I's know ob.[94]

Finnely portrays an intensely brutal prizefighting match, describing how both contestants bled and subsequently produced an "awful sight." Indeed, as opposed to intra-plantation matches for amusement purposes, "professional" slave prizefighting matches could be especially violent when big money was at stake, with the emphasis on employing any technique, including biting, to hurt the opponent as much as possible and win the contest.

However, he admitted that he enjoyed watching the fights, classing them as "'joyments on de plantation," and that Tom, the fighter, did "lak to fight" in these contests.[95] Additionally, as in the Bibb fight, the contest was not a fight to the death, and the master of Tom's opponent stepped in and ended the fight when his protégé's body started to "quiver." For the participants, prizefighting brought certain advantages. Former slave Oscar Felix Junell remarked that slaves fighting on behalf of their masters could expect certain privileges, such as reduced workloads. Other advantages could include better diet during the training periods prior to bouts, promotion to positions of authority on the plantation, respect from the slave communities, and, in rare instances, manumission, as in the case of the world-famous boxer Tom Molineaux.[96]

Fighting activities organized by slaveholders were hence not solely exploitative of enslaved men. Indeed, sociologists and anthropologists have suggested that a fighting activity such as boxing not only "exploits," it also "liberates."[97] Former featherweight champion Colin McMillan remarked, "In a world cloaked in prejudice, the ring is the one place where all men are equal. . . . To us pugilists the boxing arena is a place where we can raise our self esteem; where the short can stand tall, the weak become strong, and the shy become bold."[98] Fighting activities can thus act as a form of empowerment. In the context of slavery, the implications of this self-empowerment were significant: male fighters were able to exercise mastery over their bodies. Indeed, contrary to the claims that boxing animalizes its participants and teaches violent behavior, the discipline, strategy, strength, and movement needed in the ring require mastery of knowledge and physique. As one sociologist has claimed, "Boxing practices illustrate elements of self-control and of the need to negotiate identity through exercising agency over the body, by taking control."[99]

Closely analyzing Finnely's narrative corroborates these observations. Finnely's choice of language is telling because of the references to stamina, speed and surprise, and strength: their prominence suggests that they were specific qualities that were looked for in a match—essential qualities that were judged and celebrated and that dictated the outcome of the fight. Endurance and stamina, Finnely notes, ultimately determined the match: "Deys fight widout a rest 'til one give up or can't git up." Indeed, the account of the fight reveals that for half an hour both men were on the ground, one on top, one on the bottom, both changing positions, both "awful tired an' gittin' slow but am still fightin.'" The elements of speed and surprise were also celebrated; and these characteristics were usually Tom's trademark at the beginning of a fight: "Him stahts quick lak him always do." However, on this occasion, Tom's trademark was challenged; Finnely notes, "De udder nigger stahts jus' as quick an' dat 'sprise Tom." He narrates, "It am de fust time a niggers jus' as quick as him." Certainly, speed and surprise ultimately clinched victory for Tom. The other fighter pinned him and dealt a series of blows to his head, but, as the other fighter relaxed for an instant, Tom, "quick lak a flash, flips him off an' jumps to his feet." Tom then kicked the opponent repeatedly in the stomach until his body "quiver[ed]" and his master stepped in and called an end to the fight. Additionally, Tom's sheer strength and endurance are emphasized by his ability to come back from what seems the final barrage of blows in the match as he is pinned by his opponent. The reference to the opponent's quivering body portrays Tom as the stronger and ultimately superior fighter; he had controlled his body, through stamina, speed and surprise, and strength, whereas his opponent had failed the test, allowing his body to shake, thus signaling the end of the match.

Moreover, crucially, Tom proved he was master of his body and these qualities in the public sphere. Finnely underscores the importance of public performance with his description of the ring: "A ring am made by de fo'ks standin' 'roun' in de circle an' de niggers git in dat circle." Tom's reputation as a fighter was thus earned in the public eye of his fellow slaves and, indeed, of the whites who organized the fight. In this sphere, he could prove himself and force those detractors who doubted that he had the skill to win the match—and who commented that "Tom have met his match, him am done"—to revise their opinion. Tom's fighting skills were challenged and tested, and although Finnely admitted that that was "de clostest dat Tom ever came to gittin' whupped" that he knew of, he nevertheless answered the call to "best de udder" publicly, consequently proving himself to his peers. This idea of public display and "testing" is integral to David D. Gilmore's cross-cultural study of contemporary constructions of masculinity, which argues that masculinity is something that requires testing: it had to be proved in the presence of other men. Therefore, one's capacity to exist is determined in the public forum.[100] Gilmore's insights are especially applicable to the lives of nineteenth-century Americans. E. Anthony Rotundo has argued that a man's identity in early-nineteenth-century America "was inseparable from the duties he owed to his community"; he terms this "communal manhood." Likewise, Bertram Wyatt-Brown has argued that in the antebellum white South a man's identity was decided among "the *deme* or larger 'family' of peers and superiors called community."[101]

For enslaved men, possessing the skills and attributes of a fighter proved a vital source of self-respect and personal empowerment and a way to validate masculinity. Josiah Henson boasted in his fugitive slave narrative that he grew to be "a robust and vigorous lad" who upon reaching fifteen years of age could "run faster and farther, wrestle longer, and jump higher" than anybody else.[102] A "robust and vigorous" body like his not only endowed its possessor with pride and self-respect but also secured respect and admiration from others in the slave community. William Smith described his father as "a double-jointed man and very strong" and recounted how others would comment on his father's physique. "Man, was he strong!" said Smith; "de folks told me all about him . . . he was all muscle. Even de mawster had told de others dat dey had better not fight him, 'cause he was so strong dat he could break dere necks."[103] These "reclaimed" strong, muscular bodies could be celebrated as ideal masculine features for enslaved men, earning respect from other men and potentially attracting the attentions of enslaved women. Additionally, exhibitions of strength, speed, stamina, and surprise in the ring afforded enslaved men the opportunity to prove they possessed qualities useful for evading the patrol gangs that roamed the South.[104]

A fighter's "reclaimed" masculine body also served as a site of direct resistance to white oppression. Respondents in the WPA narratives recalled that fighters, owing to their huge builds, resisted whippings from whites and caused their owners problems. The Reverend Perry Sid Jamison, a former slave, remembered "one colored boy" who "wuz a fighter": "He wuz six foot tall and over 200 pounds" and "would not stand to be whipped by de white man."[105] Robert Falls disclosed that his father was a fighter and was "mean as a bear." He was so "troublesome" and "bad to fight" that he was sold at least four times.[106] Likewise, Wiley Childress relayed a tale about a slave named Fedd, who lived on the neighboring plantation and was "de strongest man neah dat part ob de kuntry." Fedd "wouldin' 'low nobody ter whup 'in," and one day, as "several men" appeared instructing him that they were going to whip him, "he struck one ob de mans so hahd dey had ter hab de doctuh."[107] Former slave Wallace Turnage remarked in his journal how being "an expert wrestler" gave him the courage to stand and fight his overseer. When asked by the overseer to account for his recent absence from the plantation, Turnage "spoke very saucy." Subsequently instructed to assume a prostrate position for a whipping, Turnage disobeyed and lured the overseer into a fight. The advantages of being an experienced fighter are clearly evident: "I was an expert wrestler so I could throw him as fast as I please. He was fighting all he could at last I het [held?] him so . . . we fought about two hours, and he could not do any thing with me."[108] These examples provide intriguing evidence to support the notion that "the body, so personal, was also a political entity, a site of both domination and resistance."[109] For enslaved men, the fighter's body was not necessarily exploited. Rather, his "reclaimed" body could serve as an important political site of resistance, a "symbolic and material resource" that was fiercely contested between the slave and the owner.[110]

Most important, bouts of fighting were not organized and supervised solely by the slaveholders. Enslaved men sometimes coordinated their own fights, against the wishes of owners and in spite of the threat of punishment. Glascow Norwood stated that fights took place at dances, where the participants would "tie up and fight lack mad dogs." He continued, "dey had to keep de fights a secrete, fo' de owners ob de slaves sho' didn't like no fighting 'round you all see, hit wuz like dis, dey would get crippled up and wouldn't be worth nothing to wuk."[111] Mark Oliver recalled that the slaveholders did not care how late the enslaved stayed up and danced; however, "the strictest rule they had was about fighting. They wouldn't have none of that. If you do it anyway, and somebody gets bad hurt, you be put in the stocks for that."[112] Indeed, not only did organized fighting potentially endanger the productivity of the owner's labor force by rendering contestants "worth nothing to wuk," but it could also significantly devalue the slaves as property. William Grimes stated in his narrative that on one occasion his master had recently purchased a new slave, Cato, with whom Grimes "got a fighting, and bit off his nose," shortly before the master was going to sell him. Accordingly, Grimes's actions "injured the sale of Cato, very much," and Grimes had to "beg very hard to escape being whipped" by the master, who had obviously bought Cato to sell promptly with the intention of making a quick and tidy profit.[113] Former slave Lula Jackson revealed how her mother's first husband, Myers, was killed in a wrestling bout with a younger man. Myers was "pretty old," but, nevertheless, he insisted on wrestling. Although the younger man at first refused to fight Myers due to his age, he eventually consented and successfully "threw him." Undeterred, Myers wanted to wrestle again. After initially protesting again that he did not want to fight, the younger man agreed to a second bout and proceeded to throw Myers so hard that he broke his collarbone. Myers died a week later as a result of his injuries.[114] These testimonies can be interpreted as examples of the everyday somatic politics of enslaved men. By engaging in organized fighting activities against the wishes of the owner, enslaved men exercised mastery over their own bodies and thereby contested the owner's power. Determining the fate of each other's bodies, away from the view and control of the master, amounted to a form of resistance for enslaved men. Damaged bodies equated to reduced efficiency at work and ultimately devalued the slaves as property. In more extreme cases, death caused by organized fighting resulted in a significant loss of property for the slave owner.[115] In the words of Stephanie Camp, these acts "had real and subversive effects on slaveholding mastery and on plantation productivity—both of which rested on elite white spatial and temporal control of enslaved bodies."[116]

One former slave's testimony, recorded by a WPA interviewer, gives considerable detail concerning the recreational activities of the enslaved on a Saturday afternoon. One of the "sports" that the enslaved were "very fond of" was the "free for all":

Here a ring was drawn on the ground which ranged from about 15 ft. to 30 ft. in diameter depending on the number of contestants who engaged in the combat. Each participant was given a kind of bag that was stuffed with cotton and rags into a very compact mass. When so stuffed, the bags would weigh on an average of 10 pounds, and was used by the contestants in striking their antagonist. Each combatant picked whichever opponent he desired and attempted to subdue him by pounding him over the head with the bag, which he used as his weapon of defense. And which was used as an offending weapon. The contest was continued in this manner till every combatant was counted out, and a hero of the contest proclaimed. Some times two contestants were adjudged heroes, and it was necessary to run a contest between the two combatants before a final hero could be proclaimed. Then the two antagonist would stage a battle royal and would continue in the conflict till one was proclaimed victorious.

Sometimes these Free-For-All battles were carried on with a kind of improvised boxing gloves, and the contests were carried on in the same manner as previously described. Very often, as many as 30 darkies of the most husky type were engaged in these battles, and the contests were generally attended by large audiences. Being staged during the period of favorable weather, and mostly on Saturday afternoon; these physical exhibitions were the scenes of much controversial conflict, gambling, excessive inebriation and hilarity.[117]

Although the narrative fails to explicitly state who organized these fighting contests, it does offer clues that these were likely slave-organized bouts, with the interviewer classing the contests as part of the "recreations of slaves." The revealing clue in the description is that "each combatant picked whichever opponent he desired." Unlike some of the master-controlled contests in which owners matched the contestants, the enslaved in this instance exercised a degree of agency. Furthermore, the large participation of the enslaved—thirty for the "boxing" match—and the references to the stuffed bags and padded "boxing gloves" suggest that this was not a bloody prizefight staged between two enslaved men chosen by the master but rather a communal recreational activity organized by slave communities.

Enslaved men used the free-for-all to test and prove their fighting qualities and, in due course, validate their masculinity. The contest functioned on an elimination basis. After a man picked the opponent he desired, battle ensued, and "the contest was continued in this manner till every combatant was counted out, and a hero of the contest proclaimed." In the words of one former slave, the object of such a match was to "to see who was bes' on de plantation."[118] The last man standing was crowned a hero, and when two men were adjudged heroes, it was necessary to run a contest between the two before a final hero could be proclaimed. This battle royal would decide who was ultimately victorious. Enslaved men could establish leadership roles and status among themselves and in the community in general. Those who made it to the final stages of the contests gained the highest respect and reverence among their male peers. As Frederick Douglass noted, "the great wrestler can win laurels."[119] Fighting contests among the male populations of slave communities were thus important occasions when enslaved men could assert and display distinctly gendered identities,

which were judged and validated by their peers. Additionally, male fighters were able to publically demonstrate a range of other qualities: bravery,
fairness, and expert knowledge of rules. As former slave Carter J. Jackson
stated, "the best man whipped and other one took it."[120]

Considering the African background of enslaved people is useful to
further understand the social and cultural implications of slave-organized
wrestling. Usually, African wrestling matches were held in the dry season, which began with harvesting and ended with the preparations for the
following agricultural period. Wrestling was a festive event, commonly
accompanied by music, drinking, and dancing. In Africa, traditional wrestling—performed mainly by boys or young men—served a variety of functions: it was a rite of passage for boys entering puberty, it settled quarrels,
and it was associated with marriage rituals. Intra-village wrestling contests
established male rank, leadership roles and friendship and fostered village
solidarity. Inter-village matches were also commonplace; they established
contact with other isolated villages and formed alliances, as well as emphasizing rivalry.[121]

In the antebellum American South, several examples suggest that
enslaved people—men in particular—derived similar meanings from wrestling contests. As Desch-Obi has remarked, "far from being mere leisure,"
fighting activities of the enslaved were "nothing short of African-based
community-forming and individual-empowering rituals."[122] Morris Hillyer recalled the rivalry between boys enslaved on different plantations. As
a youngster he met up with the other boys and had "regular battles." He
noted, "If I got licked in de morning I'd go home and rest up and I'd
give somebody a good licking dat evening."[123] Harry Smith's slave narrative
recounted an inter-plantation wrestling match that escalated out of control and degenerated into chaos. During corn shuckings, the slaves from
the Plum Creek plantation formed a team called the Plum Creek Tigers,
and those from Salt River named themselves the Salt River Tigers. On one
occasion, after they had been dancing and wrestling with each other, Smith
picked a fight with one of the opposite boys by asking him why he spat in
Smith's face. Each team "urged the boys on," and fighting subsequently
broke out in "dead earnest" among men from both plantations. "Men
fought all around on both sides, bunting and biting," Smith described. An
old woman's dress caught fire and dishes were smashed, while some "tore
the fences down around the cabin" and "hammered each other with the
pickets until the white men came out with guns and threatened to shoot

them if they did not stop."[124] Smith's narrative demonstrates how fighting contests not only brought men together from different plantations, thus cultivating cross-plantation alliance and friendships, but could sometimes accentuate inter-plantation rivalry and, in the process, further intraplantation solidarity and identity. Indeed, as in Africa, it is highly likely that organized fights among American slaves from the same plantation facilitated male bonding. Sociologists maintain that men engaged in sporting activities develop a kind of "covert intimacy" shaped by "doing together" rather than "mutual talk" about their inner lives. In fighting culture—boxing in particular—opponents treat each other as partners and facilitate the expression of "somatic intimacy" in which they "share their bodies, their knowledge, and their creativity."[125] Organizing their own fights, enslaved men reaffirmed the boundaries of a homosocial world that excluded women and the interference of the slaveholder. In the ring, they dramatized sex roles and, in the process, more than likely cultivated male group solidarity and identity.

But Smith's narrative raises an interesting issue: conflict. Enslaved communities were never harmonious, and conflict erupted among enslaved men over three main issues: property, courtship, and honor.[126] As in Africa, slave-organized wrestling in America settled quarrels. For example, enslaved men fought to settle courting disputes. One former female slave recalled how two men fought over her: "Dey bof' wanted me, an' couldn' decide no other way."[127] Men also defended their reputations in the ring. Lula Jackson reported how an insult could trigger off a contest: "One man would walk up to another and say 'You ain't no good.' And the other one would say, 'All right, le's see.' And they would rassle."[128] The ring thus functioned as a form of social control: disputes were resolved and interpersonal tensions were discharged.

Drinking, gambling, and wrestling played important roles in the lives of many enslaved men. Through these activities, enslaved men fashioned a unique homosocial subculture and constructed their own notions of masculinity. In these spaces, men bonded: friendships were established and affirmed, and scores were settled. Enslaved men enforced important gender, age, and status roles in the slave communities; they made contact with men enslaved on different plantations and fostered inter-plantation solidarity, as well as rivalry. In the battle over their personal lives, enslaved men refused to be emasculated. Slavery was centered on policing and controlling enslaved bodies; when enslaved men, as a result of drinking or wrestling, exercised agency over their bodies, they eroded the slaveholding authority structuring their lives and raised their self-esteem. But the male slave body was more than a profoundly personal site of contest between owner and slave: it was also a political source of resistance.

3

Beyond the Plantation

Slaveholders across the South sought to locate enslaved people in plantation space and control their mobility. As mentioned in the previous chapter, sometimes enslaved men left the plantation at night to drink, gamble, and wrestle without their owners' permission. These were dangerous acts. White patrol gangs policed the territory beyond the plantation and inflicted devastating punishment on any slave caught without permission to be there. This chapter focuses on the transgression of these spatial boundaries and examines a range of male activities that were wholly dependent on traversing into this illicit space: hunting, patrol evasion, and cross-plantation theft. Beyond the boundaries of the plantation, enslaved men created physical and symbolic boundaries of inclusion and exclusion that delineated homosocial masculine space. In this space, enslaved men established noticeable male roles. They challenged and sometimes physically fought the patrol gangs who policed these spaces, defending their honor and reputation among their peers. Some left their plantations to steal food, clothing, and money from other plantations and stores in the neighborhood. Through this risk-taking behavior, they proved themselves men. This chapter contends that by hunting, evading the patrol gangs, and engaging in cross-plantation theft, enslaved men contested the imposed spatial regulations of the slave owner, created homosocial space, and, in the process, forged a dissident homosocial masculine culture.

Hunting

From an early age, enslaved men became acquainted with the geography surrounding the plantation as a result of hunting. Almost all enslaved men hunted. Former slave Mary Johnson spoke for enslaved people across the South as she recalled her days of bondage in South Carolina: "Nigger boys in slavery when dere work was done in evening, sometime went hunting and caught rabbits, squirrels or 'possums."[1] While men hunted, women remained in their cabins spinning thread, washing clothes, cooking, and cleaning.[2] As the comments by Mary Johnson indicate, enslaved men usually hunted at night, after work, and on the weekend.[3] Slaveholders knew that allowing enslaved men to hunt served their interests: it reduced provision costs—owners could cut back on meat rations, thus forcing their slaves to hunt for subsistence purposes—and it controlled the activities of enslaved people. However, enslaved people derived many benefits from hunting that owners failed to anticipate.[4]

Male hunters supplemented the diets of enslaved people and provided for their families. According to many former slaves, food rations were generally inadequate, and so hunting was imperative.[5] Former slaves fondly recalled their fathers' hunter and provider roles. Lizzie Norfleet's father had "good dogs and did a heap of hunting," which kept the family "well supplied with possum, coons, and rabbits." He was also a good fisherman, and he "would bring home the prettiest string of fish you ever seed."[6] Nancy Settles recalled her father would come home after a successful hunt and "bring in possum and coon." "He sho could get 'em a plenty."[7] Frances Willingham described her family's domestic arrangements: her father would go hunting and "fetch in lots of 'possums, coons, rabbits, and squirrels," and her mother prepared and cooked the meat.[8]

Historians have maintained that playing the role of provider was integral to the masculine identity of enslaved men. Hunting and fishing were "fundamental features of enslaved men's sense of themselves as providers—both materially and emotionally," argues Rebecca Fraser. She adds, "Whilst slaveholding men perceived the hunt as leisure, for enslaved men it assumed much more significance in the way of providing for their families."[9] Similarly, Nicholas Proctor has suggested that, unlike for the slaveholding class, for the enslaved, hunting and notions of masculinity were rooted in "family and subsistence" rather than "fraternity and display." By sharing the game they killed, the latter played the "role of patriarch within their own family . . . assuming the role of provider." In this way, male hunters demonstrated their masculinity.[10] Provider roles certainly enhanced the masculine identity and self-worth of enslaved men. However, hunting and conceptions of masculinity among enslaved men were also anchored in "fraternity and display." Hunting functioned in similar ways to the homosocial activities of drinking gambling and wrestling: it delineated homosocial physical and symbolic boundaries. In this homosocial space, beyond plantation boundaries, hunters enjoyed the camaraderie of the hunt and displayed their hunting skills to one another.

As children, enslaved boys headed to the woods. Informants for the WPA narratives reported that younger boys did not hunt game; instead, they foraged for nuts and berries and fished. One respondent recalled that as young children they hunted for a variety of things in the woods: "grapes, muscadines, straw-berries, chinquapins, hickory nuts, calamus root, slippery elmer (elm) bark, wild cherries, mulberries, and red and black haws."[11] James Grumbles testified, "after I growed a little bigger, I went huntin' a lot. When we was jus' kids, we went fishin' most ob de time. All dat we tood along was some bait and a piece ob string dat we had tied a bent pin on. De bent pin was our hook . . . we caught sun-perch, mud cats and clearwater cats."[12] As a child, Joe High recalled seeing "the grown folks start off possum huntin' at night" while he stayed behind on the plantation.[13] In this way, elder boys and men regulated the homosocial space of the hunt. Charlie Hudson, for example, recalled being excluded from a possum hunt because of his age: "Grown boys didn't want us chillum goin' 'long 'possum huntin' wid 'em, so all right, dey tuk us way off crost de fields 'til dey found a good thick clump of bushes, and den dey would holler out dat dere was some moughty fine snipes 'round dar. Dey made us hold de poke (bag) open so de snipes could run in. Den dey blowed out deir light 'ood knot torches, and left us chillum holdin' de poke whilst dey went on huntin' 'possums."[14] Hunting could, therefore, serve as a rite of passage for enslaved boys. Elder men played important roles assisting younger boys in their transition to manhood. Acie Thomas learned "all the wood lore common to children of his time" from his elder cousin, Ed, who was "quite willing to enlighten a small boy in these matters," while Aaron Ford learned from his grandfather how to catch otters and set traps. Some enslaved fathers took their sons hunting and delegated tasks to them.[15] In this way, elder men passed on knowledge and hunting skills to the next generation and prepared boys for manhood.

Indeed, hunting did not have to be a solitary pursuit. Testimony from former slaves indicates that it was often a group experience. "Nigger mens an' boys 'ud go in crowds," recalled James Bolton, "sometimes as many as twelve at one time."[16] Group coordination was often vital for catching game such as raccoons and possums. Enslaved men sometimes hunted with specially trained dogs in order to chase a possum and force it to climb a tree. With the animal up a tree, one of the hunters climbed up in order to "shake him out."[17] John Belcher reported, "Effen one uf us had to clamb a tree we'd allus leave one man on de ground to catch em."[18] Enslaved in Chowan County, North Carolina, Allen Parker described how, with the help of torches shining from the hunters below, the climber "gets where he can see the light shining in the coon's eyes" and immediately points out the position of the animal to his fellow hunters. Then, "a sort of race begins; the man going as far out on the limb as he can with safety, and the coon going out as far as the small limb would hold him." After establishing a safe hold, the man shakes the branch so that the animal loses his grip and falls to the dogs and hunters waiting below.[19] If the animal could not be shaken out, "they would cut the tree down." And if it ran into an obstacle, such as a hollow log, "some of the hunters would get at one end of the log, and the others would guard the other end, and they would build fire to smoke the 'possum out."[20] Climbing a tree in front of one's peers, displaying skills in tracking, and shaking prey to the ground was most likely a way to command respect and status within the hunter community. After all, leadership roles emerged during the hunt. Thomas Johns, for instance, was the oldest and the "leader of de bunch" when he hunted as a slave in Alabama.[21]

Hunting in groups fostered camaraderie. Many formerly enslaved men reported the enjoyment they derived from such activities: "Me and de odder boys sho' had a big time possum huntin'," recalled Simon Stokes.[22] Willis Woodson affirmed, "All de fun we has am huntin' and fishin.'"[23] Another man fondly recalled the enjoyments shared between his fellow hunters while out on a possum hunt: "Us would build big fires an' lay 'round 'em an' tell yarns an' think o' how fine dim possums wuz a gwine taste baked wid sweet taters."[24] Similarly, George Caulton described how slaves built a big fire on the riverbank at night and fished for hours.[25] Former slaves sometimes relayed amusing tales from group hunts: "I remember one night we wuz trying to shake a possum out of a tree, and the possum missed holt an' fell right on Bill Cook's head!" recalled one former slave.[26] In the homosocial space of the hunt, enslaved men bonded. Here, huddled around a fire, far from the world of the plantation, enslaved men exchanged jokes, news, stories, and advice.

Hunters had to overcome fears of predatory animals as they entered woodlands and swamps—especially at night. Enslaved men hunted "up in dem swamps in Mississippi" where "dere war bears as big as cows," recalled Adeline Hodge.[27] Addie Vinson recalled the time a possum hunter encountered a bear while enslaved in Georgia—the hunter ran for his life.[28] Others recalled the dangers posed by alligators, panthers, and wildcats. John Walton explained how he would "hear de panthers' scream at night" as well as "hear a panther a-follerin' yo' by him pattin' his big paws along on de ground." Consequently, his mother wouldn't allow him to go out at night without a dog.[29] Another concerned mother instructed her son to stay away from the Colorado River, because it was full of alligators.[30] Hunting at night taught men not only to overcome their fear of the natural environment but also how to be masters of the local terrain.

In his autobiography, Charles Ball remarked that by regularly hunting small game in the woods, he acquired extensive knowledge of the forests beyond his master's plantation.[31] James Tubbs was able to demonstrate his knowledge of the natural environment one night while hunting; he led a group of lost boys out of the woods and back to the plantation: "Ah recollect one night we went coon huntin and de boys wuz wanderin roun and got lost. Some of de boys wuz wanderin roun tryin to git out and couldn' so ah said: 'Dar de seben star yo all jes wait and let me fine de way out and dey say all right,' 'We gwina trus yo to fine out a way out.' Went on bout 200 yards and struck our fiel.' We crawled under fence and went on, struck our coan (corn) fiel.' Den dey all reconcile wha dey is and ah had a big laff."[32] Hunting acquainted boys and men with the terrain beyond the plantation. They had to demonstrate mastery of the local environment. In Tubbs's case, his knowledge most likely afforded him a degree of trust and respect from his fellow hunters.

Patrol Evasion

Leaving the plantation boundaries to hunt meant traversing territory patrolled by whites. Enslaved men had to be granted permission by the owner to go hunting at night or hold a pass if leaving the plantation.[33] "If any ob de men wanted to break a night's rest," recalled former slave Henry Barnes, "he cud go 'possum an' rabbit huntin,' so long as he got a pass from his boss, an' wuz in de fiel' de nex' mawning on time."[34] Slave owners were determined to control the mobility of enslaved people. Virginia slaveholder Richard Eppes kept a detailed account book inscribed with plantation management advice of the following kind: "A time for everything, and everything done in its time. A place for everything, and everything kept in its place. A rule for everything, and everything done according to rule."[35] Across the

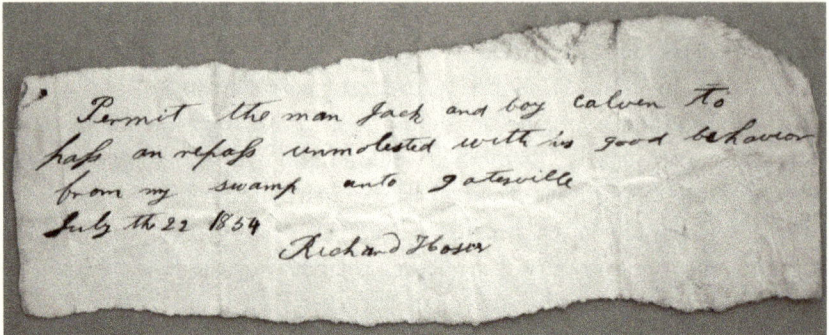

Permit the man Jack and boy Calven to pass an repass unmolested with is good behavior from my swamp anto gatesville July the 22 1854

Richard Hoser

Enslaved men were more mobile than enslaved women. Slaveholders issued passes to those who left the plantation; enslaved people were expected to produce these passes upon request by a white person. In this example, the journey destination and date were specified: Jack and a boy, Calven, were given permission to make a return journey to Gatesville on July 22, 1854, available in Gates County Criminal Actions Concerning Slaves Records. (Courtesy of the North Carolina Office of Archives and History, Raleigh, North Carolina.)

South, owners implemented rules and regulations to regulate and restrain the mobility of the enslaved.[36] "No negro shall leave the place at any time without my permission, or in my absence that of the Driver," instructed one Louisiana planter.[37] Slaves who were granted permission to leave the plantation were required to carry passes issued by the owner or manager. The first rule in the regulation book for the overseer of John Cocke's slaves stipulated, "No negro shall ever be permitted to go off the estate, on his, or her own business, without a written pass in the following form. viz. 'Permit the bearer (here name the negro.) to pass to (here name the place) and return by (here state the time of returning.) Signed this _____ day of _____ for J. H. Cocke.'"[38]

Restraints on the movements of enslaved people assumed a greater importance at night. As one advice manual claimed, the "irregularities of the negroes . . . are generally committed at night."[39] Richard Eppes, like most slaveholders throughout the antebellum South, was determined to prevent his slaves from leaving the plantation at night. Rule thirteen of his plantation advice book was unequivocal: "A horn will be sounded every night at 9 o'clock, after which every negro will be required to be at his quarters and to retire to rest; and that this rule may be strictly enforced, the manager will frequently, but at irregular and unexpected hours of the night, visit the quarters and see that all are present, or punish absentees."[40]

Similarly, on a cotton plantation in Mississippi, William Ethelbert Ervin recorded in his plantation diary that at nine o'clock every night, the horn was to be blown; those "found out of their placies" were to be punished "according to discretion."[41] Plantation owners and managers established "night watches" to enforce these regulations.[42] "A watch at night, consisting of two or more men" was crucial "to establish security and good order on the plantation," argued one Louisiana planter. He claimed, "When a regular watch is Established," it "has the due influence on the negro."[43] In March 1852, after a courthouse meeting, citizens of Buckingham County, Virginia, recommended that "all persons having slaves in their occupation or employment, should keep a vigilant patrol on their own premises, make frequent night examinations of their negro quarters, and not permit any slaves to leave the premises without written permission, specifying the place to which and the errand on which such servant is sent, and the time for his return."[44]

Local and state legislation, dating back to the seventeenth century, reinforced masters' attempts to restrict slave mobility. Collectively known as "slave codes," these laws varied from state to state, but the central principle remained consistent: slaves were defined as personal property. The slave codes protected the ownership of slave property and governed every feature of enslaved life. For example, slaves were denied the right to own property, testify against whites, or strike a white person—even in self-defense. The slave codes significantly restricted the mobility and individual liberties of enslaved people: they could not leave the plantation without authorization in the form of passes, possess alcohol or firearms, or gather in large crowds. Whites were barred from teaching the enslaved how to read or write, passing on any incendiary literature inciting insurrection, and harboring fugitive slaves. Whenever a slave insurrection occurred—or even rumors of one appeared—authorities passed more stringent and repressive slave codes and further curtailed the movements of enslaved people. In some states, authorities established courts and tribunals to enforce the slave codes; petty crimes were punished by whipping, and more serious ones were punished by imprisonment and death.[45]

Authorities across the antebellum South employed an effective weapon to enforce the slave codes: the slave patrol. Adapted from the local militia, slave patrols were composed of slaveholders and non-slaveholders who patrolled and policed designated neighborhoods and apprehended any slaves found out of place, returning them to their masters or locking them

State of North-Carolina, } Court of Pleas and Quarter Sessions.
ORANGE COUNTY. May Term, 1828.

ORDERED, that the following rules and regulations be adopted for the government of the patrols of this county.

1. There shall, after the present year, be four sober discreet men appointed as a patrol for each captain's company within this county.

2. The patrols for the present year, and afterwards, shall patrol their ---ive districts at least once in every two weeks.

3. It shall be the duty of the patrols to visit all disorderly or suspected places, or collections of negroes, within their district, that may come within their knowledge, and to suppress all rioting or disorderly conduct of negroes.

4. Any negro found off his owner's plantation, or travelling on the Sabbath or other unusual time, without a pass or permit from the owner, overseer, or person having charge of said negro, specifying where said negro is going, such negro shall be liable to be taken up by the patrol and to receive from them not exceeding fifteen lashes.

5 The patrol shall exercise their discretion whether they will inflict punishment or not on the negroes taken up without a proper pass, or without any pass at all.

6. That the clerk cause these rules to be printed in the shape of a handbill and that he furnish the same, when printed, to the sheriff, whose duty it shall be to have a copy delivered to each patroler for his direction; and further, for giving publicity to the same, to cause a copy to be set up at some public place in each captain's district in the county; and that the county trustee pay the expense of the printing.

Test, **J. TAYLOR,** *Clerk*

White patrol gangs, composed of white slaveholders and non-slaveholders, policed the mobility of enslaved people; patrols detained and whipped those found off the plantation without a pass. The organization and regulation of patrol gangs in Orange County, North Carolina, are detailed here: "Patrol Regulations from Orange County, NC, adopted May, 1828." Available in Orange County, Slave Records. (Courtesy of the North Carolina Office of Archives and History, Raleigh, North Carolina.)

up in jail.[46] Laws empowered the patrols to determine the guilt of suspected violators of the slave codes and inflict on-the-spot punishment—
often whippings. The patrols also had the power to search the dwellings of
enslaved people and to disperse slaves congregating in groups. In this way,
authorities controlled the movements of enslaved people, restricting them
to the confines of the plantation.[47] Patrols often fulfilled their duties on
horseback and in groups.[48] The scheduling of patrols varied from state to
state. In Chowan County, North Carolina, the chairman and captains of
the patrols were instructed by the county court as follows: "The Captains
of each patrol Company shall ride out their Companies at least three nights
in Two Weeks and as much oftener as the Captains may deem proper."[49]

It was mainly enslaved men—rather than women—who were granted
permission to leave the plantation. Slave owners assigned them a variety
of jobs off the plantation: skilled work, transporting goods, and relaying
messages to other plantations and local communities. Furthermore, it was
almost always the husband who was expected to visit his wife in cross-plantation marriages.[50] In accordance with the slave codes and the rules and
regulations governing plantation life, owners and managers wrote passes
permitting enslaved men to leave the plantation to work, run errands, visit
loved ones, or go hunting.[51] Those caught without passes could expect terrifying summary punishment from the patrollers. "If de patter rolls cotch you
without de pass . . . you better wish you dead 'cause you would have yourself
some trouble," remarked Green Cumby, who was enslaved in Texas.[52] Likewise, Lewis Brown commented that if caught without a pass, "the pateroles
would do the devil with you."[53] Former slaves recounted how they could
expect "39 licks with a red-heifer on the naked hide," whereupon the victim would "be tore up to where he could not hardly sit down for more than
a week."[54] Others described particularly gruesome torture scenes. Phoebe
Lyons recalled seeing the patrollers "put slaves en big hogs-heads stuck plum
full er ten-penny nails, en roll em so de nails done stuck em en tored dey
flesh."[55] One former slave described how a group of patrollers whipped an
enslaved man to death.[56] Accordingly, patrollers struck fear into the hearts
of the enslaved: "Us wuz mo' skeered er patter-rollers den any thing else,"
recalled one former slave.[57]

Despite the slave codes and the threat of these horrifying punishments,
at night, after the horn was blown, men slipped off the plantation. Henry
Green declared "De mostest reason dat sometimes de niggers out at night is
on account dey courtin' some gal whut libes on some udder place."[58] Men

left at night not only to court or visit loved ones but also to drink, gamble, wrestle, pray, dance, and exchange news with other plantations.[59] To succeed in these nocturnal activities, enslaved men had to dodge the patrols, or, if seen, they attempted to run back to their master's plantations before they could be caught and punished.[60] Such endeavors were extremely risky, but enslaved men persisted undeterred. Dempsey Jordan acknowledged he "was taking a great chance" by dodging the patrollers at night to see his girl; he knew he could "be beat nearly to-death." However, he cherished the moments when he "crawled 100 yards to her room and got in the bed with her and lay there until nearly daylight talking to her."[61] Historians have emphasized that enslaved men enhanced their masculinity by braving the patrol gangs and playing the role of visitor in courtships or cross-plantation marriages. Husbands and fathers saw themselves as "protectors and risk-takers."[62] However, by slipping off the plantation boundaries at night and evading the patrol gangs together with other men, enslaved men also proved their masculinity to one another. Anthropologists have maintained that in almost all human societies men are required to prove their masculinity by seeking out dangers and tests of courage. "Manhood is a matter of storm and stress, of challenges and trials," anthropologist David Gilmore contends. Men undertake these feats not necessarily for their own sake, but for the cause of the community—to protect it from enemies. A man must be willing to give up his life for this cause. Gilmore states, "The accepting of this very expendability . . . often constitutes the measure of manhood, a circumstance that may help explain the constant emphasis on risk-taking as evidence of manliness."[63] Evidence from the antebellum South is clear: by confronting the dangers of the patrol gangs, enslaved men protected themselves, other men, and women, and in the process forged distinct masculine identities.

Enslaved men celebrated dodging the patrols. Although Tom Holland was caught by the patrollers one night and subsequently stretched over a log and given "thirty-nine licks with a rawhide loaded with rock," he maintained that the experience "never kep' me from slippin' off 'gain"; he was simply "more careful" the next time.[64] Betty Robertson recalled her father boasting that although the patrols chased him, he gave them a "wahm reception" and "plenty of heel-dust."[65] George Caulton bragged to a WPA interviewer that by the time he was fifteen, no patrol could catch him.[66] Likewise, another former slave claimed he "could always run lak a rabbit" to ensure his escape.[67] Some enslaved men who managed to evade the patrols and return to the safety of their plantations actively taunted the patrollers.[68] Indeed, dodging the patrols became enshrined in folklore and song:

Run, nigger, run, patterroller cotch you,
Run, nigger run, 'cause it 'most de day.
Dat nigger run, dat nigger flew,
Dat nigger los' he weddin' shoe.
Over de hill and down de holler,
Patterroller cotch nigger by collar,
Dat nigger run, dat nigger flew,
Dat nigger tear he pants in two![69]

Slaves called the defiant men who braved such risks "hard-headed."[70] To prove themselves "hard-headed," enslaved men evaded the patrol gangs with other men. "If we went off without a pass we allus went two at a time," commented one former slave.[71] Sometimes, men assembled in larger groups and coordinated their efforts to evade the patrols; emboldened by their numbers, men actively resisted the patrol gangs. Stretching grapevines across the road to stop the patrollers on horseback was the most common way to resist the patrols.[72] Enslaved men who took part in these danger-ous escapades assigned themselves particular roles. Some took command and led the group; praised for their speed and planning skills, these men were called "leaders" or "captains."[73] Others "studied up" ways to "git even" with the patrols.[74] One former slave, Uncle Jackson, was given the title of "raid fox." As such, he had a distinct role: to stand out on the trail when the patrollers were looking for them and lead the patrollers "off in the wrong direction." Some groups stationed slaves in "relays" along the trail; when the patrollers appeared, the one stationed farthest out "would whistle like a bob-cat to warn the others."[75] "Lookout boys" actively baited the patrollers into the stretched grapevines:

There was ways of beating the patterollers. De best way was to head 'em off. I 'member once when we was gonna have a meetin' down in de woods near de river. Well, dey made me the lookout boy, an' then de paddyrollers come down de lane past de church—you see they was 'spectin' dat the niggers gonna hold a meetin' dat night—well, sir, dey tell me to step out f'm de woods an' let 'em see me. Well, I does, an' de paddyrollers dat was on horseback come a chasin' arter me, jus' a-gallopin' down de lane to beat de band. Well I was jus' ahead of 'em, an' when they got almost up wid me I jus' ducked into de woods. Course, the paddyrollers couldn't stop so quick an' kep' on 'roun' de ben,' an' den dere came a-screamin' an' cryin' dat make you think dat hell done bust loose. Dem ole paddyrollers done rid plumb into a great line of grape vines dat de slaves had stretched 'cross de path. An' dese vines tripped up de horses an' throwed de ole paddyrollers off in de bushes. An' some landed mighty hard, cause dey was a-limpin' roun' an cussin' an' callin' fo' de slaves to come an' help dem, but dem slaves got plenty o' sense. Dey lay in de bushes an' hole dere sides a-laughin,' but ain't none o' em gonna risk bein' seen.[76]

By fulfilling their roles in the face of danger, enslaved men proved their masculinity to one another. Riskier roles—"raid fox" or "lookout boy"—or leadership positions would have commanded particular respect. Furthermore, as the outbursts of laughing in the example above show, as men engaged in these acts together, a sense of camaraderie emerged.[77] Indeed, after a group of slaves tripped up some patrollers with grapevines one night, one former slave recalled, "You would hear them [the slaves] laughing about it when they got amongst themselves the next day."[78] Groups of men played pranks on one another while off the plantation: "Sometimes, when us boys got together one ob us would look back and shout, 'Here comes a bunch ob men!' Dere wasn't no men comin' but we'd watch de boys run jes' fo' de fun."[79] Larking around together, in this way, fostered group solidarity and camaraderie.

Enslaved men not only engaged in group trickery to foil the patrols, they also physically resisted the patrollers. "White folks and Niggers was all time quar'ellin' and fightin,'" affirmed former slave Anderson Furr.[80] Trial records from upcountry South Carolina Courts of Magistrates and Freeholders confirm that physical confrontation between slaves and patrollers was a fact of plantation life. The records also testify to the masculine nature of this pursuit: only enslaved men were brought before the court and charged with assaulting patrollers. One night in Anderson District, Marion, a slave of Col. E. S. Ervin, encountered a patrol gang and fought his way free, "unlawfully striking" one of them—a man named Richard Cockram. As Marion ran away, he hollered at the patrol gang to celebrate his victory and escape.[81] In another case from Anderson County, a patroller reported that he came across a gathering of fifteen to twenty slaves when a club was thrown at him "with considerable fury" from one of the crowd, whom he suspected was an enslaved man named Handy. According to the patroller, the crowd of slaves set their dogs on him, indicating that they were probably hunters.[82] Enslaved men fought the patrollers any way they could. At an illicitly organized slave wrestling match, Isaac Potter and "dozens" of his fellow slaves fought off patrollers by slinging hot coals and fire at them as quick and hard as possible.[83] Men did this at gatherings, former slaves testified, to allow other slaves to escape the patrols.[84] In Austin Steward's slave narrative, for example, a patrol stumbled across a slave dance attended by both enslaved men and women. Many panicked. But as the patrollers approached, "an athletic, powerful slave," named Robert, urged the slaves to stand their ground and "advised the females to lose no time in useless wailing." Robert ordered the women to seek refuge in a cabin a short distance away. The men, left behind, were "terrified at this bold act of their leader" and alarmed "at the thought of resistance." Robert, however, boldly requested that every man who felt unwilling to fight leave. Twenty-five men remained with Robert, who declared he would resist to the death. After intense hand-to-hand combat, two patrollers and six slaves lay dead— Robert was among them.[85]

Slaves like Robert sacrificed their lives to protect and defend their communities and consequently proved their masculinity. Steward's narrative celebrates Robert's heroic masculinity: he is described as a "leader," "brave," a "gigantic African, with a massive, compact frame, and an arm of great strength," who looked able to put "ten common men to flight." In addition, the demarcation of gender is explicit: women are excluded from the fighting and chastised for their "useless wailing." A strong, defiant, charismatic leader calls the men to fight. Those who are brave enough stand and fight. In the heat of battle, the bonds shared among these enslaved men must have been strong; they depended on one another for their lives. Conversely, those who chose not to stay and fight with Robert could have been subsequently ostracized in the male community. In all likelihood, they would have been deemed cowardly and effeminate—equated with the "useless wailing" women.

In another fatal case documented in the slave narratives, fierce resistance resulted in the death of a patroller in Mississippi. Andy Snow described how, one night at a slave dance, the patrollers came after a "big husky nigger man named Ned." Ned resisted the patrollers, picking one of them up and slinging him against a chimney, which killed him.[86] Perhaps the patrollers had picked on Ned because he was a "big husky" man whose superior build threatened their own sense of masculine identity—an identity shaped by honor, reputation, and fighting skills. This idea is clearly evident in a WPA narrative from a man named Morris Hillyer, formerly enslaved in Georgia:

> Jim Williams was a patroller, and how he did like to catch a nigger off de farm without a permit so he could whip him. Jim thought he was de best man in de country and could whip de best of 'em. One night John Hardin, a big husky feller, was out late. He met Jim and knowed he was in for it. Jim said, "John I'm gonna give you a white man's chance. I'm gonna let you fight me and if you are de best man, well and good." John say, "Master Jim, I can't fight wid you. Come on and give me my licking, and let me go on home." But Jim wouldn't do it, and he slapped John and called him some names and told him he is a coward [not] to fight him. All dis made John awful mad and he flew into him and give him the terriblest licking a man ever toted. He went on home but know he would git into trouble over it. Jim talked around over the country about what he was going to do to John but everybody told him dat he brought it all on hisself. He never did try to git another nigger to fight with him.[87]

The language in the passage is explicit: for the white patroller, Jim Williams, the best fighter was the "best man." Reputation was central to southern masculinity—Jim had to prove himself as the superior fighter (and man). Picking on John—a "big husky feller"—Jim attempted to exercise racial mastery and affirm his masculinity in the public sphere by fighting and defeating a strong enslaved man.

After being provoked and branded a "coward," John demonstrated that enslaved men, like their southern white counterparts, were willing to use physical violence to uphold and defend their reputations and honor. Court records illustrate how enslaved men fought the patrollers over these issues. In Fairfield District, South Carolina, a patroller claimed, before the Court of Magistrates and Freeholders, that in February 1851 "Soll the slave of Mary Mackersham did on the night the 1st day of this month use some very insulting and unbecoming language . . . to him and others who was patroling." According to Coleman, his patrol had come across Solomon, who refused to answer their questions, and, in his rage, Solomon "said that all men was made on an Equality and he was as good as any man and he would die before he would submit" to be whipped. Solomon was found guilty and sentenced to 200 lashes.[88] In Anderson District, South Carolina, Dennis, the property of C. M. Sharp, was caught in one of the slave cabins of J. W. Norris, who went to the cabin and ordered him to leave. Dennis then "commenced resistance" using "violent language" and fought off Norris with a club, threatening the master to let him go or "he would make him sorry." Norris failed for half an hour—even with the help of "two stout negroe fellows"—to capture Dennis; but eventually, with the help of others, Dennis was subdued. As he was led away, he declared "he had never been conquered by a white man nor woud damned if he would be."[89] The proclamations from these two slaves—"all men was made on an Equality and he was as good as any man," and "he had never been conquered by a white man"—indicate how enslaved men equated masculinity with reputation, honor, and the ability to physically defend oneself from white oppression. Perhaps the most famous example was Frederick Douglass's fight with Edward Covey—a poor white farmer to whom Douglass was rented out. For Douglass, the fight was the ultimate expression of slave masculinity; in his narrative, he introduces the fight thus: "You have seen how a man was made a slave; you shall see how a slave was made a man." After describing the two-hour fight—from which Covey emerged the worse off—Douglass is explicit: "The battle . . . was the turning point in my career as a slave. It rekindled the few expiring embers of freedom, and revived within me a sense of my own manhood."[90]

Cross-Plantation Theft

Men dodged the patrols to visit loved ones, engage in leisure activities, or hunt. Some, however, left the plantation to steal. Many historians have studied acts of theft committed by enslaved people. Kenneth Stampp claimed that through these acts of resistance the enslaved "formulated legal and moral codes of their own."[91] Following Stampp, Eugene Genovese employed his paternalist thesis to emphasize the ambiguities of theft. Although he argued that theft by the enslaved was a form of day-to-day resistance, he maintained that slaves experienced mixed feelings and a degree of degradation resulting from their behavior, "for their religiously informed sensibility could not offer adequate justification."[92] Alex Lichtenstein, in contrast, argued that theft was not only a form of resistance to slavery but an "assertion of economic rights that slaveowners ultimately were unable to dismiss or discourage"—a "moral economy."[93] Subsequent studies of slavery in the antebellum South include references to theft committed by enslaved people; however, they fail to examine theft and its relationship to gender.[94]

Across the antebellum South, slave owners complained in their plantation journals about thefts committed by slaves.[95] Accounts such as those of Charles Friend, a slaveholder in Virginia, were common. On June 11, 1841, he reported that his barn lock was "broken to pieces" and "2 fine shoats taken." Friend made a "diligent search" of the houses but could not retrieve them. That night, he sat up "on the watch" for his pigs. On another occasion, he recorded the theft of some corn from his barn by four enslaved men, "all of whom were soundly whiped." Toward the end of 1841, Friend reported some stolen cabbage. Furious, he matched the track left behind in the garden with one of his slave's feet and "had him up and well whiped in order to find out whether or no it was him and who was engaged with him." Friend commented, "I now think he was entirely innocent and was whiped for that which he did not do—so it is hard to know how to act in such like cases."[96]

Friend's dilemma of finding it "hard to know how to act" in such cases, emphasized the importance of effective slave management for slaveholders. Plantation instruction manuals, possessed by owners and overseers, detailed how to deal with incidents of theft committed by enslaved people. Rule six of the regulation book for the overseer of John Cocke's slaves stated "severe punishment" would be administered if any slave stole items from the plantation. Rule seven instructed the overseer to take a monthly written return of the stock of hogs on the first Saturday of every month.[97] Indeed, in an essay entitled "The Duties of an Overseer," it is claimed that the stock on the plantation required "constant attention" and that much trouble could be avoided by "adopting and enforcing a strict system." Stock checking was a "duty in which Overseers are generally most careless." The essay elaborated, "Never be induced by a course of good behavior on the part of the negroes. . . . By taking frequent strolls about the premises including of course the quarter and stock yards, during the evening and at least twice a week during the night, you will put a more effectual stop to any irregularities than by the most severe punishments. The only way to keep a negro honest, is not to trust him."[98] Similarly, managers were required to be diligent concerning tools and implements. Advice books dictated, "The implements and tools require a good deal of looking after. By keeping a memorandum of the distribution of any set of tools, they will be much more likely to be forthcoming at the end of the month."[99]

Plantation journals are valuable sources through which to investigate slave theft; however, the sources have their limitations for accurately assessing and quantifying theft. Journal entries are sometimes incomplete; they document stolen items but from time to time fail to identify the perpetrator or, indeed, the person's gender. Furthermore, plantation journal entries can be very sporadic, with gaps in months and years and a mixture of short and long entries. Other records give us a clearer picture. In South Carolina, lower courts tried slaves and free blacks for a range of offenses: from petty crimes such as drinking or gambling on the Sabbath through to theft, burglary, assault, rape, and murder. The Court of Magistrates and Freeholders was a nonjury system presided by magistrates or justices of the peace who imposed punishments varying from a few lashes to execution.[100] The most well-documented and preserved trial records from these courts come from the upcountry districts of Anderson, Pickens, Laurens, Spartanburg, Fairfield and Kershaw districts. Of these districts, Anderson District recorded the most criminal cases involving the enslaved and free black population: 429 between 1819 and 1865.[101]

In Anderson District from 1819 to 1865, 90 percent of enslaved people who stood before the Court of Magistrates and Freeholders charged with theft were male. The gender disparity in the trial records is significant and can be explained: almost every slave who appeared before the courts was summoned to do so as a result of a complaint made by a victim of crime who was not the owner of the slave. If a slaveholder experienced theft from one of his own slaves, he typically administered his own summary punishment. Recalling his boyhood growing up on a plantation in South Carolina, Daniel E. Huger Smith wrote, "It must be understood that the planter had the right of 'la basse justice et la moyenne' on his own plantation. 'La Haute Justice' was reserved to a State court. For petty crime or default the punishment was a more or less sound thrashing administered by the Driver in the presence of the Overseer or Master."[102] However, if the owner suspected that a theft had been committed on his plantation by slaves whom he did not own, he would usually issue a complaint to the courts. The following dispute between slaveholder Richard Eppes and his neighbor, Mr. Burchell, demonstrates this situation. In a copy of an October 13, 1859, letter to his neighbor, Eppes recorded that Mr. Burchell's hog had been shot; Eppes's own slave was suspected. Eppes suggested that Burchell take the slave to a magistrate: "My reasons for suggesting the tribunal of a magistrate to decide the punishment of the negro was that it ought to be free from prejudice or favor and that the negro would have justice done him whereas if he was brought before me and I did not consider the accusations and proofs sufficiently strong to justify me in punishing him I might be accused of partiality, on the other hand if I authorized Mr. Burchell to punish him being a man of strong passions and prejudices he might do it on insufficient grounds and that unmercifully."[103] Thus, cases of theft that appeared before the Court of Magistrates and Freeholders were cross-plantation thefts and thefts from local stores, houses, and farms. Unsurprisingly, enslaved men were overwhelmingly accused of these crimes; they were more mobile, familiar with the local and surrounding geography, and experienced at patrol evasion than their female counterparts. Most cross-plantation thefts occurred at night; men were particularly suited to navigate their ways beyond the plantation in the dark. With their mobility restricted, enslaved women, in contrast, engaged in opportunistic theft, many taking advantage of their work positions by stealing items they handled.[104] Hattie Sugg described how her mother "would make soap fo' Missus Nancy an steal a gourd full of it . . . to wash our Sunday clothes with."[105] Former house servant Ida Henry declared, "I would put biscuits and pieces of chicken in a sack under me dress dat hung from me waist, as I waited de table for me Mistress . . . as dey never gave de slaves none of dis sort of food."[106]

Slave owners noted the frustrations of cross-plantation theft. Virginian John Walker recorded in his plantation journal that he would only "put up" thirteen instead of twenty to twenty-four hogs "in consequence of having 14 of my this years killing hogs stolen I believe by Mrs. Fauntleroys negros."[107] Louisiana planter Bennett Barrow recorded in one of his diary entries that he had caught some slaves belonging to Captain Howell attempting to steal cotton.[108] Indeed, a petition presented in 1816 to the South Carolina Legislature complained, "There are a great number of large Plantations without any white person living thereon, the Negroes belonging thereto not being restrained are in the constant habits of Killing the stock of Cattle and Hogs of the Neighbors adjoining them, and also of the taking their Corn from their fields before it could with safety be housed."[109]

According to slave narratives, some slaveholders, on occasions, encouraged their slaves to steal stock such as chickens, hogs, and cattle from other plantations. "De masters would make us slaves steal from each of the slave owners," reported Henry Johnson. "Our master would make us surround a herd of his neighbor's cattle, round dem up at night, and make us slaves stay up all night long and kill and skin every one of dem critters, salt the skins down in layers in de master's cellar, and put de cattle piled ceilin' high in de smoke house so nobody could identify skinned cattle."[110] Slave owners punished their slaves if they were caught in the act; one master threatened his slaves, "if you get caught, I'll kill you."[111] As Johnson's testimony reveals, the proceeds of the raids were given to the master, or, on occasions, the master purchased the stolen goods from the thieves.[112] According to Eugene Genovese, slaveholders actively encouraged these acts in order to strengthen the sense among the white slaveholding family and the enslaved that their plantation was a distinct community, standing alone against outsiders. He states, "in this subtle way masters bound their slaves to their own white folks and drove a wedge between them and their neighbors, black and white."[113] This explanation appears plausible. In a case that reached the Court of Magistrates and Freeholders in Anderson District, South Carolina, on April 4, 1854, slave owner Tom N. Smith complained, "Ned the slave of William Duckworth on Sunday night . . . came to his House and went in to the Black Smith Shop Pilfering and as tho he wished to Steal some of his Iron untill his negros run him out of the Shop." The trial testimony records that the Smith slaves "rased a riot"; Ned struck Bill, the slave of a Mrs. Guiton, "2 Blows with his fist," after which the group "fell to fighting" until Mr. Smith "parted them."[114] Paternalism as an explanation, however, has its limits; if the Smith slaves had failed to prevent the theft, they could have been held accountable themselves. They were most likely motivated by self-interest rather than loyalty.[115]

Enslaved men's perceptions of masculinity motivated most cross-plantation thefts. Many former slaves reported that necessity drove many men to thievery. Inadequate rations "caused lots of trouble," reported one former slave.[116] "D' niggers 'roun' dere neber git 'nuf t' eat so dey kep' stealin' stuff all d' time," responded another.[117] Spart Quinn stated, "Lots of them would steal. They had it to do to keep from starving."[118] Through theft, enslaved men fulfilled provider roles for their families and enhanced their masculinity accordingly. Indeed, the three most stolen items by enslaved people recorded by the court in Anderson District were clothes, meat, and money—all indispensable for slave families. Other testimonies are revealing: one former slave recalled that while pregnant and trying to nurse two children, her grandmother "craved meat." In response, her grandfather stole a shoat and "had it cut up and put away."[119] In another case from Anderson

District, brought before the court in July 1840, three enslaved men were found guilty of breaking into a merchant's storehouse at night and stealing articles valued between $30 and $40. Authorities searched a series of slave cabins and found a pair of shoes in a mulatto girl's possession. The girl, when questioned, responded that her husband had given them to her "but she did now where from but after ward."[120]

Thieves not only provided their families with much-needed resources, they also distributed the spoils of their thefts to the community at large. One former slave recalled her father distributing stolen meat to slaves who "invaribly slipped over at night in search of food."[121] Another remembered how his father and uncle, who had just killed and stolen "a great big mutton[,] . . . invited company in to help eat it up."[122] Generous thieves felt a sense of self-respect, and they most likely gained admiration for their deeds, as the following testimony from Josiah Henson demonstrates:

> Sometimes, when I have seen them starved, and miserable, and unable to help themselves, I have helped them to some of the comforts which they were denied by him who owned them, and which my companions had not the wit or the daring to procure. Meat was not a part of our regular food; but my master had plenty of sheep and pigs, and sometimes I have picked out the best one I could find in the flock, or the drove, carried it a mile or two into the woods, slaughtered it, cut it up, and distributed it among the poor creatures, to whom it was at once food, luxury, and medicine. Was this wrong? I can only say that, at this distance of time, my conscience does not reproach me for it, and that then I esteemed it among the best of my deeds.[123]

Similarly, Charles Ball recalled the satisfaction he derived from sharing food with his fellow slaves. While in command of a fishery, he traded some surplus shad for some bacon, "determined, if possible, to procure such a supply of that luxury, as would enable me and all my fellow-slaves at the fishery to regale ourselves at pleasure." He boasted proudly: "Of all I ever took, I am confident, I have given away more than the half to my fellow-slaves, whom I knew to be equally needy with myself."[124] As anthropologists have noted, the sharing of food "ensures the survival of the group both socially and materially."[125] Such selfless actions by enslaved men cemented social solidarity in slave communities.

Leaving the plantation in order to embark on cross-plantation raids was extremely risky. As discussed, those who were caught could expect terrifying punishment from the patrollers. Moreover, a slave caught in the act of theft could expect to receive a whipping of up to 150 lashes depending on the magistrate and the severity of the crime.[126] Men who prevailed despite these obstacles and returned to their families and friends with stolen food or clothing certainly enhanced their self-esteem; they demonstrated their willingness to face and overcome danger to improve and protect the lives of their loved ones. In the process, they proved their masculinity to their peers, their family, and the wider community.

For support, some enslaved men embarked together on daring raids of local stores, houses, farms, and neighboring plantations. Group theft accounted for 36 percent of the cases involving slaves brought before the Court of Magistrates and Freeholders in Anderson District, South Carolina. Of these, 78 percent involved slaves from different plantations, showing a high degree of inter-plantation cooperation among enslaved thieves. In December 1857, three enslaved men from two different plantations were charged with breaking into a store one night in the village of Williamstow "by boring sundry small holes into and through the door," after which they placed their hands through the door "to remove a wooden cross bar which was the fastening of the said door" and took "a large amount of money."[127] One group of enslaved men from two different plantations was charged, in March 1856, with breaking into a plantation meat house by "digging a hole under the end & Rolling a log out," stealing fifteen to eighteen pieces of bacon.[128] Group coordination, in many cases, was vital for success. Thieves assigned look-out roles to one another.[129] Moreover, they worked together to steal a range of bulky items, such as large kegs of alcohol, heavy iron bars, and livestock.[130] In January 1865, two enslaved men were found guilty of killing and stealing a hog, weighing approximately 125 pounds, from Charles and Mary Mattison. According to trial testimony, a "considerable amount of blood" was found on the ground along with "evidence of the struggling of the dying animal."[131] To overpower a struggling hog, an extra set of hands would have been crucial. As one former slave testified, "grabbin' a pig was a sure-'nuff problem. You have to cotch him by his snoot so he won't squeal and clomp down tight while you take a knife and stick him till he die."[132] Committing these crimes together arguably strengthened solidarity among thieves. In highly dangerous circumstances, they performed assigned roles and depended on and trusted one another. Furthermore, through cross-plantation theft, thieves forged bonds of trust and secret alliances with slaves from different plantations.

Male thieves who left the plantation at night to engage in cross-plantation theft demarcated distinct physical and symbolic male spaces. Deep in the woods and beyond plantation boundaries, enslaved men prepared and divided the spoils of their theft before bringing it home to their families. May Satterfield recalled, "Sometime de men would go at night an' steal hog and sheep, burry de hair in a hole way yonder in de swamp sommers whar dey knowed de white fo'ks cudden fine."[133] Ellen Cragin remembered that after stealing a hog her father would "clean the hog and everything before he would bring him to the house."[134] Men usually buried unwanted parts or threw them in nearby rivers.[135] Josiah Henson, too, slaughtered and cut up stolen livestock "a mile or two" into the woods.[136] The swamps and woods were familiar areas for enslaved men who hunted, evaded patrol gangs, and left the plantation boundaries for work. Butchering livestock was regarded as a masculine preserve. Additionally, male thieves excluded children from their activities; they were worried that children would inform the owners of their undertakings. Former slave Delia Hill recalled that during church service the preacher actively pressed people to inform the slaveholders if they had seen anybody stealing. He would ask the children directly "what your daddy bring home to you when he come, and what he feed you chillun at night." "We scared to death to tell anything," Hill reported. "If we did de niggah get a killin, and our mammy tie up our feet and hang us upside down by our feet, build a fire under us and smoke us, scare us plum to death. . . . Lord, child, dat was an awful scare."[137] Mark Oliver recollected witnessing his father return home late one night after stealing a hog. As soon as he stepped in the door, he exclaimed, "Cover that boy's head up quick."[138] Sometimes children were excluded from enjoying the spoils of theft, owing to the fear of children informing. One former slave recalled that after her father and uncle had brought home some stolen mutton, they invited company over but gave the children nothing, "for they didn't want us to know about it, but we knowed it all the time but we knowed better than to tell it."[139] The adults would prepare and cook stolen hog while the children were in bed; another ex-slave testified: "You didn't no more dare come in there than you would stick your head in the fire."[140] In this way, male thieves played adult masculine roles and regulated space, marking boundaries of inclusion and exclusion.

The proceeds of theft brought status in slave communities. Cash, in

particular, was a "primary arbiter of wealth, status, and power," and theft
of cash enabled men to instantly acquire this prestige.[141] Money was the
third most popular stolen item recorded by the Court of Magistrates and
Freeholders in Anderson District; enslaved men stole cash in amounts rang-
ing from small amounts up to considerably large sums.[142] Records show
that enslaved men were caught attempting to change stolen $100 bills.[143]
Such large instant acquisitions would have bolstered considerably a man's
masculine identity, which was assessed, at least in part, on the ability to
provide. If money could not be stolen, then enslaved men traded stolen
goods in exchange for other commodities and money with poor whites and
free blacks.[144] Often, enslaved men traded goods among themselves: clothing, cotton, honey, turkeys, chickens, and jewelry, for example.[145] Philip
D. Morgan has argued that by bartering, trading, and exchanging goods,
slaves fostered a "collective solidarity," "sense of pride," and "collective identity."[146] Enslaved men, who conducted virtually all of this underground
trade owing to their mobility, used these trading opportunities to develop
homosocial ties. In this way, trade created business partners and had the
potential to generate instrumental male friendships. As Dylan Penningroth
has argued, "if social ties helped 'make' property, property was one of the
things that 'made' social ties."[147]

Enslaved men, however, did occasionally steal from one another. There
were only five recorded cases in Anderson District in which charges were
brought against enslaved men who stole from other slaves. In each of these,
the thief and victim lived on different plantations.[148] Stealing from other
slaves was a big taboo in slave communities. During an interview for the
American Freedmen's Inquiry Commission, when questioned whether
slaves stole from one another, former slave Harry McMillan of South Carolina responded, "Not so much; they have done it but they look upon this
change as bringing about a different state of things."[149] Fugitive slave John
Brown commented in his slave narrative, "As a rule, any one of us who
would have thought nothing of stealing a hog, or a sack of corn, from our
master, would have allowed himself to be cut to pieces rather than betray
the confidence of his fellow-slave."[150] A slave who stole from another slave
was branded "mean as master" and "just as mean as white folks," recalled
fugitive slave Lewis Clarke; this was the "lowest comparison" a slave could
make.[151]

Slaves who stole from other slaves on different plantations demonstrated that inter-plantation solidarity did not always prevail. Indeed, from

time to time, property eroded relations, causing conflict. On these occasions, enslaved men were quick to defend their property with violence—a reaction that, according to historian Jeff Forret, "points to the significance of an honor code among slaves."[152] Anthropologists have argued that "theft does not only mean the appropriation of property but is also an offence against personal and family pride." When resources in certain societies are particularly scarce, theft can threaten one's livelihood. Moreover, theft highlights that the victim has been unable to protect his family and property. "Therefore, reaction to theft is closely connected to a concept of masculinity."[153] Cases involving violence and theft brought before the courts in South Carolina demonstrate the equation some slaves made between masculinity and property. Two of the five cases of slave-on-slave theft from Anderson District, South Carolina, involved men who had attempted to reclaim property from estranged spouses. In one case, Andrew, enslaved to Thomas Duckworth, was charged with assault, housebreaking, and the theft of some clothes from the "negro house" of Andrew Oliver. Andrew argued in court that the reason he broke into the house was because "his wife had taken up with another man," and so, accordingly, he went back to get the "things there which he had given to his wife." "No man would submit to such treatment," he asserted. He had "bought the things with his own money" and had earned the money by "knocking about . . . buying & selling things." Andrew declared he would not let his wife's new man "wallow on the things he had bought."[154] Andrew's trial demonstrates how important the meager possessions of slaves were and how the provision of property was related to notions of masculinity. Andrew was furious the possessions he had worked for would be used by his wife's new man; his masculinity was being violated and undermined. In Andrew's eyes, the repossession of these goods was justified.

If male thieves were unfortunate enough to be caught, some resisted revealing the names of other suspected thieves, despite enduring horrific physical torture. On January 8, 1852, slaveholder Richard Eppes, owner of four plantations on the James River in Virginia, recorded in his diary that 150 fish had been stolen from one of his plantations. Upon discovery, he immediately ordered "all the negro men to be called up," whereupon he "measured the tracks in the house and found upon comparing them with the shoes of William, Lewis, Davy and Jim that they corresponded." Eppes gave each man "a severe whipping but could not get them to confess." He continued, "William and Jim confessed that they had stolen shad out on a former occasion but not last Saturday night. Both much frightened. Davy took his whipping without confessing anything, found him very obstinate and not minding much the lash."[155] Slaves such as William, Lewis, Davy, and Jim, subscribed to a code of silence, or, as one antebellum writer noted, a "code of honor," in an attempt to protect one another.[156] In his narrative, Charles Ball recalled a story relayed to him by another male slave, who had been caught stealing sheep: "My old master asked me if I had any accomplices in stealing the sheep. I told them none—and that it was entirely my own act—and that none of my fellow-slaves had any hand in it. This was the truth; but if any of my companions had been concerned with me, I should not have betrayed them; for such an act of treachery could not have alleviated the dreadful punishment which I know awaited me, and would only have involved them in the same misery."[157] In some cases, these codes were broken, and enslaved witnesses testified against their fellow slaves before the Court of Magistrates and Freeholders. In one instance, Alexander, slave of G. P. Pettigrew, became the chief witness in the trial of a slave named Alfred, also belonging to Pettigrew. Alexander told the court Alfred had persuaded him to go and steal some chickens and had promised to pay him "in tobacco for going with him."[158] A similar case, which led to the hanging of Willis, a slave convicted of burglary, was brought before the courts in March 1864. Charles, a slave of Jesse Hannah, told the court that Willis had "asked him to go with him to Mr. Lucks house and break open his house and git some Brandy." Charles testified he went with Willis who "took an axe and broak open the door . . . and stole out the brandy . . . they took and hid it in an old house."[159]

Conversely, however, enslaved men also protected one another in court. Just before the end of the Civil War, two male slaves belonging to Jesse W. Norris—Marsh and Pleasant—were accused of stealing a hog. During the trial, Billy—a slave also belonging to Norris—came to Marsh's defense and insisted that "he and Marsh slept together in the same bed on that night and Marsh was there in the morning when he awoke, and that he believes that he slept with him all night." Billy claimed before the court that had Marsh gotten up, "he would have known it."[160] Other witnesses at trials simply played ignorant. After some bee stands and honey went missing on a plantation belonging to Aaron Welborn, the clerk of the court recorded the following: "Harry knows nothing," Edmond "knows nothing," and Abraham's wife's testimony "amounts to nothing."[161] In another case involving Ben, a slave belonging to W. R. Burriss, who was accused of stealing ham,

bacon, and lard, the defendant claimed he had not stolen the meat but purchased it for nine dollars "from two Black men." Ben, however, would not
reveal the names of the two men, claiming that he did not know them,
and that he was not even aware of the time of month that the transaction
had taken place.[162] Perhaps he was speaking the truth, but it seems highly
unlikely that he would not even know the names of the two men to whom
he paid the handsome sum of $9. The court agreed, and he was found
guilty and sentenced to eighty-five lashes.

These records show the willingness of some enslaved men to protect
other men accused of theft and hint at a wider ethic of solidarity in the
community. Slaveholders understood the problems posed by this group solidarity; plantation manuals advised them to employ collective punishment
in a bid to break slave solidarity and to root out suspected thieves. According to Richard Eppes's plantation manual, one of the greatest difficulties
in rearing hogs was "caused by the villainy of the negroes in killing and
stealing the young hogs." The manual advised, "This can be effectually
arrested by making it an invariable rule to stop the rations of most of all
heads for one week, whenever a hog is missing and not accounted for." The
rule "should also be applied, if necessary, to protect the other kinds of stock
from depredation."[163] Indeed, on November 26, 1851, in response to two
hogs having been stolen from one of his plantations, Eppes "ordered the
entire plantation on half allowances for a week."[164] Furthermore, for Christmas 1852, Eppes collectively punished his slaves on Hundreds Plantation,
deducting three days from their Christmas holidays in response to the theft
of some of his hogs and sheep earlier that year.[165] Similarly, on a plantation in Louisiana, overseer Samuel Leigh regularly punished the enslaved
workers collectively for theft. On several occasions, he made the entire slave
workforce toil on a Sunday after a theft had been committed earlier in the
week.[166] A striking passage from Charles Ball's slave narrative demonstrates
the extraordinary attempts of enslaved men to protect one another from the
owner's wrath. After the theft of a hog, the overseer threatened to punish
all the slaves until the guilty party came forward. Nobody owned up to the
crime. The overseer ordered twenty people to lie and down and whipped
them. Still, no one admitted guilt. He returned to the first man and bru-
tally whipped him again, but the man "said not a word." It was only after
the overseer monstrously whipped the man with a cat, whose claws ripped
the flesh out of the man's back, that he admitted to the crime, and gave
the names of several others.[167] Ball's story illustrates how men attempted—

however futilely—to collectively protect one another from the owner. The code of silence was an ethical one to which enslaved men expected each other to adhere. By taking a whipping for other men, male slaves affirmed their loyalty and enhanced their identity within the male community.

Enslaved men who left the plantation to hunt, dodge the patrols, and steal for their families defied the temporal and spatial regulations controlling their lives. Men grew up aware of the geography surrounding the plantation: almost all hunted. Fathers introduced their sons to this space as they prepared them for manhood by passing down their hunting skills to the next generation. Hunting was not a solely solitary pursuit; it was often a communal activity. Together, these men created a manifestly male world, a homosocial space. It prepared them for life beyond the plantation. Leaving the plantation, however, was dangerous; when men crossed into territory patrolled by whites, they risked their lives. Dodging and fighting the patrol gangs brought enslaved men together and fostered solidarity; they had to work as a unit to successfully evade capture. In this crucible, enslaved men proved themselves to one another as protectors and defenders of their community. Men demonstrated extraordinary generosity and selflessness by stealing for their families and community; they earned respect accordingly. Accomplices in crime protected one another the best they could by maintaining a code of silence or of honor. Together, in hazardous terrain beyond the plantation boundaries, enslaved men created homosocial spaces and constructed distinct gendered roles.

4

Friendship, Resistance, and Runaways

Some of the most meaningful and satisfying relationships enslaved men experienced were their friendships with each other as together they worked, drank, wrestled, and risked the wrath of the patrol gangs off the plantation. Such friendships played central roles in their everyday lives: they gave them hope, comfort, and relief from the drudgery and horrors of their enslavement. Frederick Douglass affirmed that it was the "ardent friendship" of his "brother slaves" that helped him endure the brutality of his plantation days. These were special men. He declared, "I never loved, esteemed, or confided in men, more than I did in these."[1] Much historical writing detailing the relationships of enslaved people in the antebellum South has focused on family, courtship, and marriage. Since the revisionist historiography of the 1970s, many historians have demonstrated how enslaved people sought solace in these relationships, reclaimed their humanity, and resisted their oppression.[2] For instance, Emily West's work on slave couples in antebellum South Carolina contends that "the relationships between spouses facilitated the desire for and the development of a social space between the lives of slaves and owners and a means of resistance against oppression."[3] Such studies have radically transformed our knowledge of the cultural world of enslaved men and women. Crucially, they have forced historians to rethink how they conceptualize power and notions of resistance. However, with the sole exception of Deborah G. White's work on enslaved women, none has examined the intimate relationships shared between enslaved people of the same sex. This chapter explores the world of male friendship. Throughout the antebellum South, enslaved men regularly turned to the other men they worked, lived, and played with for daily emotional and practical support. These were important relationships, especially for those separated from their spouses in cross-plantation marriages. Moreover, in the private, intimate space of friendship, enslaved men resisted their enslavement. Some friends plotted to run away and helped each other escape. For them, the personal world of friendship was also intensely political.

Exploring such a personal and intimate aspect of enslaved life is not an easy task. As historian Larry Hudson remarked, "How can the affectional ties that existed between slaves be examined given their tendency to camouflage their personal feelings when functioning in the public world?"[4] Fortunately, some formerly enslaved men discussed the friendships they shared with other men during their enslavement in book-length autobiographical narratives, in which they used their friendships to retain their dignity and resist their enslavement. Understanding how enslaved men conceived and valued their friendships, however, is more difficult. Examining the mentalities—the worldviews—of these men requires imagination in terms of source material. The folklore of enslaved people is invaluable in this respect: it provides historians with a set of stories through which enslaved people articulated particular values and morals. But before examining this evidence, we must look at how nineteenth-century Americans understood and measured same-sex friendships.

Friendship in Nineteenth-Century America

Douglass's descriptions of his friendships with other men during his days of enslavement is certainly intense. He wrote at a time when many Americans enjoyed strong same-sex friendships. The nineteenth century was a time when many men and women inhabited separate cultural worlds. As historian Carroll Smith-Rosenberg states, "American society was characterized in large part by rigid gender-role differentiation within the family and within society as a whole, leading to the emotional segregation of women and men." In such an environment, middle-class northern women—the subject of Smith-Rosenberg's research—routinely formed intense emotional ties with other women. These friendships ranged from the supportive love of sisters, through adolescent friendship, to sensual vows of love made by adult women and became institutionalized through various rituals that accompanied significant events in a woman's life. These included the roles shared between mother and daughter, friendships at school, support for women before and after marriage, and support with childcare and sickness. Together, women shared the experiences of joy, sorrow, and grief.[5]

An emotional intensity that continued into adulthood often characterized these friendships. In letters, women addressed each other as "my
darling" and "my dearest." They openly professed their love, declaring, "I
love you with my whole soul" and "imagine yourself kissed a dozen times
my darling."[6] These intense friendships—which feminist historian Lillian Faderman termed "romantic friendships"—were idealized and actively
encouraged as long as they were not deemed sexual by wider society.[7] These
were love relationships "in every sense except the genital," argued Faderman, and were perfectly compatible with heterosexual marriage. In the
nineteenth century (unlike the twentieth), love was not necessarily equated
with sexual impulse. Accordingly, women could openly kiss, sleep together
and declare their love for one another and see their passions as nothing
more than "effusions of the spirit."[8] Moreover, in the nineteenth century,
the "passionless" woman discourse meant that women could consider their
love relationships higher in character and imbued with spiritual and moral
superiority when compared to heterosexual relationships because they
excluded male "carnal" passion.[9]

Men, too, engaged in romantic friendships. In the nineteenth century,
northern middle-class men formed intense friendships with other men in
their youth. These relationships served as important sources of support during the period of transition to adulthood—when a young man had to leave
his sheltered childhood home for the competitive public sphere. Unlike previous generations, young men could not rely on apprenticeships, family patron-
age, and family connections to ensure success. Instead, during the uncertain
changes of nineteenth-century America, young men turned to the people
close to them: other men who shared the same hopes, fears, and experiences.
Together, friends discussed daily events, career plans, gossip, and the opposite
sex.[10] Intimacy extended into physicality—it was not uncommon for close
friends to share the same bed. As one young man from the period reflected in
a letter, "we retired early and in each others arms did friendship sink peacefully to sleep."[11] Indeed, in an era with no central heating and in which many
children grew up in large families, it was common for men of all classes to
sleep together, particularly when illness or personal tragedies occurred.[12] Historian E. Anthony Rotundo has claimed that these relationships were often
"rehearsal for marriage" and would end after the young men married, became
committed to careers, and set up homes of their own. Male friendships, however, continued and were nurtured in the sociability of men's clubs, fraternal lodges, political parties, and various business associations. Rotundo has

stated, "Men tied their loyalties to those groups with a passion that equaled the passion of their youthful friendships."[13]

Romantic friendships were not the sole preserve of the middle class; working-class men and women enjoyed similar intense relationships. During the nineteenth century, it was not unusual for working-class men and women to inhabit different social and cultural worlds. A variety of same-sex relationships formed when working-class people lived in isolation from the opposite sex. For example, men forged intimate friendships in the homosocial settings of the army, navy, prison system, and, in the West, in mining and cowboy towns.[14] Some of these mirrored the intense romantic relationships of middle-class men and women. For example, historian Karen Hansen uncovered evidence of an intimate friendship between two working-class men from antebellum New England who corresponded by letter. The men had worked in a box factory together, and even though one of the friends relocated, the intense friendship survived. In a letter, one of the men wrote: "Can not forget those happy hours [th]at we spent at G. Newcombs and the evening walks; but we are deprived of that privilege now we are separated for a time we cannot tel how long perhaps before our eyes behold each other in this world."[15] Hansen argued that there was nothing in the correspondence to indicate that the two men were in any way uncomfortable about their relationship or behavior. Although evidence of such friendship is rare, owing chiefly to the lack of available source material, Hansen interpreted the discovery of these letters as demonstrating "what was possible," rather than what was "typical" in antebellum New England. She contended that other relationships of the same kind must have existed between working men because "such intimacy was not unacceptable."[16]

Southerners also enjoyed intense friendships. Many women, weary of the patriarchal nature of southern society, sought solace in same-sex friendships.[17] Men, too, despite the South's chivalrous honor culture, formed lifelong intimate friendships in the early nineteenth century. Through these friendships, southern white men articulated a gendered identity characterized by private expressive emotion and mutual affection, rather than public demonstrations of honor.[18] In southern society, regulated contact with the opposite sex fostered an emotional distance between the sexes, which stimulated bonds between members of the same sex. According to one historian, elite Virginians immersed themselves in their own version of the "female world of love and ritual."[19] Elite whites often formed friendships at university that lasted a lifetime. Friends advised each other, performed favors for each other, and were an important source of emotional strength for men navigating their way through the vicissitudes of life.[20] Some southern friends engaged in homosexual practices. Historian Martin Duberman unearthed erotic correspondence exchanged between James H. Hammond and his friend Thomas J. Withers in their early twenties. In a May 15, 1826, letter, Withers wrote to Hammond:

> I feel some inclination to learn whether you yet sleep in your Shirt-tail, and whether you yet have the extravagant delight of poking and punching a writhing Bedfellow with your long fleshen pole—the exquisite touches of which I have often had the honor of feeling? Let me say unto thee that unless thou changest former habits in this particular, thou wilt be represented by every future Chum as a nuisance. And, I pronounce it, with good reason too. Sir, you roughen the downy Slumbers of your Bedfellow—by such hostile—furious lunges as you are in the habit of making at him—when he is least prepared for defence against the crushing force of a Battering Ram.[21]

Withers's light-hearted, shameless letter led Duberman to the conclusion that male-male sexual contact in this period was not stigmatized to the degree assumed by previous historians. After all, both Hammond and Withers had ambitious plans for careers in politics; and so, if such practices were taboo, Withers's tone, Duberman hypothesized, would have demonstrated some evidence of unease and guilt. Instead, the casual letter suggested that sexual contact between men, "if not commonplace, was not wholly proscribed either."[22]

In a world characterized by the "emotional segregation of women and men," Americans, not surprisingly, turned to members of their own sex for emotional support and in the process developed intense same-sex friendships. Unfortunately, source material on romantic friendships among enslaved men in the antebellum South is notably absent. However, given the separate work, social, and cultural spaces occupied by many enslaved men and women, intense same-sex friendships—prevalent among nineteenth-century Americans from all classes—most likely existed, and indeed flourished, in slave communities.

West African Friendship

Faced with limited source material, sometimes historians have to be creative and seek clues elsewhere. The West African cultural background of enslaved people, for example, provides us with some indication of how enslaved men possibly conceptualized friendships. Numerous historians have examined the West African background of enslaved people to further their understandings of topics such as slave culture, family, gender, and resistance in the New World.[23] In his landmark study *The Myth of the Negro Past* (1941), Melville Herskovits emphasized the centrality of African culture in the New World. Attacking E. Franklin Frazier, who argued that Africans had lost their cultural heritage as a result of enslavement, Herskovits claimed that many Africanisms survived the Middle Passage and were pivotal in the development of African American culture. According to Herskovits, African culture absorbed elements of western culture while retaining "inner" African "values."[24]

Historians interested in West African culture have drawn on a variety of sources to inform their studies: European traveler accounts, African oral history, and accounts of twentieth-century anthropologists. The methodology of these historians can prove particularly useful in gauging how West Africans practiced friendship in precolonial West Africa. Many anthropologists of the twentieth century observed and recorded the function and practices of friendship in West Africa. While this research cannot be simply read back to precolonial West Africa, it is nevertheless indicative of the functions of West African friendship; moreover, it reveals the possible relationships among West Africans on the eve of the transatlantic slave trade.[25]

Friendship was central in traditional West African communities. Indeed, in the early twentieth century, Herskovits studied friendship in Dahomey (present-day Benin). He claimed, "For those interested in the background of New World Negroes, the importance of Dahomean culture derives from its situation at the very centre of the long coastal belt where the most intensive slaving operations were carried on."[26] Herskovits's study emphasized the importance of friendship in the lives of Dahomean men and women. Every man or woman was expected to have a best friend of the same sex.[27] These connections were usually formed in the playmate relationships of childhood; parents actively encouraged friendships between children. Often, friendship had its roots in adolescence. For example, when young girls reached puberty, they were withdrawn from associating with the opposite sex. During this period, members of the same sex formed strong friendships. Sometimes they engaged in homosexual practices and formed relationships, the attachments of which persisted after these experiences had been replaced by heterosexual activities in adulthood. Friendship also had its roots in the circumcision ritual: boys who had been ritually circumcised in the same group felt close to one another.[28]

Friendships, although sometimes ritualistic and ceremonial, did not lack emotional depth. Trust and mutual respect characterized them; best friends were expected to share their hopes, fears, and problems. Best friendship carried great responsibility; for example, during the Dahomean monarchy, if a person was wanted by the king's officers and had evaded capture, the officers arrested and imprisoned the fugitive's best friend. If the fugitive could not be found, the best friend was tortured—officials knew that as soon as the fugitive learned of his best friend's capture, he would give himself up to save his friend. Dahomean folklore promoted the virtues of best friendship: loyalty, risking oneself for the best friend, and putting the best friend's interests before one's own. For example, in one folktale, a man tests the friendship of three people: his father-in-law, a diviner, and his best friend, confiding in each that he had accidently shot one of the king's men while hunting. Both the father-in-law and the diviner refuse to help. Only the best friend assists the man without question, digging a grave in the woods to conceal the crime. No one, in fact, was killed—it was a test—and the tale ends: "That is why, in the life of man, of one's father-in-law, Bokonon [diviner], or best friend, a person must always be closest to the best friend. The others a person may leave to one side, but the best friend of a man, he is the first."[29]

Dahomean friendship was publicly recognized particularly at weddings or funerals, when the best friends of the celebrants or mourners assisted with the ceremonial rites. One of the most important tasks of a best friend was to act as executor of the friend's will. Over the course of a lifetime, a person gave his best friend detailed information of what he owned, where his money was hidden, and who were to be his heirs. Upon a best friend's death, the survivor dictated the will to the members of the deceased's family.[30]

Other anthropological studies of West African communities, similarly, underscore the importance of friendship. Among the Bangwa of Cameroon, for example, three types of friendship structured social relations: friendship ascribed through similar shared birthdates and birth years (*eshua*), ascribed through shared status (*eshua manze*), and acquired through mutual liking (*eshua nti* or *mbong eshua*). People of both sexes had ascribed friends. Friendships among the Bangwa permitted increased social and economic opportunity and provided valuable emotional outlets.[31] As with the Dahomeans, Bangwa folklore stressed the importance of friendship and warned strongly about being friendless. Indeed, friendship was highly valued because debts and witchcraft accusations often caused instability among kin.[32] Friends trusted each other and relayed to each other intimate personal and family details that they kept from kin. As in Dahomean friendship, a person typically acted as executor to a best friend's will. He also attended his friend's family discussions and offered impartial advice in the case of disputes. In addition, one man's friend was sometimes made godfather to the other's children.[33] The godparent was expected to look after the child's interests and play the role of confidant and advisor to his godchildren, particularly during the turbulent transition from adolescence to adulthood. The godparent was also expected to impart some degree of knowledge, such as a craft, to the child. If a man died prematurely, his friend often gained custody of his godchild. The friend managed the estate and became the heir's guardian, supervising the child's education.[34]

In some parts of West Africa, notably among the Nzema of southern Ghana, friendship was formalized through same-sex marriage, a pact reinforced through a combination of formal and informal rights and obligations. For example, friends were expected to help each other in times of debt and assist at each other's funerals. This marriage resembled a heterosexual marriage in every way except sex. A man married another man because of his character, physical beauty or prestige, or for instrumental reasons. He was expected to ask his friend's parents for permission to marry and pay bridewealth if the marriage was accepted. If the two men had female wives, the wives were required to consent to these arrangements. Same-sex marriages were socially accepted and coexisted harmoniously with cross-sex marriages.[35]

Blood brotherhood was also common throughout Africa. Perhaps the best known anthropological study of blood brotherhood was undertaken by Edward E. Evans-Pritchard in the 1930s among the Zande, a Central African people of the Nile-Uelle Divide.[36] At the time of Evans-Pritchard's writing, blood brotherhood—a formal act of friendship that men entered to fortify existing bonds of sentiment and for instrumental reasons—was sealed by a ritual act in which each participant swallowed the blood of the other.[37] The obligations of blood brotherhood were announced during the ceremony before the exchange of blood. Evans-Pritchard summarized the main points of the declaration:

A man must act always as a generous friend towards his blood brother; he must give him food and beer when he visits his homestead; he must refrain from making advances to his women; he must not refuse spears or other gifts, which he is free to part with, on the request of his blood brother; he must grant the hand of his daughter in marriage, if she is not already espoused; he must not speak evil of his blood brother to the princes; he must render him assistance in quarrels; he must do his best to protect him against vengeance and justice; he must give his blood brother the heads of any animals which he has killed in hunting, if he asks for them. Generally speaking, a man must always support his blood brother when he is in difficulties, especially when he is in legal difficulties.[38]

The obligations of blood brotherhood were substantial, but so were the practical benefits. Sometimes, blood brotherhood was employed for trading and alliances. Faced with scarce resources in their own lands, the Zande often made blood brotherhood bonds with the neighboring Mbegumba and Mberidi to exchange much-needed commodities. In this situation, blood brotherhood also included the clansmen of the two individuals. So, in theory, a man owed the same duties to the members of his blood brother's clan; however, in practice, the obligations became increasingly weaker the wider the extension. In this way, blood brotherhood promoted community cohesion.[39]

Friendship, primarily practiced between members of the same sex, was central in the lives of West Africans. Friends had to be generous, loyal, and helpful, particularly in times of need. Friends had to protect one another, even in dangerous situations, putting each other's interests before their own. Upon death, friends assumed especially important responsibilities. Friendship served the emotional needs of the individual—it was personal, expressive, and private; friends trusted and confided in one another—and it did a lot more: it provided legal, social, and economic protection.

Folklore and Friendship among Enslaved Men

By considering how West Africans and nineteenth-century Americans constructed their friendships, historians can make tentative suggestions about how enslaved men might understand and frame their own friendships. Fortunately, however, it is possible to examine the worldviews of enslaved men more closely and see how they interpreted their friendships with other men. Friendship, as Lawrence Levine has asserted, is "frequently stressed" in the folklore of enslaved people.[40] Indeed, the moralizing series of folktales collected by Charles Colcock Jones Jr. from former slaves just after the Civil War is explicit.[41] One of these tales is the story of an alligator and marsh hen—two contrasting animals who look for food in the same place and live peacefully side by side. One day, Alligator gets a crab claw stuck in his mouth and suffers excruciating pain. As Marsh-hen passes him by, Alligator begs him to remove the claw. However, Marsh-hen is afraid to trust Alligator, believing that he will kill and eat him. After much persuading, Alligator announces that he will be friends with Marsh-hen and his family for the rest of his life, as well as making all the other alligators his friends, too, if Marsh-hen helps him. After accepting his offer, Marsh-hen extracts the offending claw, and Alligator keeps his word. The story ends with Alligator and Marsh-hen living together "like the same family."[42] For the enslaved, the disrupting effects of sale and familial separation sometimes necessitated "fictive kin" arrangements, obligations rooted in kinship enjoyed by slaves unrelated to one another.[43] In the tale of the alligator and the marsh-hen, it appears that friendship and alliance activates kinship. The story also bears some similarity to the practice of blood brotherhood in African society, whereby the behavior between blood brothers included their clansmen: Alligator arranges his friendship with Marsh-hen to be extended to all the other alligators, thus forging an extended family.

The obligations of fictive kinship are markedly outlined in the story of the dying bullfrog, in which an old bullfrog is very sick and close to death. As his friends and family gather round to nurse him and take a last look at him, he calls out: "My friends, who is going to take my wife when the breath leaves this here body?" His friends holler at the top of their voices, "Me me. Me me. Me me." After this reply, the bullfrog asks another question, "Which of you is going to mind my little children?" After a pause, the response came: "Not me. Not me. Not me."[44] The story ends with a caution: many are willing to notice a pretty young widow, but they don't want to look after another man's children. Similar to the obligations of friendship in West Africa, according to the tale, a good friend is supposed to assume parental responsibility of a dead friend's young children.

Standing by one's friend in the face of danger is the moral of a story concerning two friends and a bear. The friends are on a journey together and have to cross a thick swamp full of bears and other varmints. Promising to stand together and help each other out if they are attacked, the two friends continue their journey through the swamp. While crossing the swamp, a bear jumps out and makes for them. Instead of standing by his friend, one man takes off and climbs a tree. The other plays dead in an effort to deter the bear from attacking him. After sniffing around him for a while, the bear eventually loses interest and takes off to the woods. As these events take place, his friend remains in the tree, too scared to do anything to help. Afterward, with the bear gone, he shouts down to his friend, asking what the bear had told him, because it looked like the two were having a conversation. His friend responds, "He was telling me never to trust anyone who calls himself a friend, and who runs like a coward as soon as trouble comes."[45] As in the Dahomean folktale of friendship Herskovits recorded, true friends had to help each other out whenever danger struck.

Not deceiving one's friend, and being able to trust a friend completely, occupies a central place in several folktales. In the tale of the owl and the rooster, a broken promise causes the break-up of their friendship. Much like the alligator and marsh hen tale, whereby friendship is extended to the friend's family, we learn that resulting from the breakup of friendship, the owl ends up hating the wife and children of the rooster as well as the rooster himself. The tale ends with a stark warning: "It won't do, in this world, for a man to deceive his friend."[46] "The Poor Man and the Snake" starts with a man struggling to make a meager living cutting timber in a swamp from sunrise till sundown. One day, a big snake sees him, takes pity on him, and offers to help, but only if he can keep a secret from his wife. The man accepts the snake's offer, and the snake tells him that he will give him some money the next day, but he must not tell his wife where he got it. The next day, the snake finds the man working in the swamp and crawls up to him, spitting two quarts of silver out of his belly. While giving the money to the man, the snake explicitly says he must not tell his wife how he got it, otherwise he will die a poor man. The man promises, but the snake suspects he will go back on his promise and so follows the man home. Listening from outside the man's window, the snake hears the man returning to his wife with the money. His wife is delighted and starts questioning him. The man replies that his friend had given him the money. "What friend?" the wife asks. The man answers that he had promised not to tell. However, after much begging, the man tells her everything that had happened. The wife asserts that the snake must have a belly full of silver money; she suggests the man take his axe and chop off his head and take all the money out of him. The husband agrees to her plan. The snake hears and is left angry because "the man that he had befriended had gone back on his promise and made an evil plan to kill him." The next day, the man meets the snake in the swamp, and the snake asks whether he had told his wife. The man denies having done so and swings his axe at the snake, who draws back, anticipating the man's move. The man's swing misses the snake and cuts off his own leg; he screams for help, but being in the middle of the swamp, nobody hears his cries. As the man bleeds to death, the snake says

> Didn't I tell you when you got that silver from me, that if you told your wife you would die a poor man? You promised me you would keep the secret. You went home to your wife and you showed her the money and you told her where you got it. More than that: you and she fixed a plan to kill me, me who had been your friend, and to rob me of the money I had left. Now you see the judgment that comes to you. When you tried to chop off my head, you cut your own foot off. You are going to die in these here woods. No man nor woman is ever going to find you. The buzzards are going to eat you.

The tale ends with a direct moral: "And it happened just as the snake said. The man broke his word, and he died a poor man. Anybody who goes back on his promise and tries to harm the person who has done him a favor is sure to meet up with big trouble."[47]

The tales of friendship in Jones's collection refer to friendship between male protagonists. They emphasize the importance of male solidarity and friendship and promote male friendship as an ideal bond through which to structure homosocial relationships. Significantly, in most of these folklore collections, women are depicted negatively. In "The Poor Man and the Snake," for example, the man's wife is the one who insists her husband break his promise with the snake, thus destroying the friendship between them; she is the one who hatches the evil plan to kill the snake and rob him of his money. In her study of Joel Chandler Harris's Brer Rabbit tales, historian Rebecca Griffin concludes that "overall, feminine traits are defined in negative terms." Harris's tales are told in a masculine voice and "reflect men's thinking and serve the purposes of a male audience." In some stories, women are represented as foolish, naïve and vain; in others, they are malignant, possessing magical powers that can seduce, entrap, and otherwise harm men.[48] According to Griffin, Harris's tales voice concern over the dangers of assertive female sexuality and the reversal of accepted female gender roles and identities.

In the tales collected by folklorists such as Elsie Parsons in the early twentieth century, women are portrayed as unfaithful, deceitful, and self-serving in their relationships with men; they are serial adulterers, witches, gold-diggers, and murderers.[49] In "Three Sweethearts," a woman's husband catches her sleeping with two other men. The first lover hides under the bed when the second lover pays a visit, and the second lover seeks refuge in the loft when the husband returns, suspicious of his wife's behavior. When they are discovered, the lovers escape, and the husband beats his wife. Similarly, in "Two Daddies" a man returns home to his wife, who is conducting an affair with a man she hastily hides under the bed. The lover had told the wife's little boy that he was his daddy; when the husband enters the home the boy sings: "I got two daddies now, now. I got two daddies now, now. One in de baid, an' one under de baid." The boy's song leads to the lover's capture.[50] In "Out of Her Skin," while her husband sleeps a woman practices witchcraft, turning herself into animals, such as bears and panthers, and then taking off to the woods to terrorize people. While his wife is out on a nocturnal expedition, the husband wakes to find her skin lying next to the bed, and so he applies red pepper to it. When the woman returns, she is unable to get her skin on because it burns her. The husband wakes, and she is subsequently tarred and burnt to death.[51] In "The Rich Old Man," a rich man marries, and after he loses his wealth, his wife plots to kill him. She takes him to the river with his hands tied up and runs from behind to push him into the water. However, at the last minute, the man steps aside, and she plunges into the water herself.[52]

When former slave Hector Smith was interviewed for the WPA project in South Carolina, he recalled a song passed down from his grandparents. Distrust and suspicion of women reverberated throughout:

> Some say, what make de young girls so deceivin?
> So deceivin, so deceivin.
> Some say, what make de young girls so deceivin?
> So deceivin, so deceivin.
> Way down in de lonesome valley.[53]

How do we explain this inherent distrust and suspicion toward women portrayed by Hector Smith and in folklore of the enslaved generally? It is certainly plausible, as Deborah G. White has suggested, that the residential arrangements of enslaved people fuelled distrust.[54] As mentioned, a significant number of enslaved couples lived in cross-plantation marriages and hence faced regular separation. With many men unable to count on their spouses for day-to-day practical and emotional support, it was inevitable that they bonded strongly with other men—those they resided, worked, and played with daily. Enslaved men, unsurprisingly, built their friendships on trust and loyalty. Folklore emphasizes the hallmarks of male friendship: helping and protecting one another; standing by one another, particularly in the face of danger; trusting one another; and putting friends' interests before their own. These values protected enslaved men from their debasing enslavement.

Friendships among Enslaved Men

Given the private nature of friendship, details of individual relationships are hard to find. Some slave autobiographies, however, mention male friendships and reveal the intimate world of enslaved men. These narratives indicate that slavery's racial parameters were notably absent for a number of slaves in their childhoods. Frederick Douglass recalled that as a boy enslaved in Baltimore from the age of eight to fifteen, he was close friends with his master's son, "Little Tommy." Douglass professed much love for Tommy. He had "watched over him with the care of a big brother, fighting his battles in the street, and shielding him from harm." However, after Douglass was sent away to work on the Eastern Shore of Maryland for three years, he remarked that upon his return to Baltimore, at the age of eighteen, the "loving relations" between the two boys "were broken up." In childhood, Tommy had hardly considered Douglass as inferior. However, now "the time had come when his *friend* must become his *slave*." Tommy no longer depended on Douglass for protection and felt himself "a *man,* with other and more suitable associates." This hurt Douglass, for, he reflected in his narrative, "there were few persons to whom I was more sincerely attached than to him."[55] Such boyhood interracial friendships were not uncommon and, as Douglass noted, typically ended when both parties came of age. These friendships were generally based around play activities; Lunsford Lane, for example, spent his childhood playing with the master's children: "I knew no difference between myself and the white children nor did they seem to know any in turn." However, when Lane commenced work, he soon realized the difference between his slaveholder's children and himself. He recounted, "They began to order me about, and were told to do so by my master and mistress."[56] As a child, former slave Fields Cook "never knew what the yoke of oppression was," for the black and white children fared alike. He was "entemmately associated" with a white boy, of whom he "had attached the stronges ties of affection"; but when the boys grew up, the white boy began to "raise his feathers and boast of the superiority" he held over Cook.[57] In some cases, enslaved men learned valuable skills as a result of their boyhood friendships with the sons of slaveholders. Former slave Noah Rogers recounted the "close" friendship he shared with his master's son as a child. Despite disapproval from the white community, the master's son taught Rogers to "read write and to do small sums in arithmetic."[58] John P. Parker, too, was taught to read and write by the two sons of his owner, with whom he was "on intimate terms." The two sons regularly supplied Parker with books from the family library; Parker recalled reading the Bible, Shakespeare, and the works of English poets in the hayloft when he was not required by his owner.[59]

But as boys started their harrowing sentences of lifelong labor in the field gang, it was their fellow enslaved African American workers they turned to for guidance, support, and friendship. Men, particularly those who worked in same-sex gangs, sought solace in other male workers. John Brown, born a slave in Southampton County, Virginia, recalled the traumatic separation from his mother when he was sold to a speculator: "I was so stupified with grief and fright, that I could not shed a tear, though my heart was bursting." As Brown was bundled away, his mother ran alongside him screaming and begging to be permitted to kiss him for the last time and bid him goodbye. Brown was sold to a planter named Thomas Stevens in Baldwin County, Georgia, and sent out to work as a member of a field gang in the corn fields. Traumatized and depressed by the separation from his mother, and unused to heavy field labor, he forgot his duties and worked "indifferently." Stevens flogged him severely, swearing at him, using "the most abominable oaths." Brown professed that in the face of such depravation he wanted to die. He was saved, however, by a fellow member of his field gang, John Glasgow, who felt for Brown in his grief and consoled him by regularly speaking of his own story. Glasgow had been a free black sailor based in England with a wife and two children. After having made a journey to Savannah, Georgia, for a cargo of rice, he was abducted and sold on the auction block to Thomas Stevens. Glasgow urged Brown not to cry after his parents and relatives; he assured him that if he could make it to England and conducted himself properly, people would respect him "as much as they did a white man." "These kind words from John Glasgow gave me better heart, and inspired me with a longing to get to England," reported Brown. Although he continued to receive floggings, he reported, "I got along a little better after a while." Glasgow also nursed Brown back to health after a particularly brutal physical attack from Stevens left him with a broken nose and a cut to the tendons of his right eye.[60]

In his narrative, Brown referred to Glasgow, as his "only friend." Although there are no further examples of friendship between the two, Brown chose to interrupt his narrative to dedicate an entire chapter (fourteen pages) to the personal history of Glasgow in the hope that someone might be able to help locate the whereabouts of his friend's family in England. The chapter is considerably detailed and recounts Glasgow's early life, details of his marriage and family in England, his voyage to Savannah, and the subsequent enslavement and incessant floggings and torture he experienced at the hands of Thomas Stevens. The high level of detail indicates that the two friends most likely spent many hours talking, consoling, and exchanging stories. They sustained their friendship through these conversations; sharing their traumatic experiences, the pair sought relief from the dehumanizing aspects of enslaved life. Together, they resisted Thomas Stevens's attempts to crush their spirits and aspirations. Indeed, Glasgow's stories were so powerful that Brown made repeated escapes in a bid to reach England. He acknowledged it was Glasgow who taught him "to love and to seek liberty." After a successful escape to the North, Brown crossed the ocean and settled in his friend's homeland.[61]

Male Friendship and Runaways

Brown's narrative demonstrates how friendship served the emotional needs of enslaved men. Brown was saved by the friendship he shared with Glasgow. Glasgow comforted and nursed Brown through his traumatic experiences; crucially, he gave Brown hope—a reason to live. The story of Brown and Glasgow shows how friendship provided men with a buffer against the brutal features of enslaved life. Furthermore, we see how friendship could in some cases ultimately prove subversive, directly challenging the system of slavery. In the trusted sanctuary of their friendship, Glasgow told Brown deeply personal stories of his past and encouraged him to seek freedom.

The conspiratorial characteristics of friendship surface in other narratives. Through friendship, enslaved men felt confident enough to trust one another and relay subversive thoughts and information that challenged the system of slavery. Frederick Douglass described in detail how he and his "dear friends" plotted to run away from their enslavement in Maryland. Douglass schemed with a small group of men who he lived and worked with while enslaved at William Freeland's plantation in 1835. He admitted that he was attached with "hooks of steel" to these men: "The most affectionate and confiding friendship existed between us." Regarding two men, Henry and John Harris, he remarked, "I felt a friendship as strong as one man can feel for another, for I could have died with and for them." Although he was the youngest, his experience and ability to read gave Douglass considerable influence over his friends: "They all wanted to be free, but the serious thought of running away had not entered into their minds until I won them to the undertaking." Douglass recalled the regular illicit meetings they held while they plotted to escape: "We met often by night, and on every Sunday. At these meetings we talked the matter over; told our hopes and fears, and the difficulties discovered or imagined; and, like men of sense, we counted the cost of the enterprise to which we were committing ourselves. These meetings must have resembled, on a small scale, the meetings of revolutionary conspirators, in their primary condition."[62]

Through his friendship with other men, Douglass instigated and organized an escape attempt. His language explicitly acknowledges the link between the private and intimate world of friendship and the potential "revolutionary" implications of his actions. Such evidence supports the conceptualization of slave resistance Stephanie Camp made in her study of enslaved women and everyday resistance. Camp contended that for enslaved women, "personal topics" were also "political arenas"; in personal, everyday spaces, enslaved women contested and undermined the authority and power of the slaveholder. Camp called for historians of resistance to dissolve dichotomies, arguing that "overlooking the links between the public and private—between material or political issues, on the one hand, and cultural or intimate (emotionally and physically) issues, on the other—limits our understanding of human lives in the past, especially women's."[63] She stressed that historians know a "great deal" about slave runaways and rebellion, as well as the private world of the slave quarters, such as the shape and function of slave families. However, she affirmed that less is known about the connections between the two—"about the inception and ongoing development of and changes in slaves' culture of opposition."[64] Camp's approach is particularly useful for exploring the lives of enslaved men and resistance.

Frederick Douglass's testimony, for example, blurs the distinction between one of the most private and intimate areas of enslaved male life (friendship), and an overt public act of resistance (running away). John Brown's narrative, too, intimately reveals how enslaved men, through their friendships, instigated, changed, and nurtured a culture oppositional to slavery. John Brown, initially a traumatized, depressed, and broken slave, is transformed into an inspired, hopeful, and defiant man who seeks his liberty, and eventually claims it, resulting from his friendship with John Glasgow. These narratives show the political and potentially revolutionary nature of male friendship; in private, intimate spaces, enslaved men formulated their politics.

Running away was one of the most radical and political acts of slave resistance. It was also a distinctly gendered form of resistance. Franklin and Schweninger's study of fugitive slaves estimated that 81 percent of runaways in Virginia, the Carolinas, Tennessee, and Louisiana between 1790 and 1860 were boys and men. Burdened with childcare responsibilities and less familiar with the local terrain, women were not well represented in the statistics.[65] Many enslaved men, like Douglass, plotted to run away along with other men, especially their intimate friends. Enslaved on Maryland's Eastern Shore, Isaac Mason confided his plans to escape across the Mason-Dixon Line to a young man named Joshua, only because they were "very intimate." Mason placed "the utmost confidence in him," believing he would not betray his secret. Mason's instinct was right, and Joshua, "elated over the project," pledged to go with him; the pair pooled their resources to fund their expedition.[66] William Parker and a friend, Alexander, to whom he was "greatly attached," often talked about freedom "when out of hearing of the white people, or certain ones among our fellow servants."[67] Likewise, Louis Hughes discussed freedom each time he was with one of his "fast friends."[68] These slaves, like Douglass, only discussed freedom and escape with trusted close friends. The undertaking these men contemplated was enormous, and many needed the emotional support of their friends to effect escape. James Pennington recalled the emotions that ran through his mind when he contemplated escape: "Hope, fear, dread, terror, love, sorrow, and deep melancholy were mingled in my mind together; my mental state was one of most painful distraction."[69] William Green spoke on behalf of many men when he indicated why consulting with his friend was important to him: he claimed that an escape "requires all the nerve and energy that a poor slave can bring to his support to enable him to make up his mind to leave in this precarious manner."[70]

Frederick Douglass's male friends helped him endure the horrors of slavery. He professed much love for them and conspired to run away with them. Frederick Douglass, *My Bondage and My Freedom:* part 1, *Life as a Slave;* part 2, *Life as a Freeman* (New York: Miller, Orton & Mulligan, 1855), frontispiece.

John Brown was saved by his friend John Glasgow, who comforted him after he was separated from his mother, nursed him back to health after punishment, and inspired him to run away. John Brown, *Slave Life in Georgia: A Narrative of the Life, Sufferings, and Escape of John Brown, a Fugitive Slave, Now in England* (London: W. M. Watts, 1855), frontispiece.

It was not unheard of, however, for slaves to betray one another: "It should be remembered that slaves are sometimes great enemies to each other, telling tales, lying, catching fugitives, and the like," recalled former slave William Anderson.[71] According to Frederick Douglass, slave owners had been known "to send in spies among their slaves, to ascertain their views and feelings in regard to their condition."[72] Owners also accentuated the divisions between field and house slaves on large plantations. As Henry

Bibb remarked, "the domestic slaves are often found to be traitors to their own people, for the purpose of gaining favor with their masters; and they are encouraged and trained up by them to report every plot they know of being formed about stealing any thing, or running away, or any thing of the kind; and for which they are paid."[73] The threat of betrayal thus placed an increased emphasis on the importance of friendship and trust. However, echoing folklore of the enslaved that warned of the dangers of false friendship, in some cases, friends betrayed each other's plans for escape. Leonard Black was betrayed by an "intimate" acquaintance named Henry, who told the master of his intention to run away. Henry had planned to run with Black and arranged to meet him at a certain location; he failed to show up, and, in his place, members of the master's family, along with a group of other whites, were positioned to catch Black.[74] Isaac Williams described in his narrative how a friend named Willis betrayed his plans of escape. Williams commented, "Many of the slaves themselves were treacherous to each other, and while giving the Judas kiss would betray those they professed to love."[75] The motive of the betrayer, Williams noted, was "to curry favor with the powers that be."[76] In exchange for information, "Judases" could expect to receive extra food, money, or other material rewards from their owners.[77] Acts of betrayal destroyed everything friendship stood for. Indeed, some enslaved men were simply unable to conceive that a friend would be capable of such acts. When a slave named Sandy betrayed Frederick Douglass and his friends, Douglass noted, "We all loved him too well to think it *possible* that he could have betrayed us. So we rolled the guilt on other shoulders."[78]

Nonetheless, many remained steadfastly loyal to their friends. "There are others who would die sooner than betray a friend," asserted one former slave who had escaped to Canada.[79] If some enslaved men chose not to run with their friends, they provided what assistance they could, and in some cases they utilized their contacts in the underground economy to acquire items for those planning to run away. When William Green decided to run away, he visited his "confidential friends" and made arrangements to gather as much material aid as possible in preparation for the escape.[80] George Johnson and some others "made up a purse" for a friend, Thomas, who planned to run away after learning he was to be sold.[81] William Parker's friend managed to get a written slave pass for him for five dollars.[82] A male friend of fugitive slave Israel Campbell gave him a pistol for his journey to Canada.[83] Enslaved men took bold measures to help their friends escape.

Henry Bibb recalled the pain he felt when he escaped from slavery, leaving his friends behind. Henry Bibb, *Narrative of the Life and Adventures of Henry Bibb, an American Slave, Written by Himself* (New York: Author, 1849), frontispiece.

Isaac Mason successfully escaped slavery after plotting to escape with his close friend, Joshua. Isaac Mason, *Life of Isaac Mason as a Slave* (Worcester, MA: Author, 1893), frontispiece.

William Summerson, enslaved in Charleston, South Carolina, managed to escape with his wife to Union lines on the Carolina coast during the Civil War because of his male friend. Faced with separation from his wife after he was informed that his mistress would either move him into the country or sell him, Summerson desired to escape from the city and sought the help of his enslaved friend who worked transporting goods to Charleston from a plantation seven miles outside of town. The friend agreed to hide Summerson in a rice barrel on his wagon, and thus he was able to leave the city, cross the Ashley River, and pass the numerous Confederate pickets stationed along the roads. The danger was considerable, as Summerson noted: "Every half mile for seven miles we met a rebel picket, who stopped the wagon, read the pass, and had the right to search the wagon."[84] The escape was a success, and Summerson's friend returned to the city the following day to rescue Summerson's wife the same way. During part of her journey, a Confederate soldier rode on the wagon sitting on the barrel the wife was hiding in. After the couple reunited, they walked three miles through a swamp and reached a boat Summerson's friend had left for them. Picking up another runaway slave, they managed to travel fifteen miles by boat, past a Confederate gunboat and a fort, until they reached Union boats positioned on the Stono River.[85]

Slave narratives record the affliction enslaved men experienced when leaving their friends behind. As he contemplated escape, Frederick Douglass remarked, "I had a number of warm-hearted friends in Baltimore,— friends that I loved almost as I did my life,—and the thought of being separated from them forever was painful beyond expression."[86] Henry Bibb, too, felt bad in a similar situation: "My strong attachments to friends . . . twined about my heart and were hard to break away from."[87] When Louis Hughes learned his friend Tom planned to escape, he reflected that he was "sad to see him go, for he was like a brother to me—he was my companion and friend."[88] Such passages emphasize the importance and centrality of friendship in the lives of enslaved men and the difficulties of leaving these loved ones. Indeed, sometimes the bonds between friends were so strong that many chose to run away together. Between 1790 and 1816, an average of 40 percent of runaway slaves from Virginia, North Carolina, Tennessee, South Carolina, and Louisiana escaped with the company of one or more. Between 1838 and 1860, the average for the five states had dropped to 28 percent.[89] As historian Michael Johnson has commented, group runaways "exemplified the bonds of affection, loyalty, and trust that knit the larger slave community."[90]

Men ran with their friends for emotional and practical support. Isaac Williams acknowledged the obstacles runaways faced: "A fugitive slave had everything against him, the laws of the United States, big rewards offered for his capture, and no knowledge of the country he was to pass through."

One Hundred Dollars Reward.

RANAWAY from the Subscriber, sometime in September last, four Negro Men, viz :—

ISAAC, SCIPIO, JERRY, and KASEY

ISAAC is about thirty years of age, of middle stature, spare made, with some marks of the whip upon his back. He can read a little, has some knowledge of figures and the carpenter's trade, & has a downcast look when spoken to. He had on when he went off a blue cloth coat, olive colored pantaloons, and a Castor hat.

SCIPIO is about 5 feet 10 or 11 inches high, spare made, and about the same age of Isaac.

JERRY is a stout fellow, about 6 feet high, and 26 or 27 years of age, and has a sulky look.

KASEY is about 5 feet 8 or 10 inches high, very stout, between 45 and 50 years of age, and limps a little in walking, caused by having his thigh broken.

I expect they are endeavoring to get northwardly to some non slaveholding State, as Isaac for some time had a disposition that way, and no doubt has enticed the rest away with him. I expect they were all in company with another of my negro men, who went off at the same time, and who has since been lodged in Granville Jail.

Masters of Vessels and others are hereby forwarned against harboring or carrying off said fellows. I will give the above reward for their delivery to me, or confinement in any jail, or for information so that I get them again—or Twenty-Five dollars for any one of them.

NATHAN B. WHITFIELD

Rockford, Lenoir County,
November 15th, 1826.   12 tf.

Men made up the majority of runaway slaves in the antebellum period. Some of them ran away together and turned to their trusted friends for guidance and support. Slaveholders placed advertisements in local newspapers, describing the appearance and circumstances of their fugitive slaves, offering rewards. This advertisement from a North Carolina newspaper, describes four men who have run off together. *Raleigh Register, and North-Carolina Gazette,* November 21, 1826.

Williams, therefore, chose to run away with his friend, Henry Banks: "Banks and I kept together, knowing that union was strength."[91] Hiding out in a cave during their journey, the pair discussed their next move at length. Williams declared, "I was very fortunate in having Banks for a companion, and we mutually cheered each other in those hours of gloom and despair."[92] Like friends John Brown and John Glasgow, Williams and Banks exchanged stories to keep up each other's morale. Banks told his life story—where he was born, the trials he had suffered, and an incident of betrayal during a previous escape attempt. He was "troubled with great fits of depression"; accordingly, Williams did what he could to raise his friend's spirits. Williams noted that he himself was "naturally of a more cheerful disposition, generally buoyant and light-hearted," and so he sang to Banks in a low voice to calm him down. He also helped Banks recover from a distressing encounter with a pack of dogs belonging to a slave hunter.[93] Faced with an array of obstacles during their flight to freedom, Williams and Banks used their friendship for emotional support and to boost each other's morale. Their story, according to slave folklore, appears a prime example of how friends were expected to stand together in the thick of danger. In this case, neither friend abandoned the other when trouble came.[94]

Other friendships proved instrumental during escape. John Thompson ran away with his friend, a coachman, from a neighboring plantation. Because of his work, the coachman knew the surrounding geography very well. Thompson, therefore, relied upon him for navigation.[95] James Smith escaped with the help of two companions, Zip and Lorenzo, who were sailors and hence were able to sail and navigate their way from Virginia up to Pennsylvania. The two friends "knew the country and understood where to go." Smith also suffered from a lame leg; therefore, his friends' help was crucial.[96] William Green and his friend, Joseph, needed each other when they stole a boat to escape: they shared the chore of paddling, and then one had to row while the other bailed out the water caused by a minor leak in the vessel.[97] Isaac Mason and his "intimate" friend, Joshua, pooled their resources to fund their trip. Sharing their money in this way proved beneficial to both parties, as well as to another slave, George, who had no money of his own.[98]

Fugitive men who successfully escaped and settled in the North did not forget the friends they left behind. A letter written by fugitive slave John Henry Hill to abolitionist William Still demonstrates the persistence of strong bonds of affection; Hill had been living in Canada since his escape and wrote the following: "Mr. Still, I hold in my hand A letter from a friend of South, who calls me to promise that I made to him before I left. My dear Sir, this letter have made my heart Bleed, since I Received it, he also desires of me to remember him to his beloved Brethren and then to Pray for him and his dear friends who are in Slavery."[99] Other fugitive slaves resident in Canada, interviewed by Benjamin Drew, explained how they maintained contact with friends who remained in bondage. According to Drew, fugitive slave Dan Josiah Lockhart wrote to a friend in slavery asking him to pass on messages to his wife who also remained in captivity, "assuring" his wife of his "continued affection."[100] Similarly, when George Johnson was enslaved in Virginia, he received a letter from a fugitive friend who had recently escaped to Toronto.[101] Fugitive slave Henry Brown emphasized the importance of friendship: "We love our friends more than white people love theirs, for we risk more to save them from suffering. Many of our number who have escaped from bondage ourselves, have jeopardized our own liberty, in order to release our friends, and sometimes we have been retaken and made slaves of again, while endeavoring to rescue our friends from slavery's iron jaws."[102] Antebellum newspapers recorded the efforts of fugitives who crossed back into the slave states to rescue their friends. In 1857, the *Raleigh Register* reported that a "stout and hearty negro" named Ben, who had escaped slavery six years ago, was "running off the property" of his former master in Kentucky "at every opportunity." Enraged, the slaveholder, with the help of some other men, followed a runaway male house servant from his plantation to the Kentucky side of the Ohio River, with the intention of capturing Ben, who was assisting his friends across the river. In an ambush, the slaveholder and his men captured Ben after a desperate fight, returning him to slavery. The article remarked, "Ben is not the only man who has got himself into trouble by trying to aid a friend."[103] Indeed, a year later, a story appeared in the *Liberator* that recounted the capture of a couple of fugitive male slaves who had resided in Canada and spent their time "in active correspondence with friends" still in slavery. The two men, through correspondence with their friends in slavery, attempted to rescue some eight or ten others who remained enslaved in Mason County, Kentucky. The men, however, were captured after one of their letters detailing escape plans was intercepted.[104] Louis Talbert, another fugitive slave who was resident in Canada, crossed secretly into Kentucky at night to rescue two of his sisters and friends who remained in slavery. Although he failed to rescue his sisters, he succeeded in "bringing with him four of five of his

slave friends, including two women." The value of these slaves was estimated at $37,000.[105] By risking their life and potential reenslavement, the
men who went looking for their friends in southern slaveholding territory
proved how strong the ties of friendship could be.

Friendship played central roles in the lives of enslaved men. As fugitive slave Henry Brown reflected: "A slave's friends are *all* he possesses that
is of value to him. He cannot read, he has no property, he cannot be a
teacher of truth, or a politician; he cannot be very religious, and all that
remains to him, aside from the hope of freedom, that ever present deity,
forever inspiring him in his most terrible hours of despair, is the society of
his friends."[106] As Brown's comments suggest, friendship gave enslaved men
hope. The intimate relationships they shared with other men helped them
to not only survive their enslavement but actively resist it. Many enslaved
men lived, worked, and socialized together on a daily basis. Friendship—its
values and principles—framed, shaped, and gave meaning to these men's
lives. It enabled men to endure separation from family members, and it provided daily emotional and practical support for those in cross-plantation
marriages restricted to weekly or monthly visits. To trust a friend, confide
in him, and rely on him for help, particularly in difficult situations, was a
source of strength and comfort for enslaved men. In the private world of
friendship, enslaved men instigated and created a culture oppositional to
enslavement. In these private spaces, they forged their politics.

5

Enslaved Men,
the Grapevine Telegraph,
and the Underground Railroad

When enslaved men left the plantation to work, drink, wrestle, hunt, evade the patrols and commit theft, they came into contact with other enslaved men from different plantations. As mentioned, inter-plantation activities fostered camaraderie and sometimes rivalry. This chapter explores these links in greater depth, showing how the lives of enslaved men were intertwined in a subversive inter-plantation network. Despite the huge distances separating plantations throughout the rural antebellum South, enslaved people maintained a secret system of communication that linked their communities: the grapevine telegraph, which kept enslaved communities across the South informed of news and events. Enslaved men were vital to the success of this network: they were more mobile than their female counterparts and, accordingly, more familiar with local geography. Consequently, they were also more likely to make contact with subversive, abolitionist sources. Enslaved men used the grapevine telegraph to keep informed of daily events, but they also utilized the network to hold conspiratorial cross-plantation meetings with other men. In some cases, they plotted active rebellion; in other instances, they harbored runaway slaves and ferried them northward to freedom from one plantation to the next. Individual everyday resistance in the antebellum South was intimately linked to collective acts of insurrection; thus, drawing a clear theoretical distinction between the two is misleading.[1] As Emilia Viotti da Costa states in her work on the Demerara slave rebellion of 1823, "although not every act of resistance leads to rebellion, without the daily and tenacious acts of defiance and sabotage, rebellions would have been difficult, if not impossible."[2] Through their everyday activities—work and leisure—men established strong bonds of solidarity. They used their friendships and alliances, developed in their daily lives, to collectively organize and challenge their enslavement. As Walter Johnson has contended, "collective resistance is, at bottom, a process of everyday organization, one that, in fact, depends upon connections and trust established through everyday actions."[3]

"They Are Kept in Darkness"

In his autobiography, fugitive slave Leonard Black spoke on behalf of the great majority of enslaved people: "The slaves are taught ignorance as we teach our children knowledge. They are kept in darkness."[4] Slaveholders across the South strove to keep their slaves "in darkness"; they continuously guarded their property from what they perceived to be corrupting influences.[5] Many petitions sent to southern legislatures in the antebellum period demonstrate the fears of the southern planter class, who often sought the passing of new legislation, or the reinforcement of existing laws to protect their property from subversive influences. This was particularly the case during the later antebellum period, whereby southern planters—in response to David Walker's inflammatory *Appeal to the Colored Citizens of the World* (1829), Nat Turner's revolt of 1831, and the growing abolitionist movement—sought to further isolate their slaves by halting the influx of abolitionist literature from the North.[6] For example, a petition to the Texas legislature claimed: "One of the great operating causes in corrupting the minds of the people by infusing sentiments hostile to the institution of Slavery is the free and unlicensed circulation of incendiary documents and anti-Slavery newspapers through the post offices of the State." According to the petition, slaves were interacting with "temporary sojourners" who were "voluntary or hired emissaries of northern associations; or individuals laboring to destroy slavery in the southern States, instigating desertion or conspiracy and insurrection." The petitioners asked the legislature to enact appropriate laws to combat these "evils."[7] In 1818, a group of concerned citizens complained to the Virginia legislature that crews of oyster traders were sailing down from Maryland and trading with slaves who ventured out at night to gather oysters. According to the petition, not only did the illicit trading encourage slaves to "pilfer from their masters" and "neglect their labours in the day," but the slaves were also coming into contact with whites who preached "universal emancipation," which "sanctifies in their veins the worst excitement . . . of treachery &

violence." The Maryland oyster traders were, according to the petitioners, "agents" of abolitionism: "incendiary . . . newspapers & pamphlets" were being "extensively circulated" among the slaves.[8]

Owners also sought to shield their slaves from the influence of free blacks, who they claimed instilled "views of liberty injurious to the interests of their owners" in the minds of the enslaved.[9] Free blacks, according to one appeal to the North Carolina legislature, created a "spirit of discontent" among the enslaved population of Duplin County. The appeal proposed a radical solution: free blacks should be transported to Liberia, and those who refused ought to be sold into slavery.[10] Another request, presented to the South Carolina legislature, asked the state to ban "all free Negroes and coloured people from migrating into this State." Those who had arrived within the previous five years were to be banished. According to the petitioners, the free blacks of South Carolina had established churches and schools with money from northern abolitionist societies for their own exclusive use. They were also teaching slaves to read and write.[11] Another petition from South Carolina emphasized that free blacks from the North, who arrived in Charleston on vessels from the North employed as stewards, cooks, or mariners, were responsible for introducing among the enslaved people of South Carolina "the moral contagion of their pernicious principles and opinions." According to the petitioners, there was "scarcely . . . an evil of greater magnitude" than the "constant intercourse" between these free blacks and enslaved people of South Carolina. To permit this to continue would "invite new attempts at insurrection." In the petitioners' eyes, there was only one solution: "to prevent ANY COLOURED PERSON FROM ANY PART OF THE WORLD *ever entering again into the limits of the State of South-Carolina,* by LAND OR BY WATER."[12]

Certainly, literate slaves scared southern slaveholders. In 1828, the Charleston City Council sought to enforce the law prohibiting slaves from learning how to read and write, as literate slaves were able to "carry on illicit traffic, to communicate privately among themselves and to evade those regulations that are intended to prevent confederations among them."[13] Moreover, in another appeal to the South Carolina legislature, white petitioners expressed fears that literate blacks could potentially "sap the foundation of the peace of this & all the Slave holding States," for they were able to "convey to each other throughout the different States all their plots and designs," placing whites "under all the horrors of a General insurrection."[14]

Equally, many whites were concerned about the practice of hiring out slaves. Although the arrangement often proved lucrative for slave owners, in the eyes of others it was fraught with problems. Self-hired slaves were a particular cause for concern. Many petitions to southern legislatures echoed the concerns of a group of slaveholders from Craven County, North Carolina, who, in 1831, complained that "large gangs" of self-hiring slaves, who had passes "for a month's or more duration," were habitually approaching their neighborhood to "sell, buy, traffick, and fish." According to the slaveholders, these self-hiring slaves "corrupt" their own slaves and "induce them to runaway." The petitioners implored the legislature to uphold the 1794 law prohibiting slaves from hiring out their own time, and the laws passed in 1787 and 1788 prohibiting slaves from bartering and trading.[15] Petitions from slave owners accused self-hired slaves of distributing "seditious writings & notions" among their slaves, while one appeal concluded, "Nothing is so injurious to the institution of slavery as the loose manner in which some owners maintain their authority and we deem this hiring by Slaves of their own time, either directly or indirectly as especially demoralizing to the slaves and injurious to other owners of slaves."[16]

The efforts of slaveholders to maintain their slaves' ignorance were successful in some cases. Former slave James Bolton recalled, "None er our niggers ever runned away, an' we diden' no nuthin' 'bout no Norf, twel long atter freedom done come."[17] Even when slaves heard about freedom during their enslavement, some did not know how to act: "Weuns heahs 'bout dis freedom thing but don't know what to do 'bout it," asserted Steve Robertson.[18] During the Civil War, when neighboring slaves crossed over to their plantation to inform them about how the "old man Abe" was going to set them free, Gabe Butler's family remained skeptical and fearful: "My mammy and pappy sed he might kill us," asserted Gabe Butler, "I didnt kno' what being 'free' meant."[19] When Emmett Byrd's master, Mr. Spence, informed him he was free after the Civil War, he didn't leave: "I didn't have sense to know where to go. I didn't know what freedom was," remarked Byrd.[20] However, despite the best efforts of the white ruling class, subversive news, gossip, and information on freedom leaked into slave communities. Enslaved men routinely disseminated this knowledge.

Mobile Men

As discussed, enslaved men were more mobile than women because they were presented with more hiring-out opportunities. They also regularly left plantations to visit loved ones in cross-plantation marriages, to drink, gamble, wrestle, hunt, and steal. Through these activities, they familiarized themselves with the local geography. Additionally, some enslaved men went considerably beyond their localities, working as carriage drivers, teamsters, and transporters of plantation goods.[21] The distances they traveled varied depending on the tasks and destinations; errands into nearby towns to pick up certain products for the plantation could be short in duration and completed within the day, while some entailed overnight stays.[22]

Carriage drivers could expect to drive any distance. William McWhorter told a WPA interviewer that his father, enslaved in Greene County, Georgia, was the plantation carriage driver and drove his master's family wherever they wanted to go.[23] Carrie Hudson claimed that her brother, Squire, would always drive the owner's family into town and sometimes took them from Ruckersville, Georgia, to Anderson, South Carolina, a trip of roughly thirty miles.[24] Teamsters and transporters traveled considerable distances and spent multiple days on the road. Mary Watson's father, for example, worked as teamster in the fall, hauling cotton for his master from Abbeville, South Carolina, to Augusta, Georgia, approximately sixty miles away.[25] Elizabeth W. Allston Pringle, daughter of one of the largest plantation owners in South Carolina, recalled that as a result of the Union blockade during the Civil War, her father regularly organized gangs of enslaved men to transport rice and salt along the rivers through South Carolina to the railroad. Two lighters, each crewed by a captain and a team of eight enslaved men, transported these goods up the Pee Dee River, almost the whole length of South Carolina, from Chicora Wood plantation, in Georgetown County, up to Mars Bluff, Society Hill, and sometimes Cheraw. Pringle described it as "a long, hard trip." Crews of enslaved men also transported goods from Chicora Wood up the Black River to Kingstree.[26] Slaves working on the waterways not only traveled long distances, they exercised a considerable degree of independence. Moses Grandy, for example, worked along the Albemarle Sound in North Carolina. Working as a ferryman, he was allowed to hire out his own time and charter canal boats from the Pasquotank ports of Camden, Elizabeth City, and Weeksville, through the Great Dismal Swamp up to Norfolk, Virginia. He worked on schooners and captained lighters transporting lumber out of the Great Dismal Swamp. As a ferryman, he lived away from his owner for weeks at a time, sleeping on his boat or in the lumber camps of the Great Dismal Swamp.[27]

Highly mobile enslaved men came into contact with a range of people:

Enslaved men frequently left the plantation for a variety of reasons: to maintain cross-plantation marriages, engage in leisure activities, and hunt, for example. They were also hired out more often than women. Some men traveled considerable distances transporting goods and running errands for slaveholders; in this way, they became familiar with the local geography. *Hauling Cotton to the River,* in T. B. Thorpe, "Cotton and Its Cultivation," *Harper's New Monthly Magazine* 8, no. 46 (March 1854): 460.

slaves from different plantations, free blacks, and whites, from whom they gathered dissident ideas and knowledge about freedom, often for the first time. When Charles Ball was hired out to work in the navy yard of Washington, DC, he formed an acquaintance with a free black sailor from Philadelphia, who talked about life in the free North and promised to help him escape. Ball recalled their conversations: "His description of Philadelphia, and of the liberty enjoyed there by the black people, so charmed my imagination that I determined to devise some plan of escaping . . . and making my way to the north."[28] Likewise, while hired out to a large hotel, Henry Watson met a white northerner from Boston who encouraged and assisted him to run away. The Bostonian informed him of "the security the northern states afforded for slaves, the feeling of the free people of color living there, and of the great anti-slavery movement there." This was a subject, admitted Watson, "which I was entirely ignorant of before."[29] Isaac Williams attributed his escape to his geographical mobility. During some of his "midnight wanderings," he made his way to some woods where northern men were extracting lumber. Here, two brothers from Boston "painted a vivid picture of the life, enterprise and business of the northern cities" during a "long talk" with Williams. The brothers, supporters of abolition, encouraged Williams to escape, claiming that if he escaped and reached the North, "willing hands and noble hearts" would help him. He listened attentively: he "drank all this magic tale of freedom to be gained, and listened as eagerly as a child does to a marvelous story."[30] Enslaved in Maryland, after frequent whippings and other ill treatment from his owner, James Watkins "set about obtaining every information" in his power on the subject of freedom. He regularly traveled illicitly at night two to three miles from his slave quarters to give a group of men a hand at work in some lime kilns and, in the process, "hear something about freedom." Here he encountered two Irishmen who told him about freedom in the North.[31]

Slaveholders were particularly concerned about the dissemination of these "illicit" ideas within slave communities, and they aimed to eradicate them at any cost. In a letter written to John Williams, William Pettigrew, a member of one of North Carolina's most prominent slaveholding families, discussed the problems posed by a troublesome fifty-six-year-old slave carpenter who, although engaged in faithful service for many years, had recently become "lamentably deficient" in honesty and faithfulness. Moreover, the slave had become "haunted . . . with a desire for freedom." Pettigrew complained that the slave brought "harsh strictures" against him for not granting his freedom. But what most concerned Pettigrew was the language the slave used "in the presence of his fellow servants." Pettigrew pondered whether to severely punish him, sell him farther South, or transport him to Liberia. Weighing his options, he ruled the first idea out, claiming that it would be "far more injurious" to his slaves: the slave would continue to be a "malignant enemy" in the "heart" of his establishment "poisoning the minds of all around him." Dismissing the second option as "wicked," Pettigrew resolved to transport the slave to Africa so he may "enjoy" the freedom he wanted, "perhaps not accompanied by want and sorrow, and even repentance when too late." However, he stressed that the destination of the man be kept secret from the other slaves, "otherwise a desire for freedom will take possession of them."[32]

Owners attempted to prevent the spread of subversive ideas within slave communities by policing the spatial and temporal lives of the enslaved. They specifically targeted enslaved men, who they knew were more mobile than women. Plantation management manuals emphasized the potential dangers posed by cross-plantation marriages. "Allowing the men to marry out of the plantation" gives them a "feeling of independence," asserted one instruction manual. The men are also "exposed to temptation from meeting and associating with negroes from different directions, and with various habits & vices."[33] For this reason, slaveholders banned notorious enslaved men from entering their plantations. On May 5, 1838, Robert Rives, a plantation owner in Virginia, wrote a letter to Floyd L. Whitehead, complaining about one of Whitehead's slaves. He declared, "I am so afraid of the corrupting influence of Milo on my negroes that I have directed none of them shall see him and particularly that they shall not go on your plantation."[34] Likewise, after a failed attempt to run away from his enslavement, James Watkins wrote in his autobiography that he was forbidden by neighboring planters to associate with their slaves, "lest I should contaminate them."[35] Slaveholder Richard Eppes sought to hire out a troublesome slave, Sandy, away from one of his plantations on the James River, Virginia, because he "exerted a bad influence" on the other slaves. Writing a month after Lincoln's election, and with rumors of secession and civil war circulating, Eppes was convinced this was the safest thing to do to quash potential unrest on his plantation.[36] Many slave owners forbade slaves to meet in groups: "We were not allowed to gather in groups for conversation for fear we were plottin' to escape, or cause trouble of some kind," remarked a former Virginia slave.[37] Isaac Williams said, "Slave owners were so fearful of an insurrection among the slaves, that if three or four colored men gathered together on a Sunday and entered into any earnest conversation, they were sentenced to receive thirty-nine lashes on Monday morning."[38] In his narrative, Charles Ball recalled: "All over the south, the slaves are discouraged, as much as possible, and by all possible means, from going to any place of religious worship on Sunday. This is to prevent them from associating together, from different estates, and distant parts of the country; and plotting conspiracies and insurrections. On some estates, the overseers are required to prohibit the people from going to meeting off the plantation, at any time, under the severest penalties."[39] Indeed, in the aftermath of Nat Turner's slave rebellion, legislatures across the South passed laws prohibiting slaves from congregating in groups.[40] Virginia passed laws banning both enslaved people and free blacks from preaching or conducting religious gatherings. Enslaved people were only allowed to attend religious meetings accompanied by whites. Free blacks were persecuted in the state—many fled Southampton County. In the wake of the rebellion, the militia and patrol systems were expanded and strengthened across the South.[41] Slaveholders reacted earnestly to rumor, gossip, and the spread of "corrupting" influences by enslaved men; they knew this communication was potentially subversive. Indeed, on the subject of rumor among subaltern people, historian Ranajit Guha has commented, "An unmistakable, if indirect, acknowledgement of its power is the historically known concern for its suppression and control on the part of those who in all such societies had the most to lose by rebellion."[42]

Enslaved Men and the Grapevine Telegraph

Despite slaveholders' best efforts, enslaved people maintained an illicit inter-plantation grapevine telegraph. Former slave George Washington Albright recollected, "We slaves knew very little about what was going on outside our plantations, for our owners aimed to keep us in darkness. But sometimes, by grapevine telegraph, we learned of great events."[43] Enslaved men were the key operators of the grapevine telegraph; men who transported goods and ran errands for their masters carried messages, news, and seditious material from one plantation to another. "When the white folks wrote notes to each other," recalled former slave Square Irvin, "who so ever carried the note, picked up all the news he could gather both going and coming."[44] According to Booker T. Washington, during the Civil War, the slaves on his plantation often "got knowledge of the results of great battles before the white people received it." He stated:

> This news was usually gotten from the colored man who was sent to the post-office for the mail. In our case the post-office was about three miles from the plantation and the mail came once or twice a week. The man who was sent to the office would linger about the place long enough to get the drift of the conversation from the group

of white people who naturally congregated there, after receiving their mail, to discuss the latest news. The mail-carrier on his way back to our master's house would as naturally retail the news that he had secured among the slaves, and in this way they often heard of important events before the white people at the "big house," as the master's house was called.[45]

In some rare cases, enslaved men exchanged letters. Literate slaves were uncommon, so this was not the typical means of communication; however, it did occur. In Richmond County, Virginia, Elias Harroll, an enslaved carpenter owned by Colonel Carter of Sabine Hall, wrote a letter to his friend, explaining that he had run away due to excessive ill treatment at the hands of Coleman Smith, the man he was hired out to. Smith had intercepted the letter and written to Carter, demanding to know whether the allegations Elias made in the letter were true. The letter read:

> Dear friend, I will now take this opportunity of writing you a few lines to inform you, that I now am all right, and I have seen my master and I showed myself to him and he was very much hutted & he sent right off after one of his overseers to look at me with him for a Witness for he says that he never seen nobody whipt in such away in his life and he said he would have been much better satisfied if Smith hader brought me home and put me down & told him that he would not pay him for my hire, then to whip me in the way that he did & he told his overseers that any man that would whip a hired servant in that he was a Dam Raskill he did not car who he was & he told me that he was not going to think about send me back to Smith nor wood employ me himself because if he did employ me he would have to lone my hire but he told me to try & take care of myself for he wood not must making him pay my hire for five hundred Dollars.
>
>   I do not want you to trouble yourself about me for I am safe in my glorious hiding place.
> Elias Harroll.[46]

In this case, communication stretched beyond the confines of the plantation and extended to runaways. Harroll knew that his friend would be concerned about his welfare, so he emphasized that he was safe. In this way, friends stayed in touch and reassured one another of their well-being. The majority of slaves, however, were illiterate, so enslaved men took stolen newspapers or seditious material to the few literate slaves in the neighborhood. For example, men traveled miles carrying stolen papers for literate slave Henry Clay Bruce to read to them at night.[47] Enslaved men regularly passed information to other plantation communities when they visited their wives in cross-plantation marriages. "Dey only way any news wuz carried wuz through a pass ter go see a girl from anuther plantation," remarked Jeff Calhoun.[48] In this way, the slaves preserved the "grapevine way," recalled Louis Davis; "when we made these visits, we exchanged all the news we heared."[49] At night, enslaved men also illicitly communicated with other plantations without passes. The dangers of engaging in this subversive activity were clear, as one former slave declared: "We wasn't to carry news from one plantation to anoder. Kill you shore. What was done on one plantation had to stay right dar."[50] Despite the threat of the patrol gangs, slaves "would git each other word by sending a man round way late at night."[51] As a result of the grapevine telegraph, numerous slave communities "kept up pretty good with what was going on."[52] Through the grapevine, enslaved men communicated major events to slave communities throughout the South: the Emancipation Proclamation, developments during the Civil War, as well as forthcoming slave sales.[53] Some managed to follow national politics. For example, former slave Henry Clay Bruce recalled having followed the presidential election of 1856, in which John C. Frémont stood as the first presidential candidate for the new Republican Party. Bruce and his fellow slaves "expected to be set free if Frémont was elected."[54] In his slave narrative, James Curry recalled, similarly, how slaves became aware of a presidential election involving Van Buren: "The slaves also from neighboring plantations hold frequent intercourse with each other, and then they cannot help hearing white people talk. For instance, just before the last presidential election, there came a report from a neighboring plantation, that, if Van Buren was elected, he was going to give all the slaves their freedom. It spread rapidly among all the slaves in the neighborhood, and great, very great was the rejoicing."[55]

For enslaved people, the slave grapevine was a pivotal form of oppositional discourse. As James C. Scott has contended, for people denied access to institutionalized political dialogue, short of rebellion, the site of rumor and gossip becomes "*the* site of public political discourse."[56] In his work charting the history of African American political mobilization, Steven

Hahn argued that in societies such as the antebellum South, among enslaved people rumor was a "political weapon." For Hahn, rumor is "cloaked in anonymity" and "flows through established channels of everyday life." It is subject to "continuous improvisation and embellishment, thereby activating and energizing (in effect politicizing) those who become involved in its circuits."[57] Through the daily operation of the grapevine, enslaved men maintained their politics and in some cases plotted insurrection. Day-to-day resistance became revolutionary.

In the narrative of William Webb, through the grapevine network, enslaved men professed their loyalties to one another and maintained an underground inter-plantation organization collectively resisting the institution of slavery. Together, they forged an alliance that had revolutionary implications. Webb recalled the turmoil that swept the South during the presidential election of 1856. It was the first time, recounted Webb, that black people were aware that "another Nation" wanted them to be free.[58] In Mississippi, where Webb was enslaved, despite the threat of capital punishment for holding clandestine meetings, enslaved men from the surrounding areas gathered secretly to discuss the steps they should take to secure their freedom. At these meetings, the men took turns standing up and addressing their peers. They debated whether to rebel and embark on a killing spree or wait another four years for the next president. They held their initial meeting at a secret location fourteen miles from where Webb was enslaved; they protected themselves by stationing a guard of men, and established a signal in case patrol gangs were spotted. To secure trust, the men swore an oath to keep their meetings secret. Webb warned them not to break the oath: if anyone broke it, the others "would put him in a bag with a rock tied around his neck and sink him in the creek." They designated the initial location of their meeting the "headquarters," where "all news" was to be sent; from there, instructions could be sent out to enslaved men.

At a subsequent meeting, Webb proposed establishing an inter-state, inter-plantation network of enslaved men. In each state, "kings" were to be established, and they would then "appoint a man to travel twelve miles, and then hand the news to another man, and so on." Webb's idea was simple: if enslaved people decided to rebel, they could do so simultaneously across the states. The men elected "Old Uncle Ned" the King of their band in Mississippi, for he knew the surrounding country well. When the son of William Webb's owner married a girl from Kentucky, Webb accompanied the young master to work there. Upon settling in Kentucky, he immediately organized

In the antebellum period, enslaved men, in defiance of the spatial and temporal constraints of plantation life, met up in secret off the plantation to socialize, organize, and plot. This illustration shows a group of enslaved men holding a secret meeting in the woods and swamps of the South during the Civil War. *Fugitive Slaves, 1862,* in *Le Monde Illustré* 9 (1862): 9.

a band of men from among the local plantations, just like he had done in Mississippi. After appointing a "head man," John, he singled out twelve men, each of whom he gave a little bag of roots and instructed to shake the bags in the direction of their master's house every morning. He told them that the possession of these roots was to be kept a secret from the other slaves. After the men had met regularly and established trust, Webb discussed the issue of freedom with them the same manner as in Mississippi: they debated whether to rise up and rebel, or wait for the next elections.[59] By organizing an inter-plantation network in this way, Webb claimed to have had "friends all over the country" and received news from different States "in a very short time." Indeed, just before the Civil War, he maintained that the "blessed news" of Lincoln "flew from one State to another."[60]

Webb's inter-plantation network was a distinctly male homosocial organization. Women, when mentioned, were tasked with preparing food for the men after the underground gatherings. Not only were women excluded from the meetings, there appears to have been a lack of trust between the sexes. After a meeting, which culminated in a supper prepared by the women, the women wanted to discuss freedom with Webb. He initially rejected the request: "I told them I did not know that I could talk to them as I would wish to."[61] Male solidarity, therefore, underpinned the secret collusion and diffusion of subversive information. Trust shaped the day-to-day relationships of enslaved men, but it did a lot more: it effected collective resistance to slavery. As Webb's narrative shows, through their inter-plantation network, men conspired to rebel.

Indeed, almost all of the slave rebellions and plots of the first half of the nineteenth century were planned, led, and organized by enslaved men. For example, out of the 236 slaves tried for insurrection in Virginia between 1785 and 1865, only 2 were female.[62] During the antebellum period, it was exclusively enslaved men who collectively organized the three major slave rebellions and conspiracies: Gabriel Prosser (1800), Denmark Vesey (1822) and Nat Turner (1831).[63] Examining the Gabriel Prosser conspiracy, historian James Sidbury has emphasized that the rebels spent most of their time in male homosocial spaces; the associations they formed "bore a strong resemblance to a secret fraternal society." Trial testimony of the Prosser conspiracy reveals that enslaved men drank and gambled with other men in homosocial settings. Moreover, cross-plantation marriages served to further divide men and women. Men traveled together to visit their wives weekly. The sexes occupied different worlds in daily life. Indeed, the same distrust evident in Webb's narrative surfaces during the trial of the rebels: one recruiter was instructed to "keep the business secret, and not divulge to a *woman*."[64] Gabriel's men undertook oaths of secrecy and fidelity similar to Webb and his men. Furthermore, joining the rebels meant affirming one's manhood. Several recruiters made direct appeals to masculinity; they tried to shame men into joining the cause by asking if they were men.[65] Enslaved men and women, according to Sidbury, "defined the spatial parameters of their lives in different ways." Their day-to-day world was different, and "Gabriel's conspiracy was organized in the masculine sphere" accordingly.[66]

Similarly, enslaved men, and a few free black men, were involved in the Denmark Vesey conspiracy. Conspirators in Charleston held subversive meetings and discussed freedom in a traditionally male space: the artisan workshop, which served as an important rendezvous for enslaved men to pass time with other men and socialize with other workers. According to trial testimony in the Vesey case, enslaved men gathered at one shop "for the purpose of combining and confederating in the intended insurrection." They also met at an isolated farm several miles outside of Charleston, where they stored weapons, conducted meetings and ceremonies, and engaged in Gullah rituals that fostered a rebellious masculine camaraderie. The persistence of West African practices in Vesey's conspiracy, such as the *poro* (a Mende word meaning "the great secret society of men"), may have further

Enslaved men organized nearly every slave conspiracy and rebellion that took place during the first half of the nineteenth century. Organized insurrection depended on the bonds nurtured among men in their everyday homosocial activities. *Nat Turner & His Confederates in Conference,* in Orville J. Victor, *History of American Conspiracies: A Record of Treason, Insurrection, Rebellion, &c. in United States of America, From 1760 to 1860* (New York: James D. Torrey, 1863), 397.

facilitated the male homosocial organization of conspiracy.[67] Also, in 1822 West Africa and South Carolina were both intensely patriarchal places, and Vesey was building an army—such organizations did not include women. He may also have excluded women because he wished to protect families from the dangers of involvement.[68] Ultimately, however, enslaved men participated in Vesey's conspiracy—and others—because they were more mobile than enslaved women. Burdened with domestic and childcare responsibilities, enslaved women did not enjoy the autonomy of enslaved men. Crucially, in the Vesey case, enslaved women did not practice skilled artisanal trades and were hence excluded from the male space of the workshop.

Enslaved Men and the Underground Railroad

Enslaved men used their mobility and knowledge of local geography to engage in another collective act of resistance: assisting fugitive slaves to escape from slavery. Men used their contacts in the grapevine telegraph to funnel slaves to freedom in the North along an "underground railroad" operated almost entirely by enslaved people in the antebellum South. In his fugitive slave narrative, former slave Andrew Jackson explained how runaways found their way north: "Slaves know much more about this matter than many persons are aware. They have means of communication with each other, altogether unknown to their masters, or to the people of the free states." According to Jackson, "even the route of some who have escaped is familiarly known to the more intelligent ones."[69]

The Underground Railroad has fascinated both historians and the general public for many years. Perhaps the most influential work on the Underground Railroad is Wilbur H. Siebert's *The Underground Railroad*.[70] Published in 1898, Siebert's research chronicled numerous stories of a chain of safe houses and routes run by abolitionists and used by fugitive slaves in their escape northward. However, in 1961, Larry Gara's *Liberty Line* criticized Siebert's methodology, which was based on white abolitionist recollections. Gara claimed Siebert exaggerated the existence of the Underground Railroad; he argued that it was not a well-organized extensive network. Indeed, according to Gara, for most of their escapes through the South, fugitives had to make their own arrangements and help themselves. Assistance was often only available to those who had accomplished the most difficult parts of their journey and reached the borderlands of the North. "It was the slaves themselves," argued Gara, "who took things into their own hands, planned their escapes, and during the greater part of their journeys arranged for or managed their own transportation, without the assistance of the legendary underground railroad."[71] Since the publication of Gara's book, scholars have emphasized the role of the African American community in assisting fugitive slaves to escape. However, many of these works focus on the roles of free African American communities in the borderland areas and the North.[72] We currently know a lot about the roles of white abolitionists and free blacks in the Underground Railroad; however, much less is known about the role enslaved communities themselves played in effecting their own freedom. Historians, including Gara, have only touched on the subject of slaves assisting one another to escape their bondage.[73] Many of the examples cited by historians record the assistance free or enslaved relatives offered to fugitives; very little attention has been dedicated to the help enslaved communities gave to unknown fugitives.[74] The following discussion will show that enslaved communities helped these fugitives in their journey northward to freedom and, in the process, operated an Underground Railroad themselves. Above all, it will explain how enslaved men were crucial to the Railroad's success.

While on the run, fugitive slaves deliberated over whether to reach out to strangers for assistance. They knew that whites, free blacks, and other slaves were all capable of betrayal. While on the run, Isaac Williams declared to his friend Banks, "There are lots of wolves in sheep's clothing, and we will have to be very careful to whom we speak." Both men knew this only too well, having been betrayed in previous escape attempts.[75] The pass system of the antebellum South meant that, by law, any white person could request to see African Americans' free papers or slave passes. Fugitive slaves, accordingly, tried to avoid contact with whites. When William Anderson, a fugitive from Mississippi, trusted a white man who had promised to help him, he was swiftly betrayed, captured, and returned to his owner for a reward of more than a hundred dollars.[76] Such sums of money were huge for poor whites and incentivized them to turn runaways in; consequently, many fugitive slaves, like Andrew Jackson, remarked, "I had learned to look upon every white man as my foe, and dared not pass near to any one."[77]

It was more logical, instead, for fugitive slaves to reach out to fellow African Americans. Some free blacks proved trustworthy and helped them. William Grimes managed to escape with the help of a black northern sailor who concealed him on a ship bound for New York.[78] A free black man gave John Thompson directions and advised him which areas to avoid during his escape.[79] Isaac Williams and his companion, too, were given directions from a black man; also, a gang of black lumberjacks gave them food as they followed the railway track from Washington, DC, to Baltimore. Williams commented:

> Generally in speaking to the colored people we met in this manner, I would first study the expression of their faces and try to judge whether they would be false or not. If, on inspection I was favorably impressed, I would be perfectly frank with them and say that we were trying to reach the free states and if they wanted to betray us they could do so. This appealing to their better nature and placing confidence in them, often won them over to our cause. At heart they were all on our side, and it was only self-interest that made them our enemies.[80]

Not all encounters were favorable. On one occasion, for instance, as Williams and his runaway friends approached a free black at Morrisville, Virginia, to ask for food and shelter, the man attempted to lure them into a trap and alerted a group of whites. Williams, sensing that something was not right, fled the scene with his friends. He later learned from a black family, who provided them with food and shelter, that this particular man had often captured runaway slaves for money.[81] Free blacks had their own reasons to distrust runaways. If they were caught helping them, they could expect severe punishment. For example, in 1843, a mulatto man was convicted, by the Frederick County court in Maryland, of assisting runaways—ten to twelve—and sentenced to five years and six months imprisonment.[82] When fugitive John Andrew Jackson asked a free black who worked on a ship bound for Boston if he could hide in the vessel, the man replied, "Yes . . . but don't you betray me! Did not some white man send you here to ask me this?"[83] The mutual distrust between runaway and stranger forced William Wells Brown to conclude, "I had long since made up my mind that I would not trust myself in the hands of any man, white or colored. The slave is brought up to look upon every white man as an enemy to him and his race; and twenty-one years in slavery had taught me that there were traitors, even among colored people."[84]

These "colored people" included enslaved people. William Grimes, for example, was betrayed when he asked a slave named George to help him escape. George initially helped, giving him a jacket and some bread, but then informed the overseer of Grimes's plans.[85] Likewise, Henry Bibb and his runaway accomplice, Jack, were betrayed by a domestic slave on a large plantation when they stopped and asked her for some food—she immediately sounded the alarm, calling for her master.[86] Unsurprisingly, some slaves treated runaways from neighborhoods other than theirs with suspicion and turned them in. Outside the neighborhood, they had few friends and relatives to trust. According to historian Anthony E. Kaye, runaways from different neighborhoods "were deeply suspicious figures, suspicious of other slaves and the objects of other slaves' suspicions."[87] Nonetheless, many slaves exhibited remarkable solidarity and, despite the danger, provided runaways with food and shelter.[88] Many assisted fugitives from outside of their communities. Fugitive slave James Curry suffered from continual hunger as he fled from North Carolina through Virginia, Maryland, and toward Pennsylvania. Whenever he asked slaves for food during his long journey, he was "never refused, if they had food to give."[89] Similarly, Moses Roper found assistance from an enslaved stranger as he escaped from Marianna, Florida, to Savannah, Georgia, where he boarded a vessel to the North.

After barely eating for three to four days, as he crossed the Chattahoochee River into Georgia, Roper was given food by an elderly male slave.[90] When John Thompson escaped from a plantation in southern Maryland, the slave community near Rockville concealed him and provided him with food as he fled to Pennsylvania.[91]

The farther fugitives fled from their homes, the more they became disorientated; they were, according to runaway slave Lewis Clarke, "ignorant of the world."[92] Frederick Douglass, enslaved near the Mason Dixon line, on the eastern shore of Maryland, reflected on his escape northward: "The real distance was great enough, but the imagined distance was, to our ignorance, much greater." Douglass's geographical knowledge was certainly poor. He declared, "I really did not know that there was a state of New York or a state of Massachusetts. I had heard of Pennsylvania, Delaware, and New Jersey, and all the southern states, but was utterly ignorant of the free states."[93] If runaways were skilled enough to navigate their way north using the North Star, geographical awareness remained an obstacle: "I have no knowledge of distance or direction. I know that Pennsylvania is a free state, but I know not where its soil begins, or where that of Maryland ends," reported James Pennington in his fugitive slave narrative. "My only guide was the *north star,* by this I knew my general course northward, but at what point I should strike Penn, or when and where I should find a friend, I knew not."[94] Fugitive slave John Brown demonstrated the most woeful lack of navigation skills during his escape from his brutal enslavement in Georgia. As he reached the banks of the Ohio River, he headed to New Orleans, intending to seek refuge in Britain—which he heard was "only just across the water."[95]

Enslaved men, however, used their geographical knowledge and mobility to guide and direct runaway slaves throughout the South. As Jourden Banks and his band neared the Ohio River, they were fortunate to cross paths with a local enslaved man who informed them of their location, which direction to take, and advice on the situation in Illinois:

We gained valuable information from him in regard to our whereabouts, and the proper way to conduct ourselves. He informed us that we were about forty miles from the river; and if we crossed at the point where the road would strike, we would find ourselves in Missouri. He directed us to what he called the iron bank road, which he said would bring us to a place called Padauka. He also warned us that when we got into Illinois we would be as much in danger of being taken, nearly as much as in the Slave States. He stated that he himself had once escaped from his master, and after being in Illinois three days he was arrested and taken back.[96]

During the Civil War, in November 1863, Hannibal A. Johnson, a lieutenant in the Third Maine Infantry, escaped from a Confederate prison with three other officers in Columbia, South Carolina. Aiming to rejoin Union lines in Knoxville, Tennessee, the band of men set out in darkness, during a storm, with no compasses or stars to guide them. After trudging through woods for what seemed like twenty miles, the men found they had been traveling in a circle and were merely one and a half miles from their prison camp in Columbia. Setting out again, hungry, and unable to find the right road or direction, the party became desperate. Fortunately, they encountered "a family of trusty negroes" who gave them food and shelter and, the following day, concealed them in the woods, promising to find them a guide. As the soldiers waited, the slave women gave them food twice. That evening, a slave named Frank took them twenty-two miles to another plantation. Here, slaves again supplied the Union soldiers with food and gave them shelter. In this way, moving from one plantation to another, the soldiers were led to a location near Pickensville, South Carolina, close to the North Carolina state line, where they met up with a band of Confederate deserters and Union sympathizers. Johnson admitted his soldiers were entirely dependent on the slaves for food, shelter, and navigation.[97]

In Johnson's story, enslaved people rescue Union soldiers during the Civil War. However, the tale also illustrates what was possible during the antebellum period: enslaved people could assist fugitive slaves in their quest for freedom. Johnson's narrative shows how enslaved men and women both assisted fugitives: women prepared and cooked food for them, while men used their navigational skills to guide them onward to freedom. Furthermore, the narrative reveals the extensive nature of this underground network. According to Johnson, his men were aided by a continual network of thirty different guides, of whom Johnson noted the gender of twenty-three: all were enslaved men.[98]

Some enslaved men, like Arnold Gragston, capitalized on their mobility in extraordinary ways. Gragston was enslaved on the Kentucky side of the Ohio River to a "pretty good man" named Mr. Tabb, who owned a boat and afforded his slave a significant degree of mobility. "He used to let me go all about," reported Gragston. "It was 'cause he used to let me go around in the day and night so much that I came to be the one who carried the runnin' away slaves over the river." According to Gragston, during his enslavement, he transported two to three hundred slaves across the Ohio River to Ripley, Ohio. He had never intended to get involved in these bold operations; he only made his first trip after an old woman, enslaved on a nearby plantation, asked him to escort a pretty slave girl across the river. After this first journey, he took some time getting over the "scared feelin'." He soon found himself, however, "goin' back across the river, with two and three people, and sometimes a whole boatload," three and four times a month. He stated, "After I made a few trips I got to like it, and even though I could have been free any night myself, I figgered I wasn't gettin' along so bad so I would stay on Mr. Tabb's place and help the others get free. I did it for four years." He eventually escaped with his wife to Ripley, making for the house of prominent abolitionist John Rankin.[99] Similar to Gragston's story, another man, enslaved near the Ohio River and allowed the use of a boat, helped a fugitive slave, this one named Rachel, escape. Familiar with the area because his master permitted him to cross the river to trade, he guided Rachel to a free black settlement on the free side of the Ohio River, near Madison.[100]

Formerly enslaved people who lived north of the Ohio River were active members of the Underground Railroad. Just a stone's throw from Arnold Gragston across the river, lived John Parker, a former slave who had purchased his freedom and settled on the banks of the Ohio River in Ripley. After settling there, he helped hundreds of slaves escape their bondage, guiding and ferrying them across the river. He later wrote a narrative recording his exploits.[101] According to Parker, this borderland region experienced "incessant warfare" between the "friends and enemies of the fugitive."[102] Once the runaways were secure on the Ohio side of the river, Parker liaised with prominent members of the Underground Railroad in Ripley, such as John Rankin, and together they escorted fugitives farther north. Parker was part of an extremely sophisticated underground network that stretched deep into Kentucky; he regularly communicated with mobile enslaved men from that state. On one occasion, he learned that a group of fugitive slaves was hiding in the woods there, some twenty miles from the Ohio River. The fugitives, from central Kentucky, were unable to move because their leader, who had been navigating the expedition, had been captured. The man who delivered Parker the news was an enslaved coffin-maker from Kentucky who had crossed the Ohio River in a stolen boat. Parker remarked, "It was one of those 'grape vine' dispatches, given by word of mouth from one friend to another until it mysteriously got across the river." Parker immediately set out to rescue the fugitives, accompanying the Kentucky slave back to the other side of the river. The slave took Parker to another enslaved man, who guided him to the fugitives. Deep in the woods, Parker and his guide found the ten fugitives, who included two women accompanying their husbands. Despite their being pursued by various slave patrols, Parker successfully led the fugitives to the Ohio River and ferried all but two across the river.[103] Parker's narrative shows how the grapevine network, illicitly maintained by enslaved men within the South, crossed over to the North and included contacts with active abolitionist African Americans. John Parker probably knew Arnold Gragston; after all, Gragston knew John Rankin and was aware of the abolitionist activity in Ripley.

Enslaved men who helped fugitives actively challenged their own enslavement. These acts, however, were not merely hidden, individual, everyday acts. They were intensely political actions. When enslaved men collectively guided runaways to freedom, they actively contributed to the abolition of slavery. As historian James Oakes has noted, during the years preceding secession, runaways "were essential to abolitionist propaganda" and "helped transform the simple act of escape into a politically explosive fugitive slave controversy."[104] During the Civil War, the political consequences of such resistance were revolutionary, as the continual stream of fugitive slaves fleeing to Union lines forced the Union to consider emancipation as a war aim.[105]

Despite the distances that separated them, enslaved men maintained regular links with other men enslaved on different plantations. In daily homosocial spaces, they drank, gambled, wrestled, and hunted, and they used their contacts to pioneer and maintain the grapevine telegraph that kept enslaved communities informed of news, gossip, rumors, and antislavery ideology. Through this resistance, enslaved men formulated a radical politics: they plotted rebellion, and they harbored runaway slaves and funneled them to freedom. Organized insurrection and the operation of the Underground Railroad depended on the solidarities, trust, and friendships that were nurtured through day-to-day male homosocial activities. Everyday resistance and rebellion were interrelated; the covert, informal acts of enslaved men were deeply political and challenged the foundations of the slaveholding South.

Epilogue

After his first escape attempt failed, Frederick Douglass found himself bound together with his four male coconspirators—John and Henry Harris, Charles Roberts, and Henry Bailey—and forced to march barefooted on a dusty road toward a jail in Easton, Maryland, a journey of fifteen miles. It was a hot day, and the five men were deprived of hats to protect them from the sun and were fastened to three strong horses ridden by armed men and dragged through crowds of people who hurled insults at them. Some yelled out that the slaves should be hanged, others exclaimed that they should be burned, and still others shouted out that the men ought to have their "hides" torn off. The only sympathetic looks the men received that day were from enslaved people at work in the fields. Douglass lamented, "Where is now the God of justice and mercy?" He recalled, "Our hopes were all blasted at one blow." In this moment of despair, however, he affirmed that the one thing he could count on was the "dear friends" he was tied to. They did not blame him for involving them in the escape attempt; in fact, Douglass remarked that as they were dragged through the angry crowds, he and his friends were "a band of brothers" who were "never dearer to each other" than at that time. Douglass noted that the most painful thought the men had to endure was the likely separation that would occur as they were sold off to the Deep South as punishment. Although they were finally released by their owners and not sold, Douglass wrote: "My friends were separated from me, and apparently forever. This circumstance caused me more pain than any other incident connected with our capture and imprisonment. Thirty-nine lashes on my naked and bleeding back would have been joyfully borne, in preference to this separation from these, the friends of my youth."[1]

In this passage, and throughout his narrative, Douglass underscored the importance of his male friends. He recalled them with affection, and, as we see in this example, he affirmed how central these homosocial relationships were to his emotional well-being, particularly in the darkest hours of his enslavement. The pain of his separation from his friends is striking, a poignant reminder of how male interdependence was a significant fact of enslaved life. The men revered the homosocial world they created; in the company of other men, they raised their self-esteem, forged meaningful friendships, and constructed masculine identities.

As historian James Sidbury has stated, "gender identities remained powerful determinants of the ways they [enslaved people] experienced life."[2] For enslaved men, this was particularly true. Those on large plantations labored all day together in same-sex work gangs, and those employed in industry found themselves cut off from plantation life, living and working in a distinct male homosocial world. In such environments, enslaved men fashioned unique homosocial work cultures. The social spaces enslaved men occupied were also distinctive; by drinking, gambling, and wrestling together, they affirmed their own masculine identities, independent from the slaveholder. They treasured their precious time and chose to spend it with other men. Beginning in boyhood, they prepared one another for a world beyond the plantation boundaries. Deep in the woods, far from their owners' gazes, they carved out space for themselves—a masculine space. To be men, they had to master the natural environment. They used the forest to hunt and feed their families, but here they also learned how to coordinate their efforts and test their bravery, resolve, and ability to fight and evade the white patrol gangs. Enslaved manhood was earned in these treacherous spaces. By dodging the patrols, men could visit loved ones enslaved on neighboring plantations and play the masculine roles of provider and protector. Friendships were also formed, sometimes broken, and sometimes preserved for life. Enslaved men treasured these relationships; they helped the men survive the brutalizing rhythms of plantation life. Friends comforted one another and gave each other something to live for: hope. They could trust in one another and vent their frustrations together. This was an intensely personal and private world, but it was also political: friends conspired together to resist their enslavement and run away. Enslaved men created an all-male subculture that extended beyond plantation boundaries. Utilizing their mobility, they maintained links with other men enslaved on neighboring plantations. In this way, in their everyday spaces, men funneled fugitive slaves to freedom and plotted to overthrow the system of slavery. The visible, organized, and collective world of slave rebellion was clearly linked to the intimate, hidden, and private spaces enslaved men created. As historian Emilia Viotti da Costa asserts, "It was in daily resistance that slaves reinforced their commitment to their 'rights' and tested the limits of their masters' power. It was in daily resistance that slaves' resentment grew, that bonds of solidarity were strengthened, that networks and leaders were formed, and individual acts of defiance were converted into collective protest."[3]

Frederick Douglass's story eventually had a happy ending. On his second escape attempt, Douglass reached New York disguised as a free black sailor and commenced a remarkable career as an abolitionist, social reformer, writer, and statesman. He noted the joy of arriving in New York: "It was a moment of the highest excitement I ever experienced. . . . I felt like one who had escaped a den of hungry lions." Yet, his feelings were bittersweet. Although ecstatic about reaching the free state of New York, he admitted he was "again seized with a feeling of great insecurity and loneliness." He had escaped a life of enslavement and misery; however, he had also left behind his friends and community: "There I was in the midst of thousands, and yet a perfect stranger; without home and without friends."[4] Douglass's "band of brothers" had broken up. The men who had been central throughout his life—the men he had loved—were now gone.

Acknowledgments

It is an absolute pleasure to thank the many people who have made this book possible. First, let me start by thanking Rebecca Fraser. Her inspiring teaching and enthusiasm nurtured my interest in American history while I was an undergraduate student at the University of Wales, Aberystwyth. This book would not have been possible without Rebecca; she helped me formulate the initial ideas of my PhD thesis, from which this book developed. As I embarked on my postgraduate research at the University of Warwick, I found a new mentor, Rebecca Earle. Rebecca has been a source of steadfast support. She has diligently read countless drafts of my work and engaged with every aspect of this project. From the beginning, she believed in my work and gave me the confidence to develop my ideas. She has been inspirational—without her, there would be no book. I would also like to thank Tim Lockley, who co-supervised my postgraduate work. Tim has consistently expressed confidence in my work and supported me. I would also like to acknowledge the help I received from Stephanie Camp during the early stages of this project. I was saddened and shocked to hear about her recent death. I never met Stephanie, but she kindly communicated with me via email and provided me with extensive feedback on my plans for this book; her suggestions helped me considerably. As this book shows, her work has had a profound impact on me.

The Department of History at the University of Warwick has supported me throughout my studies. I have also benefitted from discussions among delegates at the annual conferences of the British American Nineteenth Century Historians (BrANCH). Special thanks to David Brown, who drew my attention to some of the WPA sources used in this book. Thanks, also, to Emily West, who read drafts of this manuscript and provided me with valuable suggestions and comments. I am grateful, too, for the anonymous readers who read drafts and helped me improve it. Many thanks to Erin Holman, my copy editor, who improved the manuscript significantly. Anne Dean Dotson and the staff at the University Press of Kentucky were very supportive and encouraging throughout the publication process.

This book could not have been written without the generous scholarship I received from the Arts and Humanities Research Council (AHRC). I was also fortunate enough to be awarded a scholarship to take part in an AHRC-sponsored program that funded a select number of British postgraduates to conduct research at the Library of Congress, in Washington, DC, as a resident fellow at the John W. Kluge Center, where I spent many happy months. The staff at the center was extremely kind and supportive. Mary Lou Reker routinely went out of her way to help me. Jurretta Heckscher shared her research with me and helped me track down some very useful primary source material, and she selflessly gave up her time to take me on a charming tour around the library stacks. I have enjoyed and benefitted from the companionship of the fellows at the Kluge Center. Christine Johnson and Samuel James read portions of this book and provided me with useful feedback. Matthew Adams helped me locate some valuable nineteenth-century newspapers. Marcy Dinius shared her expertise on Frederick Douglass. Staff members at the Manuscript Division of the Library of Congress were especially accommodating and fun to work with. Patrick Kerwin and Joe Jackson helped me navigate through masses of source material relating to slavery; both kept up my morale as I plowed through countless microfilm reels of Kenneth Stampp's *Records of Antebellum Plantations.*

My visits to various archives in the South were made possible through the generosity and assistance of others. Before I set out, Jeff Forret gave me invaluable advice on slave records housed in the state archives of North and South Carolina. I was extremely fortunate to grab a ride from Washington, DC, down to Columbia, South Carolina, from Mary Guibert. Connie Schulz welcomed me, and other scholars, into her home in Columbia for three weeks during the summer. Stephen and Jeanne-Marie Kenny gave me rides everywhere in Columbia. Charles Lesser regularly drove me to the state archives and was a fountain of knowledge on the various manuscript collections housed there. Steve Tuttle helped me find my way through the Court of Magistrates and Freeholders records. My research in North Carolina benefitted from an Archie K. Davis Fellowship from the North Caroliniana Society. The staff at the Southern Historical Collection, Chapel Hill, and the staff in the state archives in Raleigh were very cooperative and hospitable as I conducted my research in North Carolina. Special thanks to Marty and Marta Matthews, who welcomed me into their home in Raleigh with true southern hospitality. They went out of their way to accommodate me: Marty gave me rides everywhere and introduced me to his work at the Division of State Historic Sites, as well as his truly comprehensive Frank Sinatra CD collection. Marty gave me a memorable guided tour of Stagville, where the original quarters of enslaved people still stand today.

I'd also like to extend my thanks to members of the staff at Nottingham Trent University; in particular, Amy Fuller, Lizbeth Powell, Jenny Woodley, Nick Hayes, John McCallum, and Kevin Gould. They have been incredibly supportive since I joined the team in 2012. Finally, I want to extend my deepest gratitude to my family and friends. I want to thank Alastair Brown for keeping me sane throughout this project. Thora is a very special person whose love has sustained me every step of this journey. My sister, Claudia, continues to be a source of inspiration. My parents deserve a special mention. I am lucky to have such wonderful parents; this book would not have been possible without their love, support, and sacrifice. I know they are proud of what I have achieved and what it represents for our family. My grandmother passed away as I neared the completion of this book. Her indomitable spirit was legendary: I have yet to meet anyone else over the age of eighty who smokes non-filter cigarettes, drives a convertible Mercedes, and visits the gym more than once a week. I fondly recall the war stories she told me as I grew up—my introduction to oral history. As a child, she was fortunate enough to be stationed at the American airbases in Britain during the war—her father was in the Royal Air Force. She frequently described, in vivid detail, the food supplied by the Americans: pancakes, maple syrup, bacon, and chocolate. For an English girl in an era of rationing, these items were heavenly. I wish I could have given my grandmother a copy of this book so that she could see what I have been doing all these years. I dedicate this book to her.

Some of the arguments made in this book appeared earlier in article form. See "To See Who Was Best on the Plantation: Enslaved Fighting Contests and Masculinity in the Antebellum South," *Journal of Southern History* 76, no. 4 (November 2010): 901–22. Used by permission of the *Journal of Southern History*. See also "'No Band of Brothers Could Be More Loving': Enslaved Male Homosociality, Friendship, and Resistance in the Antebellum American South," *Journal of Social History* 46, no. 4 (Summer 2013): 872–95. Used by permission of Oxford University Press.

Notes

Abbreviations

NCDAH	North Carolina Department of Archives and History, Raleigh.
RASP	Kenneth Stampp, ed., *Records of Ante-bellum Southern Plantations from the Revolution through the Civil War,* ser. A–N (Bethesda, MD: University Publications of America, 1985–2001).
RSFB	Loren Schweninger, ed., *Race, Slavery, and Free Blacks,* ser. 1, Petitions to Southern Legislatures, 1777–1867 (Bethesda, MD: University Publications of America, 1999).
SASI	Charles B, Dew, ed., *Slavery in Ante-Bellum Southern Industries* (Bethesda, MD: University Publication of America, 1991).
SCDAH	South Carolina Department of Archives and History, Columbia.
SHC	Southern Historical Collection, University of North Carolina, Chapel Hill.

Introduction

1. *Life and Times of Frederick Douglass,* 151.

2. Lussana, "No Band of Brothers," 872–95; Foster, "Sexual Abuse of Black Men," 445–64; Lussana, "To See Who Was Best on the Plantation," 901–22; Rebecca Fraser, "Negotiating Their Manhood: Masculinity amongst the Enslaved in the Upper South, 1830–1861," in Plath and Lussana, *Black and White Masculinity,* 76–94; Forret, "Conflict and the 'Slave Community,'" 551–88; Edward E. Baptist, "The Absent Subject: African American Masculinity and Forced Migration to the Antebellum Plantation Frontier," in Friend and Glover, *Southern Manhood,* 136–73.

3. See for example, Pflugrad-Jackisch, *Brothers of a Vow*; Glover, *Southern Sons;* Friend and Glover, *Southern Manhood;* Wyatt-Brown, *Shaping of Southern Culture;* Greenberg, *Honor and Slavery;* Wyatt-Brown, *Southern Honor.*

4. Frazier, *Negro Family.*

5. Stampp, *Peculiar Institution,* 340, 343, 344.

6. Elkins, *Slavery,* 130.

7. Moynihan, *Negro Family.*

8. Gutman, *Black Family,* 45, 186–92.

9. Ibid., 186–92.

10. Genovese, *Roll, Jordan, Roll,* 491–92, 450, 482–94.

11. Blassingame, *Slave Community,* 179.

12. Kolchin, "Reevaluating the Antebellum Slave Community," 581.

13. White, *Ar'n't I a Woman?* 153. White chose the term "matrifocal" to describe the slave family rather than the word "matriarchy" (defined as a society dominated by women, in which "some, if not all of the legal powers relating to the ordering and governing of the family-power over property, over inheritance, over marriage, over the house are lodged in women rather than men." [Ladner, *Tomorrow's Tomorrow,* 41]). White explained: "Matrifocality is a term used to convey the fact that women *in their role as mothers* are the focus of familial relationships. It does not mean that fathers are absent; indeed two-parent households can be matrifocal. Nor does it stress a power relationship where women rule men. When *mothers* become the focal point of family activity, they are just more central than are fathers to a family's continuity and survival as a unit." White, "Female Slaves," 256 (emphasis in original). For a further discussion of matrifocality in slave communities, see Claire Robertson, "Africa into the Americas?" in Gaspar and Hine, *More Than Chattel,* 9–20.

14. Patterson, *Rituals of Blood,* 27.

15. Ibid., 4, 32.

16. Dunaway, *African-American Family,* 270; see esp. "Theoretical Reprise," 268–87.

17. Dusinberre, *Them Dark Days,* 118; see esp. chap. 4, "Unhappy Families."

18. West, *Chains of Love,* 44, 46.

19. Ibid., 45. Cross-plantation marriages were especially common on small plantations throughout the antebellum South because the small numbers of enslaved people resident on individual holdings forced slaves to find partners off the plantation. Additionally, historians have suggested that enslaved people chose cross-plantation marriages as a result of the rules of exogamy in the slave community—for example, the ban of marriage to first cousins. Living in such marriages meant that men did not have to witness the daily abuse of their spouses or loved ones. And as men were expected to perform the role of visitor, cross-plantation marriages offered them extended social worlds, as well as breaks from their daily routines. Enslaved women may have preferred the arrangement because it gave them greater domestic power. In his quantitative analysis of the WPA narratives, Paul D. Escott calculated that 27.5 percent of slave marriages throughout the antebellum South were cross-plantation marriages. According to Brenda Stevenson, 72 percent of slaves who resided on George Washington's five farms in Virginia were in cross-plantation marriages. Recently, Diane Mutti Burke's research on slavery in Missouri concluded that 57 percent of slave marriages were between men and women who resided on different holdings. See Escott, *Slavery Remembered,* 50–52; Stevenson, *Life in Black and White,* 212, 222, 229–33; Burke, *On Slavery's Border,* 200–201.

20. Fraser, *Courtship and Love,* 73–75.

21. Fraser, "Negotiating Their Manhood," 81–85; Fraser, *Courtship and Love,* 69–79.

22. Fraser, "Negotiating Their Manhood," 77.

23. Kimmel, *History of Men,* 38; Tosh, "What Should Historians Do with Masculinity?" 185; Gilmore, *Manhood in the Making,* 222–23.

24. Kimmel, *Manhood in America,* 7.

25. Gilmore, *Manhood in the Making,* 11–12.

26. Michelle Z. Rosaldo, "Woman, Culture, and Society: A Theoretical Overview," in Rosaldo and Lamphere, *Woman, Culture, and Society,* 28.

27. Glover, *Southern Sons,* 3.

28. Wyatt-Brown, *Southern Honor,* xii, xv.

29. Gorn, "Gouge and Bite," 42; Ownby, *Subduing Satan,* 13; Lindman, "Acting the Manly Christian," 395.

30. See for example, Camp, *Closer to Freedom;* Morgan, *Laboring Women;* Schwalm, *Hard Fight for We;* Gaspar and Hine, *More Than Chattel;* Morton, *Discovering the Women in Slavery;* Jacqueline Jones, "Race, Sex, and Self-Evident Truths: The Status of Slave Women during the Era of the American Revolution," in Hoffman and Albert, *Women in the Age,* 293–337; Fox-Genovese, *Within the Plantation Household;* Jones, *Labor of Love;* White, *Ar'n't I a Woman?*

31. Scott, *Gender and the Politics of History,* 42.

32. White, *Ar'n't I a Woman?* 119, 132–33, 154, 141.

33. White, "Female Slaves," 255.

34. Walker, *Walker's Appeal,* 35, 70.

35. Baptist, "Absent Subject," 138–39.

36. In this way, the book develops Stephanie Camp's theoretical approach. See Camp, *Closer to Freedom,* 3.

37. Scott, *Weapons of the Weak,* xvi. "The hidden transcript is not just behind-the-scenes griping and grumbling; it is enacted in a host of down-to-earth, low profile stratagems designed to minimize appropriation. In the case of slaves, for example, these stratagems have typically included theft, pilfering, feigned ignorance, shirking or careless labor, footdragging, secret trade, and production for sale, sabotage of crops, livestock, and machinery, arson, flight, and so on." Scott, *Domination and the Arts of Resistance,* 188.

38. Johnson, "On Agency," 118.

39. Stephanie M. H. Camp and Edward E. Baptist, introduction to Baptist and Camp, *New Studies,* 3.

40. Miller, *Out of the Past,* xix. For more on the challenges of writing gay history, see Duberman, Vicinus, and Chauncey, *Hidden from History.* For recent works documenting gay life in the twentieth century American South, see Howard, *Men Like That;* Johnson, *Sweet Tea.*

41. See John Blassingame, introduction to Blassingame, *Slave Testimony,* xliv–xlv, liii.

42. Spindel, "Assessing Memory," 259.

43. Edward E. Baptist, "'Stol' and Fetched Here': Enslaved Migration, Ex-slave Narratives, and Vernacular History," in Baptist and Camp, *New Studies,* 247.

44. West, *Chains of Love,* 7.

45. Lantz, "Family and Kin," 670.

46. Rawick, Hillegas, and Lawrence, *American Slave,* supp. ser. 1; Rawick, *American Slave,* supp. ser. 2.

47. Musher, "Contesting 'The Way,'" 2–4, 14.

48. Escott, *Slavery Remembered,* 6–7.

49. Fraser, *Courtship and Love,* 16.

50. See for example, Phillips, *American Negro Slavery;* Stampp, *Peculiar Institution;* Elkins, *Slavery.*

51. Yuval Taylor, introduction to Taylor, *I Was Born a Slave,* xv–xxxviii.

52. Ibid., xvi.

53. Blassingame, *Slave Community,* 368.

54. Gilbert Osofsky, "Puttin' On Ole Massa: The Significance of Slave Narratives," in Osofsky, *Puttin' On Ole Massa,* 21.

55. Blassingame, *Slave Community,* 367.

56. Blassingame, introduction to *Slave Testimony,* xviii.

57. Blassingame provides an interesting biographical sketch of numerous editors of the slave narratives. See ibid., xvii–lxv.

58. Ibid., xxv; West, *Chains of Love,* 9; Taylor, introduction to *I Was Born a Slave,* xvii.

59. Bascom, "Four Functions of Folklore," 342–49.

60. Notable studies of enslaved people that have utilized folklore include Blassingame, *Slave Community;* Genovese, *Roll, Jordan, Roll;* Levine, *Black Culture and Black Consciousness;* Joyner, *Down by the Riverside;* Stuckey, *Slave Culture;* Gomez, *Exchanging Our Country Marks;* Rebecca Fraser, "Courtship Contests"; Fraser, *Courtship and Love;* Rucker, *River Flows On;* Young, *Rituals of Resistance.*

61. Levine, *Black Culture and Black Consciousness,* 80.

62. Stuckey, "Through the Prism of Folklore," 418, 419, 436.

63. Rawick, Hillegas, and Lawrence, *American Slave,* supp. ser. 1, vol. 10, pt. 5, p. 2182.

64. Rawick, *American Slave,* vol. 3, pt. 4, pp. 68–69.

65. Rawick, Hillegas, and Lawrence, *American Slave,* supp. ser. 1, vol. 11, pp. 36, 38, 39; Rawick, *American Slave,* vol. 16 (KY), 117; Rawick, Hillegas, and Lawrence, *American Slave,* supp. ser. 1, vol. 1, p. 312; Rawick, *American Slave,* supp. ser. 2, vol. 5, pt. 4, p. 1504.

66. See Susan Millar Williams's foreword in the recently retitled edition of Jones's collection, Jones, *Gullah Folktales from the Georgia.* Joel Chandler Harris's first published collection of folktales was *Uncle Remus: His Songs and Sayings.* Harris's subsequent collections included *Nights with Uncle Remus, Daddy Jake the Runaway and Short Stories Told after Dark by Uncle Remus; Uncle Remus and His Friends: Old Plantation Stories, Songs and Ballads with Sketches of Negro Character.*

67. For more on the history of the Gullah people, see Pollitzer, *Gullah Peo-*

ple. For a classic study of the Gullah language and its links to Africa, see Turner, *Africanisms.*

68. Stampp, "Rebels and Sambos," 368.

69. Dickson, "'John and Old Master' Stories," 419.

70. Gilbert Osofsky, "A Note on the Usefulness of Folklore," in Osofsky, *Puttin' On Ole Massa,* 46.

71. Loren Schweninger collected the petitions referred to in this study as part of his project *Race, Slavery, and Free Blacks* (RSFB). See Schweninger, *Race, Slavery, and Free Blacks,* ser. 1, Petitions to Southern Legislatures, 1777–1867; Schweninger, *Race, Slavery, and Free Blacks,* ser. 2, Petitions to Southern County Courts, 1775–1867; Schweninger, *Southern Debate over Slavery,* vol. 1; Schweninger, *Southern Debate over Slavery,* vol. 2; Schweninger, introduction to RSFB, ser. 1, xi.

72. Camp, *Closer to Freedom,* 8–9. See also Osofsky, "Puttin' On Ole Massa," 14.

1. Enslaved Men and Work

1. White, *Ar'n't I a Woman?* 121.

2. Parish, *Many Faces,* 17; Brown and Webb, *Race in the American South,* 125–26; Cooper and Terrill, *American South,* 1:215.

3. Morgan, "Work and Culture," 563–99.

4. Olmsted, *Journey in the Seaboard Slave States,* 433. See also Allston, *South Carolina Rice Plantation,* 346. For an insightful example of how slaveholders classified and valued enslaved men and women in this way, see the inventory of enslaved men and women reproduced as "Master Bruce Inventories His Slave Property," in Rose, *Documentary History,* 337–44.

5. Joyner, *Down by the Riverside,* 59.

6. Philip D. Morgan, "Task and Gang Systems: The Organization of Labor on New World Plantations," in Innes, *Work and Labor,* 189–220.

7. Rawick, *American Slave,* vol. 18, p. 217.

8. Rawick, Hillegas, and Lawrence, *American Slave,* supp. ser. 1, vol. 5, p. 402.

9. Rawick, Hillegas, and Lawrence, *American Slave,* supp. ser. 1, vol. 9, pt. 4, pp. 1513–14.

10. Rawick, *American Slave,* supp. ser. 2, vol. 5, pt. 4, p. 1554.

11. Fox-Genovese, *Within the Plantation Household,* 175.

12. Cooper and Terrill, *American South,* 1:218; Berlin, Favreau, and Miller, *Remembering Slavery,* 72.

13. Kolchin, *American Slavery,* 101, 243.

14. Fox-Genovese, *Within the Plantation Household,* 172–76; West, *Chains of Love,* 80–88; Dunaway, *Slavery in the American Mountain South,* 55; White, *Ar'n't I a Woman,* 120–21; White, "Female Slaves," 250–51; Kolchin, *American Slavery,* 103; Weiner, *Mistresses and Slaves,* 12–13; Jones, *Labor of Love,* 17.

15. Weiner, *Mistresses and Slaves,* 13.

16. Kolchin, *American Slavery,* 101.

17. Follett, *Sugar Masters,* 50–51; Michael Tadman, "Demographic Cost of Sugar," 1543–44, 1554.

18. Moody, *Slavery on Louisiana Sugar Plantations,* 45.

19. Russell, *My Diary North and South,* 262.

20. Franklin A. Hudson Diary, October 18, November 24, 1856, May 20, 1857, J, pt. 5, reel 12–13, RASP.

21. Franklin A. Hudson Diary, December 8, 1853, November 1, 1854, September 15, October 18, 21, November 3, 20, 21, 24–26, 1856, February 14, May 20, 1857, March 5, 11, April 9, 27, June 11, November 7, 12, December 17, 1859, J, pt. 5, reel 12–13, RASP. See also Bayside Plantation Records, September 6, 27, 1861, J, pt. 5, reel 6, RASP.

22. *Plantation Diary of the Late Valcour Aime,* 164–65, 171–74. For more on Valcour Aime, see Toledano, "Louisiana's Golden Age," 211–24.

23. Lorena S. Walsh, "Slave Life, Slave Society, and Tobacco Production in the Tidewater Chesapeake, 1620–1820," in Berlin and Morgan, *Cultivation and Culture,* 177–78, 186–87; Walsh, *Motives of Honor,* 622–23; Morgan, *Slave Counterpoint,* 173–74.

24. Charles Friend Diary, November 24, 26–28, 30, December 6, 31, 1841, January 1, 1842, February 19, 21, March 5, April 4, 1842, Friend Family Papers, M, pt. 3, reel 18, RASP.

25. Charles Friend Diary, December 13, 1841, January 2, 1842, Friend Family Papers, M, pt. 3, reel 18, RASP.

26. Charles Friend Diary, December 13, 1841, January 2, February 23, 24, 26, March 28, April 5, 1842, Friend Family Papers, M, pt. 3, reel 18, RASP.

27. James Hervey Greenlee Diary, April 4, 5, 8, 17, 20, July 29, October 10, 1848, J, pt. 14, reel 3, RASP.

28. Fox-Genovese, *Within the Plantation Household,* 174.

29. Ronald L. F. Davis, "The Plantation Lifeworld of the Old Natchez District: 1840–1880," in Durant and Knottnerus, *Plantation Society and Race Relations,* 166; Jones, *Labor of Love,* 17; O'Donovan, *Becoming Free in the Cotton South,* 36.

30. Libby, *Slavery and Frontier,* 41–42; Diary of Leven Convington, March 30, April 1–4, 6–8, May 4, 5, 8, 1829, February 18, 19, 20, 22–27, March 1, 2, 5, 6, 8, 1830, in Phillips, *Plantation and Frontier,* 231–44; William Ethelbert Ervin Diary, January 6, 11, 14, 19, 20–25, 1842, J, pt. 6, reel 17, RASP; Olmsted, *Journey in the Backcountry,* 48.

31. Sydnor, *Slavery in Mississippi,* 12; Hughes, *Thirty Years a Slave,* 39–43.

32. Olmsted, *Journey in the Backcountry,* 81.

33. O'Donovan, *Becoming Free in the Cotton South,* 35–37.

34. John Edwin Fripp Diary, March 31, May 12, 14, 15, June 13, August 24, September 8, November 4, 6, 7, 16, 20, 28, December 9, 10, 1857, January 5, 6, 27–29, February 2, 3, 19, 27, March 4, 11, April 21, May 7, 17, August, 10, 17–21, September 11, 1858, John Edwin Fripp Papers, J, pt. 3, reel 25, RASP.

35. Berry, *"Swing the Sickle,"* 19–21.

36. Olmsted, *Journey in the Seaboard Slave States,* 434.

37. Heyward, *Seed from Madagascar,* 28–29; Clifton, *Life and Labor on Argyle Island,* 142; Allston, *South Carolina Rice Plantation,* 326–27.

38. Pringle, *Woman Rice Planter,* 79.

39. Heyward, *Seed from Madagascar,* 31; Schwalm, *Hard Fight for We,* 19–21, 23–24; Carney, *Black Rice,* 110.

40. Heyward, *Seed from Madagascar,* 30; Clifton, *Life and Labor on Argyle Island,* 94; Grant, *Planter Management,* October 25, 1848, p. 112, July 16, November 16–30, 1840, p. 159, May 9–13, 1854, p. 289; Allston, *South Carolina Rice Plantation,* 303, 318, 327; Joyner, *Down by the Riverside,* 45.

41. Allston, *South Carolina Rice Plantation,* 346 (emphasis in original).

42. Grant, *Planter Management,* September 26, 1842, p. 95, October 10, 1855, p. 123; Allston, *South Carolina Rice Plantation,* 270–71, 303, 316–20, 323–24, 326.

43. Clifton, *Life and Labor on Argyle Island,* 91, 94.

44. Olmsted, *Journey in the Seaboard Slave States,* 430–32.

45. West, *Chains of Love,* 88.

46. Rawick, *American Slave,* vol. 7 (OK), 314; Rawick, *American Slave,* vol. 11 (AR), pt. 7, p. 163; Rawick, *American Slave,* vol. 2, pt. 2, p. 101; Rawick, *American Slave,* vol. 8, pt. 2, p. 217; Rawick, *American Slave,* vol. 12, pt. 1, p. 113; Rawick, *American Slave,* vol. 14, pt. 1, p. 445.

47. See Starobin, *Industrial Slavery,* 3–34.

48. Lewis, *Coal, Iron, and Slaves,* 7.

49. Starobin, *Industrial Slavery,* 14–15.

50. See for example, Louisa Furnace Account Books, 1831–1860, in Dew, *Slavery in Ante-Bellum Southern Industries,* ser. B, reel 21–22 (SASI); Negro Account Book, Etna Furnace, 1854–1856, Weaver-Brady Papers, D, pt. 1, reel 35, SASI.

51. Dew, "Disciplining Slave Ironworkers," 396–98.

52. Lewis, *Coal, Iron, and Slaves,* 28–29, 33, 192; Dew, "David Ross," 196–98; Dew, "Disciplining Slave Ironworkers," 395.

53. Dunaway, *Slavery in the American Mountain South,* 129–30.

54. Lewis, *Coal, Iron, and Slaves,* 169.

55. Ibid., 171.

56. Lewis, *Black Coal Miners,* 5.

57. Jeremiah T. Jones Account Book, 1853–1854, Jeremiah T. Jones Papers, A, reel 4, SASI; Lewis, *Coal, Iron, and Slaves,* 119–20.

58. *Fayetteville Observer,* March 26, 1855; *Daily National Intelligencer,* March 23, 1855; Starobin, *Industrial Slavery,* 45–47.

59. Buckley, *Danger, Death, and Disaster,* 28–29; Scott, *Domination and the Arts of Resistance,* 134–35; Callahan, *Work and Faith,* 103.

60. Callahan, *Work and Faith,* 103; Tallichet, *Daughters of the Mountain,* 5.

61. Glass, "Miner's World," 443.

62. Ibid., 430, 442.

63. Starobin, *Industrial Slavery,* 23–24. For more on the gold mines of North Carolina, see Green, "Gold Mining," 1–19.

64. According to Glass, this statistic differed from those of most antebellum American mining communities whereby a higher percentage of the population consisted of single men who shared boardinghouses. Glass, "Miner's World," 442–43.

65. Outland, "Slavery, Work, and the Geography," 30–31, 42. See Olmsted's account of his encounter with workers in the naval stores industry in Olmsted, *Journey in the Seaboard Slave States,* 338–51.

66. James Redding Grist Business Records, December 24, 1860, A, reel 7, SASI; Outland, "Slavery, Work, and the Geography," 36, 43.

67. For evidence of this separation see, for example, William J. Parham to James R. Grist, May 1, 1854, James Redding Grist Business Records, Correspondence ser., A, reel 6, SASI; J. Nevitt to B. May, February 9, 1853, William B. Rodman Papers, Correspondence, box 5, North Carolina Division of Archives and History, Raleigh (NCDAH).

68. Outland, "Slavery, Work, and the Geography," 46.

69. Starobin, *Industrial Slavery,* 25–26.

70. Olmsted, *Journey in the Seaboard Slave States,* 153.

71. Registration of Slaves to Work in the Great Dismal Swamp from 1847–1861, NCDAH. In 1847, the law in North Carolina required that any slave working in the Great Dismal Swamp was recorded in this manner. Ratified on January 18, 1847, the law aimed "to provide for the apprehension of runaway slaves in the Great Dismal Swamp and for other purposes." It stated that "many slaves belonging to persons residing or having plantations in the neighborhood of the great dismal swamp, have left the service of their masters and taken refuge in the said swamp" and that they "remain setting at defiance the power of their masters, corrupting and seducing other slaves, and by their evil example and evil practices, lessening the due subordination, and greatly impairing the value of slaves in the district of country bordering on the said great dismal swamp." One of the solutions proposed in section one of the act called for all slaves working in the Dismal Swamp to be registered in a book and made known and identified by "every peculiar mark or description," and that it was necessary for the slave to hand in to the employer a permit with a copy of this information. *Laws of the State of North Carolina . . . 1846–47,* 109–13. Further evidence that the laborers who worked in lumber were exclusively male can be seen by going through the receipts of hired out slaves to the Great Dismal Swamp Land Company. See Great Dismal Swamp Land Company Records, Receipts, reel 20–21, A, SASI. See also the passes given to Dismal Swamp slave workers in fol. "Permission for Negroes to Work," box 2, Gates County Criminal Actions Concerning Slaves, NCDAH.

72. Roper, *Narrative of the Adventures and Escape,* 16.

73. Registration of Slaves to Work in the Great Dismal Swamp from 1847–

1861, NCDAH. The boy of twelve is described on page 308, the man of sixty on page 19.

74. Olmsted, *Journey in the Seaboard Slave States*, 154.

75. Ruffin, "Observations Made during an Excursion," 518.

76. Marrs, *Railroads in the Old South*, 57–58. See for example "Names of Negroes Hired to Work the Central Railroad" complied January 1, 1852, Hawkins Family Papers, B, reel 18, SASI, and the "Negroes Account of Work" lists compiled February 1859, Hawkins Family Papers, B, reel 20, SASI.

77. Trelease, *North Carolina Railroad*, 34.

78. Fannie Berry in Perdue, Barden, and Phillips, *Weevils in the Wheat*, 39.

79. Redpath, *Roving Editor*, 125–26.

80. Cecelski, *Waterman's Song*, 109.

81. Starobin, *Industrial Slavery*, 28–29.

82. Advertisement for slaves to work on the James River and Kanawha Canal in Cocke Family Papers, E, pt. 4, reel 70, fr. 51, RASP.

83. *Narrative of the Life of Moses Grandy*, 35.

84. Although he acknowledged that "most canal work camps were all male," David Cecelski found an example of a few women and children living at a work camp in Juniper Bay, North Carolina. Although records do not specify their work duties, one can speculate that the women worked as cooks and the children supplied drinking water to the workers. Cecelski, *Waterman's Song*, 110.

85. Iverson L. Twyman to John Austin, January 2, 1851, Austin-Twyman Papers, L, pt. 4, reel 2, RASP.

86. Cecelski, *Waterman's Song*, 112–13.

87. Starobin, *Industrial Slavery*, 26–27; Cecelski, *Waterman's Song*, 99; Olmsted, *Journey in the Seaboard Slave States*, 351–55.

88. Cecelski, *Waterman's Song*, 58, 81.

89. Ball, *Slavery in the United States*, 298, 303–4.

90. According to Robert, this ratio varied in several tobacco manufacturing centers. By 1860, for example, 99 percent of men worked in the Richmond factories, whereas in Petersburg the figure was 67 percent. Robert, *Tobacco Kingdom*, 197; Barnes, *Artisan Workers*, 163; Wade, *Slavery in the Cities*, 35; Starobin, *Industrial Slavery*, 165; *Narrative of Henry Box Brown*, 41–42.

91. Robert, *Tobacco Kingdom*, 204.

92. Starobin, *Industrial Slavery*, 165.

93. Stealey, "Slavery and the Western Virginia Salt Industry," 111–13.

94. Hopkins, *History of the Hemp Industry*, 25, 136.

95. Lander, "Slave Labor in South Carolina Cotton Mills," 166; Miller, "Fabric of Control," 486.

96. Wade, *Slavery in the Cities*, 116–19.

97. White, *Ar'n't I a Woman?* 128.

98. Kolchin, *American Slavery*, 109.

99. Dusinberre, *Them Dark Days*, 197.

100. Kolchin, *American Slavery,* 105; Fogel and Engerman, *Time on the Cross,* 39–40. Charles Joyner calculated that on the Laurel Hill and Hagley plantations of South Carolina, roughly 70 percent of all slaves were unskilled field laborers. Joyner, *Down by the Riverside,* 60–63. Philip Morgan has calculated that by the end of the eighteenth century, 25 percent of enslaved men in the Lowcountry were skilled workers and 35 percent of enslaved men in the Chesapeake were skilled. Morgan, *Slave Counterpoint,* 205–11.

101. Joyner, *Down by the Riverside,* 59–60.

102. Berry, *"Swing the Sickle,"* 17.

103. Morgan, *Slave Counterpoint,* 204–54; Joyner, *Down by the Riverside,* 61–89; Dunaway, *Women, Work, and Family,* 106–9; Follett, *Sugar Masters,* 118, 120–29, 135–38; Moody, *Slavery on Louisiana Sugar Plantations,* 54–64; Kulikoff, *Tobacco and Slaves,* 396–420; Fogel and Engerman, *Time on the Cross,* 39–51; Dusinberre, *Them Dark Days,* 275–81; West, *Chains of Love,* 90–94; Stevenson, *Life in Black and White,* 196–205; Berry, *"Swing the Sickle,"* 35–51; Jones, *Labor of Love,* 18; Fox-Genovese, *Within the Plantation Household,* 146–91; Weiner, *Mistresses and Slaves,* 13–22; Genovese, *Roll, Jordan, Roll,* 388–94.

104. Rawick, *American Slave,* vol. 12, pt. 2, p. 141.

105. Rawick, Hillegas, and Lawrence, *American Slave,* supp. ser. 1, vol. 8, pt. 3, p. 816.

106. Rawick, *American Slave,* vol. 13, pt. 4, p. 196.

107. Rawick, *American Slave,* vol. 10, pt. 6, pp. 240–41. For other hiring out examples, see Rawick, *American Slave,* vol. 16 (MD), 66; Rawick, Hillegas, and Lawrence, *American Slave,* supp. ser. 1, vol. 1, p. 40; Rawick, Hillegas, and Lawrence, *American Slave,* supp. ser. 1, vol. 4, pt. 2, p. 454.

108. Heyward, *Seed from Madagascar,* 112.

109. Pringle, *Chronicles of Chicora Wood,* 13.

110. Devereux, *Plantation Sketches,* 23–24.

111. John W. Blassingame, "Status and Social Structure in the Slave Community: Evidence from New Sources," in Owens, *Perspectives and Irony,* 142, 150–51.

112. Rawick, Hillegas, and Lawrence, *American Slave,* supp. ser. 1, vol. 9, pt. 4, p. 1665; Rawick, *American Slave,* vol. 13, pt. 4, p. 199.

113. Rawick, Hillegas, and Lawrence, *American Slave,* supp. ser. 1, vol. 10, pt. 5, p. 2367.

114. Rawick, Hillegas, and Lawrence, *American Slave,* supp. ser. 1, vol. 3, pt. 1, p. 113.

115. Rawick, *American Slave,* supp. ser. 2, vol. 4, pt. 3, pp. 1056–57; Rawick, *American Slave,* supp. ser. 2, vol. 6, pt. 5, p. 2036.

116. Rawick, *American Slave,* vol. 2, pt. 2, p. 272.

117. Rawick, *American Slave,* vol. 6 (AL), 9.

118. Rawick, *American Slave,* vol. 17, pp. 22–23.

119. Rawick, *American Slave,* vol. 8, pt. 2, p. 85.

120. Jacobs, *Incidents in the Life of a Slave Girl,* 11.

121. Rawick, *American Slave,* supp. ser. 2, vol. 4, pt. 3, pp. 1056–57.

122. Morgan, *Slave Counterpoint,* 215.

123. Rawick, *American Slave,* vol. 7 (OK), 143.

124. Rawick, *American Slave,* vol. 10, pt. 6, p. 244. See also Rawick, *American Slave,* vol. 9, pt. 3, p. 370; Heyward, *Seed from Madagascar,* 112.

125. Devereux, *Plantation Sketches,* 22–24.

126. Rawick, *American Slave,* vol. 7 (OK), 314; Rawick, *American Slave,* vol. 11 (AR), pt. 7, p. 163; Rawick, *American Slave,* vol. 2, pt. 2, p. 101; Rawick, *American Slave,* vol. 8, pt. 2, p. 217; Rawick, *American Slave,* vol. 12, pt. 1, p. 113; Rawick, *American Slave,* vol. 14, pt. 1, p. 445.

2. Enslaved Men and Leisure

1. Rawick, Hillegas, and Lawrence, *American Slave,* supp. ser. 1, vol. 10, pt. 5, pp. 2314–15.

2. Scott, *Weapons of the Weak,* xv.

3. For a similar theoretical approach to study enslaved women, see Camp, *Closer to Freedom,* 3.

4. Rawick, *American Slave,* vol. 3, pt. 3, p. 272.

5. Rawick, *American Slave,* vol. 16 (MD), 7; Rawick, *American Slave,* vol. 16 (OH), 22, 87.

6. Rawick, *American Slave,* vol. 6 (IN), 107.

7. Griffin, "Goin' Back Over There," 100.

8. Rawick, *American Slave,* supp. ser. 2, vol. 5, pt. 4, p. 1843.

9. See for example, Rawick, Hillegas, and Lawrence, *American Slave,* supp. ser. 1, vol. 3, pt. 1, p. 170; Rawick, *American Slave,* vol. 14, pt. 1, p. 213.

10. It is worth noting that, when compared to modern patterns of consumption, by the antebellum period Americans were drinking substantial amounts of alcohol. William J. Rorabaugh's study concluded that between 1800 and 1830, annual per capita consumption of distilled spirits reached five gallons, a rate triple that of drinking patterns recorded in the 1970s. Rorabaugh, *Alcoholic Republic,* 8.

11. Rawick, *American Slave,* supp. ser. 2, vol. 3, pt. 2, p. 739.

12. Rawick, *American Slave,* vol. 3, pt. 3, p. 230. References to apple, peach, and pear orchards appear in many plantation papers. For a few examples, see Charles Friend Diary, February 15, 1842, Friend Family Papers, M, pt. 3, reel 18, RASP; Richard Eppes Diary, November 30, 1859, Eppes Family Muniments, M, pt. 3, reel 13, RASP; William Writ Henry Account Book, November 27, 1861, Henry Family Papers, M, pt. 5, reel 34, RASP; James Hervey Greenlee Diary, March 23, 29, 1848, J, pt. 14, reel 3, RASP.

13. Rorabaugh, *Alcoholic Republic,* 13–14.

14. Rawick, Hillegas, and Lawrence, *American Slave,* supp. ser. 1, vol. 10, pt. 5, pp. 2366–67; Rawick, Hillegas, and Lawrence, *American Slave,* supp. ser. 1, vol. 8, pt. 3, p. 821.

15. Rawick, *American Slave,* supp. ser. 2, vol. 1, p. 9.

16. Rawick, *American Slave*, vol. 16 (VA), 22; Rawick, Hillegas, and Lawrence, *American Slave*, supp. ser. 1, vol. 1, p. 245; Rawick, Hillegas, and Lawrence, *American Slave*, supp. ser. 1, vol. 8, pt. 3, p. 1098; Rawick, Hillegas, and Lawrence, *American Slave*, supp. ser. 1, vol. 10, pt. 5, p. 2007; Rawick, *American Slave*, vol. 6 (AL), 327; Rawick, *American Slave*, vol. 16 (TN), 50.

17. Rawick, *American Slave*, vol. 12, pt. 2, p. 142.

18. Rawick, *American Slave*, vol. 2, pt. 1, p. 310; Rawick, *American Slave*, supp. ser. 2, vol. 9, pt. 8, p. 3655.

19. Richard Eppes Diary, June 15, 1858, Eppes Family Muniments, M, pt. 3, reel 13, RASP. Eppes noted in his June 15, 1858, entry that he "promised 6 ¼ ¢ a day to all those who drew no whiskey." This is certainly one explanation as to why three men took none during the harvesting.

20. Rawick, *American Slave*, supp. ser. 2, vol. 9, pt. 8, p. 3822.

21. Rawick, *American Slave*, supp. ser. 2, vol. 5, pt. 4, p. 1843.

22. Rawick, Hillegas, and Lawrence, *American Slave*, supp. ser. 1, vol. 6, pt. 1, pp. 59–60.

23. Rawick, Hillegas, and Lawrence, *American Slave*, supp. ser. 1, vol. 3, pt. 1, p. 86.

24. Rawick, *American Slave*, vol. 4, pt. 1, p. 206; see also pt. 2, p. 61.

25. Rawick, *American Slave*, vol. 4, pt. 2, p. 234.

26. Rawick, *American Slave*, vol. 7 (OK), 111.

27. Rawick, *American Slave*, vol. 3, pt. 3, pp. 94–95.

28. Rawick, *American Slave*, supp. ser. 2, vol. 2, pt. 1, p. 373. See also Rawick, *American Slave*, vol. 18, p. 146; Rawick, *American Slave*, vol. 7 (OK), 21; Rawick, *American Slave*, vol. 8, pt. 1, p. 331.

29. Rawick, *American Slave*, vol. 2, pt. 2, p. 309 (emphasis in original); Rawick, *American Slave*, vol. 18, p. 36; For work on the trade between slaves and poor whites, see esp. Lockley, "Trading Encounters," 25–48; Forret, "Slaves, Poor Whites," 783–824.

30. Rawick, *American Slave*, supp. ser. 2, vol. 5, pt. 4, p. 1448.

31. Rawick, *American Slave*, vol. 3, pt. 3, p. 222.

32. Rawick, *American Slave*, vol. 18, p. 80.

33. Rawick, Hillegas, and Lawrence, *American Slave*, supp. ser. 1, vol. 6, pt. 1, p. 280.

34. Lemle and Mishkind, "Alcohol and Masculinity," 213.

35. Mary Douglas, "A Distinctive Anthropological Perspective," in Douglas *Constructive Drinking*, 4, 8.

36. Akyeampong, *Drink, Power, and Cultural Change*, 15, 30, 15, 25.

37. Rawick, *American Slave*, vol. 16 (TN), 22.

38. Rawick, *American Slave*, vol. 2, pt. 2, p. 201.

39. For examples of enslaved women drinking, see Camp, *Closer to Freedom*, 87–89, 61; Rawick, *American Slave*, vol. 18, p. 146; Rawick, *American Slave*, vol. 5, pt. 4, pp. 19–20.

40. Rawick, *American Slave,* vol. 16 (KY), 6.

41. Rawick, *American Slave,* supp. ser. 2, vol. 2, pt. 1, p. 392.

42. Rawick, *American Slave,* vol. 13, pt. 4, p. 62.

43. See for example, Anderson District, Court of Magistrates and Freeholders, Trial Papers, microfilm reel C2916, cases 103, 104, microfilm reel C2917, cases 166, 169, 170, 185, microfilm reel C2919, cases 327, 371; Spartanburg District, microfilm reel C2920, case 86, microfilm reel C2921, cases 166, 178 (all held at South Carolina Department of Archives and History, Columbia [SCDAH]).

44. Rawick, *American Slave,* vol. 2, pt. 1, p. 28.

45. Rawick, *American Slave,* vol. 14, pt. 1, p. 157.

46. See for example, Anderson District, Court of Magistrates and Freeholders, Trial Papers, microfilm reel C2916, cases 103, 104, microfilm reel C2918, cases 210, 218, microfilm reel C2919, cases 294, 295, 313, 314, 327, 354, SCDAH.

47. Kershaw District, Court of Magistrates and Freeholders, Trial Papers, 1802–1861, fols. 84, 118, box 2, SCDAH.

48. Laurens District, Court of Magistrates and Freeholders, Trial Papers, 1808–1865, fol. 58, box 1, SCDAH.

49. Ibid.

50. Anderson District, Court of Magistrates and Freeholders, Trial Papers, microfilm reel C2919, case 354, SCDAH. See also case 312.

51. Irving Kenneth Zola, "Observations on Gambling in a Lower-Class Setting," in Herman, *Gambling,* 22.

52. Wyatt-Brown, *Southern Honor,* 340.

53. Rawick, Hillegas, and Lawrence, *American Slave,* supp. ser. 1, vol. 9, pt. 4, pp. 1432–33.

54. Anderson District, Court of Magistrates and Freeholders, Trial Papers, microfilm reel C2919, case 327, SCDAH. For other cases involving gambling and conflict, see Anderson District, Court of Magistrates and Freeholders, Trial Papers, microfilm reel C2919, cases 312, 313; Spartanburg District, Court of Magistrates and Freeholders, Trial Papers, microfilm reel C2921, cases 135, 136, 137, SCDAH.

55. Rawick, *American Slave,* vol. 14, pt. 1, p. 213.

56. Heath, "Some Generalizations about Alcohol and Culture," in Heath, *International Handbook,* 352.

57. Netting, "Beer as a Locus of Value," 376. For a list of studies on alcohol and drinking in African communities undertaken by anthropologists in the twentieth century, see Partanen, *Sociability and Intoxication,* 32–33.

58. Rawick, Hillegas, and Lawrence, *American Slave,* supp. ser. 1, vol. 8, pt. 3, p. 1129.

59. Anderson District, Court of Magistrates and Freeholders, Trial Papers, microfilm reel C2916, case 103, microfilm reel C2917, cases 170, 185, microfilm reel C2919, cases 327, 371, SCDAH.

60. Anthropologists have identified similar occurrences in African cultures.

See for example, Ndolamb Ngokwey's study of drinking among the Lele people in the Kasai region of the Congo. Ngokwey stated, "The individual who tends to drink too much will be warned by the other members of the group against the negative behavioral disruptions which accompany drunkenness." Ndolamb Ngokwey, "Varieties of Palm Wine among the Lele of the Kasai," in Douglas *Constructive Drinking*, 118. Netting, "Beer as a Locus of Value," 382; Kenneth Christmon, "Historical Overview of Alcohol," 321–24.

61. Rawick, *American Slave*, supp. ser. 2, vol. 10, pt. 9, p. 4242.

62. Rawick, *American Slave*, supp. ser. 2, vol. 7, pt. 6, p. 2825.

63. Rawick, *American Slave*, vol. 12, pt. 1, p. 348.

64. Anderson District, Court of Magistrates and Freeholders, Trial Papers, microfilm reel C2919, case 371, SCDAH. See also Anderson District, Court of Magistrates and Freeholders, Trial Papers, microfilm reel C2917, case 185, SCDAH.

65. Rawick, Hillegas, and Lawrence, *American Slave*, supp. ser. 1, vol. 8, pt. 3, p. 1232.

66. Richard E. Boyatzis, "Drinking as a Manifestation of Power Concerns," in Everett, Waddell, and Heath, *Cross-Cultural Approaches*, 265.

67. Rawick, *American Slave*, vol. 3, pt. 3, p. 134.

68. Rawick, *American Slave*, supp. ser. 2, vol. 8, pt. 7, p. 3020.

69. Camp, "Pleasures of Resistance," 543–44.

70. Jones, *Religious Instruction of the Negroes*, 138.

71. Petition of P. A. L. Smith et al. to the Virginia General Assembly, January 1860, microfilm reel 22, fr. 454, RSFB, ser. 1. See also petition of E. S. Arnold et al. to the Legislature of Virginia, January 1854, microfilm reel 22, fr. 90, RSFB, ser. 1.

72. Olmsted, *Cotton Kingdom*, 301.

73. Petition of Citizens of Wilkinson County to the Mississippi Senate and House of Representatives, ca. 1852, microfilm reel 3, fr. 520, RSFB, ser. 1.

74. Rawick, *American Slave*, vol. 12, pt. 1, p. 260.

75. Christmon, "Historical Overview of Alcohol," 326.

76. Scott, *Domination and the Arts of Resistance*, 121–22, xiii.

77. Turner, *Confessions of Nat Turner*, 11–12.

78. Scott, *Domination and the Arts of Resistance*, 199.

79. Rawick, *American Slave*, supp. ser. 2, vol. 9, pt. 8, p. 3448; Rawick, *American Slave*, vol. 18, p. 15; Rawick, *American Slave*, vol. 17, p. 134; *Narrative of William Hayden*, 20. For a study of the play of slave children, see Wiggins, "Play of Slave Children," 21–39.

80. Rawick, *American Slave*, supp. ser. 2, vol. 5, pt. 4, p. 1478.

81. *Narrative of the Life and Labors of the Rev. G. W. Offley*, 11; See also Rawick, *American Slave*, vol. 17, p. 134; Robert Ellett in Perdue, Barden, and Phillips, *Weevils in the Wheat*, 84.

82. Rawick, Hillegas, and Lawrence, *American Slave*, supp. ser. 1, vol. 10, pt. 5, p. 2361.

83. Rawick, *American Slave*, supp. ser. 2, vol. 9, pt. 8, p. 3758.

84. *Narrative of the Life and Adventures of Henry Bibb*, 23.

85. Greenberg, *Honor and Slavery*, 34–35.

86. Desch-Obi, *Fighting for Honor*, 99.

87. Rawick, *American Slave*, vol. 14, pt. 1, p. 406.

88. Rawick, *American Slave*, supp. ser. 2, vol. 5, pt. 4, p. 1886.

89. Rawick, *American Slave*, vol. 18, p. 255.

90. Rawick, *American Slave*, vol. 12, pt. 2, p. 85.

91. Rawick, *American Slave*, vol. 18, p. 255.

92. Rawick, *American Slave*, vol. 9, pt. 4, p. 173.

93. Rawick, *American Slave*, supp. ser. 2, vol. 7, pt. 6, p. 2659.

94. Rawick, *American Slave*, supp. ser. 2, vol. 4, pt. 3, pp. 1344–47.

95. Ibid., 1344–45.

96. Desch-Obi, *Fighting for Honor*, 99–100. For a brief description of Tom Molineaux's life and his famous fights in 1810 and 1811 with English champion Tom Crib, see "Tom Molineaux, Black Pioneer in Sport," in Wiggins and Miller, *Unlevel Playing Field*, 9–13.

97. Sugden, *Boxing and Society*, 189.

98. Quoted in ibid., 190.

99. Woodward, "Rumbles in the Jungle," 11.

100. Gilmore, *Manhood in the Making*, 11–12.

101. Rotundo, *American Manhood*, 2; Wyatt-Brown, *Southern Honor*, xii.

102. *Life of Josiah Henson*, 7.

103. Rawick, *American Slave*, supp. ser. 2, vol. 9, pt. 8, pp. 3690–91.

104. Fraser, "Negotiating Their Manhood," 76–94; Fraser, *Courtship and Love*, 69–87.

105. Rawick, *American Slave*, vol. 16 (OH), 52.

106. Rawick, *American Slave*, vol. 16 (TN), 13.

107. Ibid., 9. During the interview, Childress revealed that Fedd eventually ran away and on his travels met a white man who "know'd he wuz a good fighter." The white man placed a $250 bet on a fight between Fedd and a black man from an ironworks. Fedd proved a good bet and killed his opponent in the contest. For another incident of a "fighter" lashing out at an overseer, see *Life of William Grimes*, 37.

108. "Journal of Wallace Turnage," in Blight, *Slave No More*, 218–19.

109. Camp, *Closer to Freedom*, 62.

110. Camp, "Pleasures of Resistance," 544.

111. Rawick, Hillegas, and Lawrence, *American Slave*, supp. ser. 1, vol. 9, pt. 4, p. 1657.

112. Ibid., 1663–64.

113. Grimes, *Life of William Grimes*, 28. Although it is not clear whether Cato sustained these injuries in an organized bout of wrestling or whether the conflict was a spontaneous act of violence, the narrative nevertheless offers suggestion that

Grimes had fought before in a wrestling capacity. Indeed, he noted in his narrative that when he fought a fellow slave named Moses, he had cut off his hair "as close as possible, for the purpose of having the advantage." Ibid., 14.

114. Rawick, *American Slave,* vol. 9, pt. 4, p. 12.

115. Indeed, not only would the slave owner lose the life and property of the slave killed in the ring, but he would also most likely lose the life of the slave responsible for the death through the ensuing protocols of capital punishment.

116. Camp, "Pleasures of Resistance," 538.

117. Rawick, *American Slave,* vol. 16 (KY), 114–15.

118. Rawick, *American Slave,* vol. 15, pt. 2, p. 365.

119. Douglass, *My Bondage and My Freedom,* 253.

120. Rawick, *American Slave,* supp. ser. 2, vol. 5, pt. 4, p. 1886.

121. Sigrid Paul, "The Wrestling Tradition and Its Social Functions," in Baker and Mangan, *Sport in Africa,* 23, 36, 41.

122. Desch-Obi, *Fighting for Honor,* 92–93.

123. Rawick, *American Slave,* vol. 7, pt. 1, p. 142.

124. Smith, *Fifty Years of Slavery,* 62–63. For a similar incident, see also Rawick, *American Slave,* vol. 18, p. 106.

125. Michael A. Messner, "Like Family: Power, Intimacy, and Sexuality in Male Athletes' Friendships," in Nardi, *Men's Friendships,* 232; Laurence de Garis, "'Be a Buddy to Your Buddy': Male Intimacy, Aggression, and Intimacy in a Boxing Gym," in McKay, Messner, and Sabo, *Masculinities, Gender Relations, and Sport,* 104.

126. Forret, "Conflict and the 'Slave Community,'" 551–88.

127. Armstrong, *Old Massa's People,* 160.

128. Rawick, *American Slave,* vol. 9, pt. 4, p. 12.

3. Beyond the Plantation

1. Rawick, *American Slave,* vol. 3, pt. 3, p. 56. In her study of South Carolina, historian Emily West used WPA narratives to calculate that 96.9 percent of former male slaves hunted, while not one woman fished or hunted. West, *Chains of Love,* 100.

2. Rawick, *American Slave,* supp. ser. 2, vol. 10, pt. 9, p. 3935; Rawick, *American Slave,* vol. 4, pt. 1, p. 286; Rawick, *American Slave,* vol. 2, pt. 1, p. 152.

3. Rawick, *American Slave,* supp. ser. 2, vol. 5, pt. 4, p. 1525; Rawick, *American Slave,* vol. 2, pt. 1, p. 241. Rawick, *American Slave,* vol. 13, pt. 4, pp. 76, 198.

4. Scott Giltner, "Slave Hunting and Fishing in the Antebellum South," in Glave and Stoll, *"To Love the Wind and the Rain,"* 24–25, 28.

5. Rawick, *American Slave,* vol. 12, pt. 1, p. 302; Rawick, *American Slave,* vol. 8, pt. 2, p. 24.

6. Rawick, Hillegas, and Lawrence, *American Slave,* supp. ser. 1, vol. 9, pt. 4, p. 1640.

7. Rawick, *American Slave,* vol. 13, pt. 3, p. 233.

8. Rawick, *American Slave,* vol. 13, pt. 4, p. 154.

9. Fraser, "Negotiating Their Manhood," 81, 83.

10. Proctor, *Bathed in Blood,* 145, 157.

11. Rawick, *American Slave,* vol. 2, pt. 2, pp. 266–67.

12. Rawick, *American Slave,* supp. ser. 2, vol. 5, pt. 4, p. 1618; Rawick, Hillegas, and Lawrence *American Slave,* supp. ser. 1, vol. 1, pp. 427, 64.

13. Rawick, *American Slave,* vol. 14, pt. 1, p. 412.

14. Rawick, *American Slave,* vol. 12, pt. 2, pp. 223–24.

15. Rawick, *American Slave,* vol. 17, p. 328; Rawick, *American Slave,* vol. 2, pt. 2, p. 75; Rawick, Hillegas, and Lawrence, *American Slave,* supp. ser. 1, vol. 2, pp. 48–49.

16. Rawick, Hillegas, and Lawrence, *American Slave,* supp. ser. 1, vol. 3, pt. 1, p. 77; Rawick, *American Slave,* supp. ser. 2, vol. 10, pt. 9, p. 4143.

17. Rawick, *American Slave,* supp. ser. 2, vol. 1, p. 28.

18. Rawick, Hillegas, and Lawrence, *American Slave,* supp. ser. 1, vol. 6, pt. 1, p. 112.

19. Parker, *Recollections of Slavery Times,* 48–50.

20. Rawick, *American Slave,* vol. 13, pt. 4, p. 75.

21. Rawick, *American Slave,* supp. ser. 2, vol. 6, pt. 5, p. 1962.

22. Rawick, *American Slave,* vol. 16 (VA), 45.

23. Rawick, *American Slave,* vol. 5, pt. 4, p. 215.

24. Rawick, Hillegas, and Lawrence, *American Slave,* supp. ser. 1, vol. 9, pt. 4, p. 1432.

25. Rawick, Hillegas, and Lawrence, *American Slave,* supp. ser. 1, vol. 3, pt. 1, p. 172.

26. Rawick, Hillegas, and Lawrence, *American Slave,* supp. ser. 1, vol. 5, p. 74.

27. Rawick, Hillegas, and Lawrence, *American Slave,* supp. ser. 1, vol. 1, p. 185.

28. Rawick, *American Slave,* vol. 13, pt. 4, p. 101.

29. Rawick, *American Slave,* supp. ser. 2, vol. 10, pt. 9, pp. 3948–49.

30. Rawick, *American Slave,* supp. ser. 2, vol. 5, pt. 4, p. 1618.

31. Ball, *Fifty Years in Chains,* 163.

32. Rawick, *American Slave,* vol. 10, pt. 6, p. 354.

33. Rawick, *American Slave,* vol. 5, pt. 3, p. 167; Rawick, *American Slave,* supp. ser. 2, vol. 9, pt. 8, p. 3887; Rawick, *American Slave,* vol. 15, pt. 2, p. 277; Rawick, Hillegas, and Lawrence, *American Slave,* supp. ser. 1, vol. 1, p. 451.

34. Rawick, Hillegas, and Lawrence, *American Slave,* supp. ser. 1, vol. 1, p. 41.

35. Richard Eppes Diary; see the advice given in "Plantation and Farm Instruction, Regulation, Record, Inventory and Account Book," which precedes the diary entries of January 4–December 31, 1858, M, pt. 3, reel 13, RASP. For more on how time was regulated for the enslaved in the antebellum South, see Smith, *Mastered by the Clock.*

36. See Camp, *Closer to Freedom,* esp. chap. 1.

37. Barrow, *Plantation Life,* 406. See also rule ten in the "Cornhill" Plantation Book of John Blount Miller and John F. Furman, McDonald Furman Papers, F, pt. 2, reel 9, RASP, and rule three in William Ethelbert Ervin Diary, October 31, 1847, J, pt. 6, reel 17, RASP.

38. Regulation Book for Overseer, January 1828, Cocke Family Papers, E, pt. 4, reel 19, RASP.

39. Richard Eppes Diary, "Plantation and Farm Instruction, Regulation, Record, Inventory and Account Book," preceding entries of January 4–December 31, 1858, M, pt. 3, reel 13, RASP. See also rule five in the "Cornhill" Plantation Book of John Blount Miller and John F. Furman, McDonald Furman Papers, F, pt. 2, reel 9, RASP.

40. Richard Eppes Diary, "Plantation and Farm Instruction, Regulation, Record, Inventory and Account Book," preceding entries of January 4–December 31, 1858, M, pt. 3, reel 13, RASP.

41. William Ethelbert Ervin Diary, October 31, 1847, J, pt. 6, reel 17, RASP.

42. Plantation Journal, 1857–1858, Robert Ruffin Barrow Papers, J, pt. 5, reel 2, RASP. Robert Ruffin Barrow had two men on "night watch" every night.

43. Barrow, *Plantation Life,* 410.

44. Petition of Citizens of Buckingham County to the Virginia Legislature, ca. March 1852, microfilm reel 22, fr. 376, RSFB, ser. 1.

45. Franklin and Moss, *From Slavery to Freedom,* 124–26.

46. For examples of slaveholders assuming patrol duty, see Roswell King Jr. Diary, August 12, September 9, October 2, 10, 1839, I, pt. 2, reel 20, RASP; Circular letter for a slave patrol committee dated August 1853, Pettigrew Family Papers, J, pt. 2, reel 22, RASP; Richard Eppes Diary, November 30, 1851, M, pt. 3, reel 12, RASP. For examples of poor whites on patrol, see Rawick, *American Slave,* vol. 2, pt. 1, p. 68; Rawick, Hillegas, and Lawrence, *American Slave,* supp. ser. 1, vol. 11, p. 133; Rawick, *American Slave,* vol. 7 (OK), p. 66. For insights into the duties of the patrols see Petition of Citizens of Wilkinson County to the Mississippi Senate and House of Representatives, ca. 1852, microfilm reel 3, fr. 520, RSFB, ser. 1; Petition of William Whitfield et al. to the Representatives of Wayne and Lenoir Counties, North Carolina, ca. December 1830, microfilm reel 6, fr. 279, RSFB, ser. 1; Petition of Citizens of Sussex County, Delaware to the Delaware Senate and House of Representatives, ca. 1818, microfilm reel 1, fr. 440, RSFB, ser. 1.

47. Genovese, *Roll, Jordan, Roll,* 618–19; Hadden, *Slave Patrols;* Fry, *Night Riders in Black Folk History;* Stampp, *Peculiar Institution,* 214–15.

48. Rawick, Hillegas, and Lawrence, *American Slave,* supp. ser. 1, vol. 2, p. 158.

49. "Rules for the Government of the Patrols," November Term 1846, Chowan County Slave Records Criminal Actions Concerning Slaves, box 33: Miscellaneous Slave Records, 1730–1861, NCDAH.

50. Camp, *Closer to Freedom,* 28; West, *Chains of Love,* 37, 58; Fraser, *Courtship and Love,* 70–71.

51. Richard Eppes Diary, December 30, 1858, June 4, 1859, M, pt. 3, reel 13, RASP; John Nevitt Diary, February 5, 12, 1831, J, pt. 6, reel 3, RASP.

52. Rawick, *American Slave,* vol. 4, pt. 1, p. 260.

53. Rawick, *American Slave,* vol. 8, pt. 1, p. 294.

54. Rawick, *American Slave,* supp. ser. 2, vol. 9, pt. 8, p. 3678.

55. Rawick, Hillegas, and Lawrence, *American Slave,* supp. ser. 1, vol. 5, p. 403.

56. Rawick, *American Slave,* vol. 18, p. 193. See also an overseer's correspondence of May 18, 1817, which recounts the beating of enslaved men by a patrol in John Ball Sr. and John Ball Jr. Papers, F, pt. 2, reel 2, RASP; Richard Eppes Diary, September 2, 1859, M, pt. 3, reel 13, RASP.

57. Rawick, *American Slave,* vol. 13, pt. 3, p. 68; Rawick, *American Slave,* vol. 4, pt. 1, p. 158.

58. Rawick, *American Slave,* vol. 9, pt. 3, p. 94.

59. Rawick, Hillegas, and Lawrence, *American Slave,* supp. ser. 1, vol. 3, pt. 1, p. 7; Rawick, Hillegas, and Lawrence, *American Slave,* supp. ser. 1, vol. 11, p. 316; Rawick, *American Slave,* vol. 10, pt. 5, p. 335; Rawick, *American Slave,* vol. 8, pt. 1, p. 318; Rawick, *American Slave,* vol. 7 (OK), 146.

60. Rawick, *American Slave,* vol. 9, pt. 3, p. 94.

61. Rawick, *American Slave,* supp. ser. 2, vol. 6, pt. 5, p. 2161. Because many enslaved men left the plantation boundaries to court women or maintain cross-plantation marriages, some slaveholders were intensely opposed to allowing enslaved men to marry off the plantation. See, for example, Plantation Journal, January 6, 1836, Regulations for the year 1838, Hugenin and Johnston Family Papers, Southern Historical Collection, University of North Carolina, Chapel Hill (SHC); Frank Steel to Anna Steel, December 15, 1859, Steel Letters, J, pt. 6, reel 29, RASP; Barrow, *Plantation Life,* 406, 408.

62. West, *Chains of Love,* 59.

63. Gilmore, *Manhood in the Making,* 57, 121.

64. Rawick, *American Slave,* vol. 4, pt. 2, p. 145.

65. Rawick, *American Slave,* supp. ser. 2, vol. 3, pt. 2, p. 839.

66. Rawick, Hillegas, and Lawrence, *American Slave,* supp. ser. 1, vol. 3, pt. 1, p. 171.

67. Rawick, Hillegas, and Lawrence, *American Slave,* supp. ser. 1, vol. 1, p. 87.

68. Some slave owners forbid patrollers to enter their property. Rawick, Hillegas, and Lawrence, *American Slave,* supp. ser. 1, vol. 11, p. 316; Rawick, *American Slave,* vol. 13, pt. 3, p. 5.

69. Rawick, *American Slave,* supp. ser. 2, vol. 2, pt. 1, p. 304.

70. Rawick, Hillegas, and Lawrence, *American Slave,* supp. ser. 1, vol. 3, pt. 1, p. 185; Rawick, Hillegas, and Lawrence, *American Slave,* supp. ser. 1, vol. 9, pt. 4, p. 1440.

71. Rawick, *American Slave,* vol. 4, pt. 2, p. 145.

72. Rawick, *American Slave,* vol. 16 (MD), 49–50; Rawick, *American Slave,*

vol. 6 (IN), 62–63; Rawick, Hillegas, and Lawrence, *American Slave,* supp. ser. 1, vol. 9, pt. 4, pp. 1748–49; Rawick, *American Slave,* vol. 8, pt. 2, p. 172; Rawick, *American Slave,* vol. 13, pt. 4, p. 80; Rawick, Hillegas, and Lawrence, *American Slave,* supp. ser. 1, vol. 3, pt. 1, p. 8.

73. Rawick, *American Slave,* vol. 9, pt. 4, pp. 220–21; Ishrael Massie in Perdue, Barden, and Phillips, *Weevils in the Wheat,* 208.

74. Rawick, *American Slave,* vol. 10, pt. 5, p. 335; Rawick, *American Slave,* vol. 16 (VA), 12.

75. Beverly Jones in Perdue, Barden, and Phillips, *Weevils in the Wheat,* 181–83.

76. West Turner in Perdue, Barden, and Phillips, *Weevils in the Wheat,* 290.

77. Fraser, "Negotiating Their Manhood," 85–86.

78. Rawick, *American Slave,* vol. 8, pt. 2, p. 182.

79. Rawick, *American Slave,* supp. ser. 2, vol. 6, pt. 5, p. 2215.

80. Rawick, *American Slave,* vol. 12, pt. 1, p. 350.

81. Anderson District, Court of Magistrates and Freeholders, Trial Papers, microfilm reel C2918, case 237, SCDAH.

82. Anderson District, Court of Magistrates and Freeholders, Trial Papers, microfilm reel C2917, case 190, SCDAH.

83. Rawick, Hillegas, and Lawrence, *American Slave,* supp. ser. 1, vol. 9, pt. 4, p. 1743.

84. Rawick, Hillegas, and Lawrence, *American Slave,* supp. ser. 1, vol. 3, pt. 1, pp. 7–8; Rawick, *American Slave,* supp. ser. 2, vol. 10, pt. 9, p. 4157; Rawick, Hillegas, and Lawrence, *American Slave,* supp. ser. 1, vol. 8, pt. 3, p. 826.

85. Steward, *Twenty-Two Years a Slave,* 33–39.

86. Rawick, Hillegas, and Lawrence, *American Slave,* supp. ser. 1, vol. 10, pt. 5, p. 2001.

87. Rawick, *American Slave,* vol. 7 (OK), 142–43.

88. Fairfield District, Court of Magistrates and Freeholders, Trial Papers, 1839–1865, fol. 27, box 1, SCDAH.

89. Anderson District, Court of Magistrates and Freeholders, Trial Papers, microfilm reel C2918, case 226, SCDAH.

90. *Narrative of the Life of Frederick Douglass,* 65–66, 72.

91. Stampp, *Peculiar Institution,* 125.

92. Genovese, *Roll, Jordan, Roll,* 608.

93. Lichtenstein, "That Disposition to Theft," 433. Drawing on the theory developed by E. P. Thompson, Lichtenstein defined "moral economy" as the "notion that an oppressed group or class develops an autonomous conception of their economic and social rights, essentially drawing a line across which the ruling class cannot legitimately step." When the ruling class attempts to redefine or erode these rights by law, the subordinate classes protest and react by staging food riots, smuggling, poaching, theft, etc. This behavior, defined as criminal by the ruling classes, is typically understood as legitimate by the subordinates. Ibid., 415–16.

94. See, for example, Schwarz, *Twice Condemned,* 217; Dusinberre, *Them Dark*

Days, 140–42; Franklin and Schweninger, *Runaway Slaves,* 79–83; Follett, *Sugar Masters,* 147–49; Megginson, *African American Life,* 130–32; Forret, *Race Relations at the Margins,* 74–114.

95. See, for example, David Gavin Diary, November 3, 1855, J, pt. 3, reel 10, RASP; John Walker Plantation Journal, October 18, 1830, John Walker Papers, J, pt. 9, reel 32, RASP; A. Ledoux & Co. Plantation Journal, January 27, February 3, April 6, May 18, 25, June 1, 1856, I, pt. 1, reel 9, RASP; John Nevitt Diary, August 27, 1830, J, pt. 6, reel 3, RASP; Richard Eppes Diary, November 26, 1851, January 8, October 7, December 1, 1852, September 12, 1853, October 16, 1853, December 4, 1855, December 14, 1857, January 18, 1858, September 21, 24, 1859, January 20, September 3, 1860, M, pt. 3, reel 12–13, RASP.

96. Charles Friend Diary, June 11, 1841, July 14, 1846, December 13, 1841, Friend Family Papers, M, pt. 3, reel 18, RASP.

97. "Regulations to be followed by overseers," Cocke Family Papers, January 1828, E, pt. 4, reel 19, RASP. See also "Cornhill" Plantation Book of John Blount Miller and John F. Furman, McDonald Furman Papers, 1827–1873, F, pt. 2, reel 9, RASP.

98. "The Duties of an Overseer," Elley Plantation Book, 1855–1856, N, reel 10, RASP.

99. Ibid. See also Richard Eppes Diary, "Plantation and Farm Instruction, Regulation, Record, Inventory and Account Book," preceding entries of January 4–December 31, 1858, M, pt. 3, reel 13, RASP; Rawick, *American Slave,* vol. 13, pt. 4, p. 333, rule fifteen.

100. Housed in the state archives of South Carolina are trial records for fourteen antebellum districts: Anderson, Camden, Clarendon, Fairfield, Greenville, Kershaw, Laurens, Marlboro, Pickens, Richland, Spartanburg, Sumter, Union, and York. For more on the background and workings of the South Carolina Court of Magistrates and Freeholders, see Henderson, "Slave Court System in Spartanburg County," 31–37; Lipscomb and Jacobs, "Magistrates and Freeholders Court," 62–65.

101. Anderson District, Court of Magistrates and Freeholders, Trial Papers, microfilm reels C2916–19, C2775, SCDAH.

102. Daniel E. Huger Smith, "A Plantation Boyhood," in Huger, *Carolina Rice Plantation,* 65.

103. Richard Eppes to Mr. Burchell, October 13, 1859, Richard Eppes Diary, M, pt. 3, reel 13, RASP. See also John Nevitt Diary, August 27, 1830, J, pt. 6, reel 3, RASP; A. Stanley to John Gray Blount, March 10, 1838, John Gray Blount Papers, NCDAH; Rawick, *American Slave,* vol. 10, pt. 6, p. 105.

104. Paul D. Escott undertook a quantitative analysis of the WPA narratives in his examination of enslaved life. From the interviews he calculated the sex of those who engaged in theft: 53.3 percent male, 26.7 percent female, and 20 percent both male and female involved. Unfortunately, he did not stipulate whether these thefts occurred on or off the plantation. However, given the percentage of women

who engaged in theft, it is plausible that most of these thefts were committed by enslaved people against their own masters. Escott, *Slavery Remembered,* 90.

105. Rawick, Hillegas, and Lawrence, *American Slave,* supp. ser. 1, vol. 10, pt. 5, p. 2076.

106. Rawick, *American Slave,* vol. 7 (OK), 136.

107. John Walker Plantation Journal, October 18, 1830, John Walker Papers, J, pt. 9, reel 32, RASP.

108. Barrow, September 15, 1840, diary entry, *Plantation Life,* 211.

109. Petition of Richard Dawson Sr. et al., Beaufort District to South Carolina Assembly, ca. 1816, in Schweninger, *Southern Debate over Slavery,* 1:51. See also petition of Sanders Glover et al., Amelia Township, to South Carolina Assembly, 1816, in Schweninger, *Southern Debate over Slavery,* 1:55–56; Petition of Citizens of Charles City and New Kent Counties to Virginia Assembly, 1831, in Schweninger, *Southern Debate over Slavery,* 1:136; Petition of Harvey Dean et al. to the Tennessee Legislature, ca. December 1847, microfilm reel 14, fr. 166, RSFB, ser. 1; Petition of George H. Burwell et al. to the Senate and House of Delegates of Virginia, ca. January 1860, microfilm reel 22, fr. 438, RSFB, ser. 1.

110. Rawick, *American Slave,* vol. 11, pt. 7 (MO), 208; Rawick, *American Slave,* vol. 13, pt. 4, p. 185; *Narrative of Henry Box Brown,* 27–29.

111. Rawick, *American Slave,* vol. 12, pt. 2, p. 52; Rawick, *American Slave,* vol. 9, pt. 3, p. 290.

112. Rawick, *American Slave,* vol. 17, p. 291.

113. Genovese, *Roll, Jordan, Roll,* 605.

114. Anderson District, Court of Magistrates and Freeholders, Trial Papers, microfilm reel C2918, case 268, SCDAH.

115. See Forret, "Conflict and the 'Slave Community,'" 565.

116. Rawick, *American Slave,* supp. ser. 2, vol. 8, pt. 7, p. 3136.

117. Rawick, *American Slave,* supp. ser. 2, vol. 2, pt. 1, p. 89.

118. Rawick, Hillegas, and Lawrence, *American Slave,* supp. ser. 1, vol. 9, pt. 4, p. 1771.

119. Rawick, *American Slave,* vol. 8, pt. 1, p. 238.

120. Anderson District, Court of Magistrates and Freeholders, Trial Papers, microfilm reel C2916, case 114, SCDAH.

121. Rawick, *American Slave,* vol. 13, pt. 3, p. 180. See also Rawick, *American Slave,* vol. 18, pp. 11–12.

122. Rawick, *American Slave,* vol. 18, pp. 137–38.

123. *Life of Josiah Henson,* 9–10.

124. Ball, *Slavery in the United States,* 300, 305.

125. Counihan, *Anthropology of Food and Body,* 13.

126. See, for example, Anderson District, Court of Magistrates and Freeholders, Trial Papers, microfilm reel C2918, case 281, microfilm reel C2919, case 296, SCDAH. The number of lashes given to slaves found guilty of theft varied enormously. In only three cases was the death penalty applied for theft; one of these

was tried on March 18, 1861, and the rest were tried during the Civil War. See Anderson District, Court of Magistrates and Freeholders, Trial Papers, microfilm reel C2919, case 363, microfilm reel C2775, cases 375, 410, SCDAH.

127. Anderson District, Court of Magistrates and Freeholders, Trial Papers, microfilm reel C2919, case 322, SCDAH.

128. Anderson District, Court of Magistrates and Freeholders, Trial Papers, microfilm reel C2919, case 298, SCDAH.

129. Spartanburg District, Court of Magistrates and Freeholders, Trial Papers, microfilm C2921, case 225, SCDAH.

130. Anderson District, Court of Magistrates and Freeholders, Trial Papers, microfilm reel C2775, case 410, 424, microfilm reel C2916, case 43, microfilm reel C2918, case 223, SCDAH.

131. Anderson District, Court of Magistrates and Freeholders, Trial Papers, microfilm reel C2775, case 424, SCDAH.

132. Rawick, *American Slave,* supp. ser. 2, vol. 3, pt. 2, p. 630.

133. May Satterfield in Perdue, Barden, and Phillips, *Weevils in the Wheat,* 245.

134. Rawick, *American Slave,* vol. 8, pt. 2, p. 47.

135. Rawick, *American Slave,* vol. 13, pt. 4, p. 185.

136. *Life of Josiah Henson,* 9.

137. Rawick, *American Slave,* vol. 11, pt. 7, p. 181. See also Rawick, *American Slave,* vol. 12, pt. 2, p. 235.

138. Rawick, Hillegas, and Lawrence, *American Slave,* supp. ser. 1, vol. 9, pt. 4, p. 1664. See also Rawick, *American Slave,* vol. 7 (OK), 348.

139. Rawick, *American Slave,* vol. 18, pp. 137–38.

140. Rawick, *American Slave,* vol. 18, p. 9.

141. Larry E. Hudson, "'All that Cash': Work and Status in the Slave Quarters," in Hudson, *Working toward Freedom,* 77.

142. Anderson District, Court of Magistrates and Freeholders, Trial Papers, microfilm reel C2916, cases 3, 58, 91, microfilm reel C2918, case 253, microfilm reel C2919, case 354, microfilm reel C2775, case 412, SCDAH.

143. Anderson District, Court of Magistrates and Freeholders, Trial Papers, microfilm reel C2917, case 157, microfilm reel C2775, case 392, SCDAH.

144. For examples of slaves trading with poor whites, see Olmsted, *Cotton Kingdom,* 83; Rawick, *American Slave,* vol. 7 (OK), 112; Lockley, *Lines in the Sand,* chap. 3. For evidence of slaves trading with free blacks, see Rawick, *American Slave,* vol. 18, p. 285; Anderson District, Court of Magistrates and Freeholders, Trial Papers, microfilm reel C2916, cases 13, 67, SCDAH.

145. Anderson District, Court of Magistrates and Freeholders, Trial Papers, microfilm reel C2917, cases 137, 178, microfilm reel C2918, cases 214, 232, microfilm C2919, cases 307, 349, microfilm reel C2775, case 389, SCDAH.

146. Morgan, "Ownership of Property by Slaves," 404.

147. Penningroth, *Claims of Kinfolk,* 11.

148. Except in two cases where enslaved men were accused of stealing from free

blacks, and the five cases in which enslaved men were accused of stealing from other slaves, the evidence suggests that all other cases of theft tried in Anderson District were committed by enslaved people against property-owning whites. For the two cases of theft where enslaved people had stolen from free blacks, see Anderson District, Court of Magistrates and Freeholders, Trial Papers, microfilm reel C2918, case 209, microfilm reel C2919, case 299, SCDAH. For the five cases of slave-on-slave theft, see Anderson District, Court of Magistrates and Freeholders, Trial Papers, microfilm reel C2917, cases 129, 142, microfilm reel C2918, cases 221, 283, microfilm reel C2919, case 310, SCDAH.

149. Robert Smalls, interviewed for the American Freedmen's Inquiry Commission, 1863, in Blassingame, *Slave Testimony*, 381.

150. Brown, *Slave Life in Georgia*, 83.

151. *Narratives of the Sufferings of Lewis and Milton Clarke*, 119.

152. Forret's recent work used the Court of Magistrates and Freeholders trial papers in upcountry South Carolina to examine cases of conflict between slaves arising over theft of property. Forret, "Conflict and the 'Slave Community,'" 562–65, 576.

153. Aimar Ventsel, "Pride, Honour, Individual and Collective Violence: Order in a 'Lawless' Village," in Benda-Beckmann and Pirie, *Order and Disorder*, 41.

154. Anderson District, Court of Magistrates and Freeholders, Trial Papers, microfilm reel C2917, case 129, SCDAH. In another case from Anderson District, Edward, enslaved to Ezekiel Murphy, stole five dresses belonging to his estranged wife, Margaret, the slave of J. Duckworth. According to trial testimony, Edward "mad[e] threats that if Marget did not do him any good that she Should not do Any one Else any good." Anderson District, Court of Magistrates and Freeholders, Trial Papers, microfilm reel C2918, case 283, SCDAH.

155. Richard Eppes Diary, January 8, 1852, M, pt. 3, reel 12, RASP.

156. Long, *Pictures of Slavery in Church and State*, 197.

157. Ball, *Slavery in the United States*, 112.

158. Anderson District, Court of Magistrates and Freeholders, Trial Papers, microfilm reel C2918, case 214, SCDAH. See also microfilm reel C2919, case 327.

159. Anderson District, Court of Magistrates and Freeholders, Trial Papers, microfilm reel C2775, case 410, SCDAH.

160. Anderson District, Court of Magistrates and Freeholders, Trial Papers, microfilm reel C2775, case 424, SCDAH.

161. Anderson District, Court of Magistrates and Freeholders, Trial Papers, microfilm reel C2775, case 391, SCDAH.

162. Anderson District, Court of Magistrates and Freeholders, Trial Papers, microfilm reel C2775, case 387, SCDAH.

163. Richard Eppes Diary, "Plantation and Farm Instruction, Regulation, Record, Inventory and Account Book" preceding entries of January 4–December 31, 1858, M, pt. 3, reel 13, RASP. See also Tattler, "Management of Negroes," *Southern Cultivator* 8 (November 1850): 162–64, reprinted in Breeden, *Advice among Masters*, 83.

164. Richard Eppes Diary, November 26, 1851, M, pt. 3, reel 12, RASP.

165. Richard Eppes Diary, December 24, 1852. Eppes recorded the thefts in his diary on October 7, and December 1, 1852, M, pt. 3, reel 13, RASP.

166. A. Ledoux & Co. Plantation Journal, January 27, February 3, April 6, May 18, 25, June 1, 1856, I, pt. 1, reel 9, RASP.

167. Ball, *Slavery in the United States*, 365–67. See also Rawick, *American Slave*, supp. ser. 2, vol. 3, pt. 2, p. 643.

4. Friendship, Resistance, and Runaways

1. *Life and Times of Frederick Douglass*, 151.

2. See, for example, Gutman, *Black Family*; Genovese, *Roll, Jordan, Roll*; Blassingame, *Slave Community*; Malone, *Sweet Chariot*; Hudson, *To Have and to Hold*; West, *Chains of Love*; and Fraser, *Courtship and Love*.

3. West, *Chains of Love*, 3.

4. Hudson, *To Have and to Hold*, 166.

5. Smith-Rosenberg, "Female World of Love and Ritual," 9, 2, 14.

6. Ibid., 4–6.

7. Faderman, *Surpassing the Love of Men*, 16. Although Elizabeth Mavor was the first to use the term "romantic friendship"—in her study of two eighteenth-century women, Eleanor Butler and Sarah Ponsonby, who eloped together—it was not until the publication of Faderman's work in 1981 that the term entered widespread usage. See Mavor, *Ladies of Llangollen*.

8. Ibid., 16–17, 16, 19. Some historians, however, remain unconvinced by Faderman's claim that romantic friendships were totally asexual. See Vicinus, *Intimate Friends*, xv; Moore, "Something More Tender Still," 499–520.

9. Cott, "Passionlessness," 233.

10. Rotundo, "Romantic Friendship," 1, 3.

11. Ibid., 5.

12. Donald Yacovone, "Abolitionists and the 'Language of Fraternal Love,'" in Carnes and Griffin, *Meanings for Manhood*, 94.

13. Rotundo, "Romantic Friendship," 19.

14. D'Emilio and Freedman, *Intimate Matters*, 121, 124.

15. Karen Hansen, "'Our Eyes Behold Each Other': Masculinity and Intimate Friendship in Antebellum New England," in Nardi, *Men's Friendships*, 48.

16. Ibid., 52, 52–53, 54. Hansen has also argued that such intimate relationships existed between working-class women. See Hansen, *Very Social Time*, 55–56.

17. Anya Jabour, "Female Families: Same-Sex Love in the Victorian South," in Friend and Jabour, *Family Values in the Old South*, 91. For more on intimate female friendships in the antebellum South, see Farnham, *Education of the Southern Belle*, 155–67; Cashin, *Our Common Affairs*; Anya Jabour, "'College Girls': The Female Academy and Female Identity in the Old South," in Clayton and Salmond, *"Lives Full of Struggle and Triumph,"* 74–92; Jabour, *Scarlett's Sisters*.

18. Jabour, "Male Friendship and Masculinity," 83–111.

19. Melinda S. Buza, "'Pledges of Our Love': Friendship, Love, and Marriage among the Virginian Gentry, 1800–1825," in Ayers and Willis, *Edge of the South*, 29.

20. See, for example, Jeffrey, "Our Remarkable Friendship," 28–58.

21. Martin Duberman, "Writhing Bedfellows in Antebellum South Carolina: Historical Interpretation and the Politics of Evidence," in Duberman et al., *Hidden from History*, 155.

22. Ibid., 160–61.

23. See for example, Blassingame, *Slave Community;* Genovese, *Roll, Jordan, Roll;* Wood, *Black Majority;* Levine, *Black Culture and Black Consciousness;* Raboteau, *Slave Religion;* Joyner, *Down by the Riverside;* Stuckey, *Slave Culture;* Creel, *"A Peculiar People";* Gomez, *Exchanging Our Country Marks;* Morgan, *Slave Counterpoint;* Thornton, *Africa and Africans;* Heywood, *Central Africans and Cultural Transformations;* Hall, *Slavery and African Ethnicities;* Young, *Rituals of Resistance;* Desch-Obi, *Fighting for Honor.*

24. Herskovits, *Myth of the Negro Past,* 298.

25. Jason R. Young's recent research used twentieth-century anthropological research to inform his discussion of African religion in the Kongo and the Lowcountry South. Young, *Rituals of Resistance,* esp. 23.

26. Herskovits, *Dahomey,* iv.

27. Melville Herskovits, "The Best Friend in Dahomey," in Cunard, *Negro Anthology,* 627.

28. Ibid., 629.

29. Ibid., 628.

30. Ibid., 629–30.

31. Robert Brain, "Friends and Twins in Bangwa," in Douglas and Kaberry, *Man in Africa,* 215–16.

32. Brain, *Friends and Lovers,* 35.

33. Brain, "Friends and Twins in Bangwa," 221.

34. Ibid., 223.

35. Brain, *Friends and Lovers,* 63–64.

36. Although Evans-Pritchard's study focused on the Zande of Central Africa, blood brotherhood has been extremely common throughout the whole of the African continent, especially in West Africa. Harry Tegnaeus's study of blood brotherhood mentioned many West African tribes that practiced blood brotherhood. The following list is by no means exhaustive, but it gives an indication of how widespread the practice was in West Africa. Tegnaeus notes the existence of blood brotherhood in Cameroon (Bassa, Koko, Bangwa, Dualla, Ndjunge, and Basakomo), the northern tribes of Nigeria (including the Basa, Baushi, Igara, Kamuku, Kakanda, Igbira, Apa, Gwari, Kpoto, Ngwoi, Zumper, and Tiv), and the societies of the Upper Cross River region (the Nde and neighboring tribes). Among the Ekoi and Ibibio and all over the Niger Delta differ-

ent tribes were bound together; for example, the Uwet were allied by blood to the Efik. The people of the Kwa River in the vicinity of Old Calabar practiced blood brotherhood, so did the Yoruba people of Dahomey (present-day Benin), various tribes situated in Ghana (Anlo-Ewe, Tallensi), and the Mande, Khasonke, Malinke, and Soninke. Tegnaeus also claims that blood brotherhood was common among the *poro* secret societies of the Slave Coast (the coastal areas of present-day Togo, Benin, western Nigeria, and the Bight of Benin). Tegnaeus, *Blood-Brothers,* 119–45.

37. Edward E. Evans-Pritchard, "Zande Blood Brotherhood," in Pritchard, *Social Anthropology,* 259.

38. Ibid., 274–75.

39. Ibid., 279.

40. Levine, *Black Culture and Black Consciousness,* 93.

41. Jones, *Gullah Folktales.*

42. For the ease of the reader, I have reworded the quotations from the original Gullah dialect into standard English. The original reads: "Buh Alligatur, him keep eh wud. Ebber sence, Buh Mash-hen kin walk bout de mash an de ribber, an buil nes, an ketch fiddler an shrimp all round Buh Alligatur, an eh yent try fuh bodder um. Dat de way Buh Alligatur an Buh Mash-hen come fur lib togerruh luk same fambly." Ibid., 26.

43. Gutman, *Black Family,* 216.

44. My translation. For original dialect, see Jones, *Gullah Folktales,* 144.

45. My translation. For original dialect, see ibid., 74.

46. My translation. For original dialect, see ibid., 37.

47. The "Poor Man and the Snake" is conveniently reproduced and converted into standard English from the Gullah dialect in Abrahams, *African American Folktales,* 130–32. For original dialect, see Jones, *Gullah Folktales,* 46–50.

48. Griffin, "Courtship Contests," 794, 776.

49. President of the American Folklore Society from 1919 to 1920 and an associate editor of the *Journal of American Folklore* from 1918 until 1941, Elsie Parsons traveled extensively, collecting a wealth of folktales, riddles, and songs from informants across the West Indies and the American South. Her findings appeared in numerous issues of the *Journal of American Folklore* and were published as *Folk-Tales of Andros Island, Bahamas; Folk-Lore from the Cape Verde Islands; Folk-Lore of the Sea Islands, South Carolina;* and *Folk-Lore of the Antilles, French and English.* Many scholars have since praised her work; in a memorial issue dedicated to Parsons, Melville J. Herskovits commented that the bulk of her contributions were so important to folklore that "no significant work can be done in the future without using them as a base." Herskovits, "Some Next Steps," 1. For more on the life of Elsie Parsons, see Chambers, "Indefatigable Elsie Clews Parsons," 180–98.

50. Smiley, "Folk-Lore from Virginia," 372–73. See also Parsons, "Tales from Guilford County, North Carolina," 186, 199.

51. Bacon and Parsons, "Folk-Lore from Elizabeth City County, Virginia," 285.

52. Parsons, *Folk-Lore of the Sea Islands, South Carolina,* 75, cited in Garner, "Black Ethos in Folktales," 60.

53. Rawick, *American Slave,* vol. 3, pt. 4, p. 107.

54. White, *Ar'n't I a Woman?* 132.

55. Douglass, *My Bondage and My Freedom,* 138, 152, 307–8 (emphasis in original).

56. *Narrative of Lunsford Lane,* 6–7.

57. Bratton, "Fields's Observations," 78–80.

58. Rawick, Hillegas, and Lawrence, *American Slave,* supp. ser. 1, vol. 9, pt. 4, p. 1878. See also *Narrative of the Life and Labors of the Rev. G. W. Offley,* 11.

59. Parker, *His Promised Land,* 71.

60. Brown, *Slave Life in Georgia,* 15, 23, 24, 230–31, 29–30.

61. Ibid., 72. See chapter 4 for the account of John Glasgow, which is also appended to the end of Brown's narrative in the form of a declaration made before a Notary Public of the City of London, 228–40. Brown justifies the inclusion of the declaration "in order that any person disposed, to make inquiries respecting John Glasgow's English wife and family, may have legal evidence on which to proceed." Ibid., 228.

62. Douglass, *Life and Times of Frederick Douglass,* 151, 157, 154, 158.

63. Camp, *Closer to Freedom,* 3.

64. Ibid., 9, 3, 94.

65. Franklin and Schweninger, *Runaway Slaves,* 210. Freddie Parker found that 82.2 percent of runaways in North Carolina between 1775 and 1835 were male. J. Blaine Hudson calculated that before 1850, 80 percent of runaways in Kentucky were male; this figure decreased to 72.6 percent after 1850. Genovese claimed that 81 percent of runaways in the antebellum South were male. Parker, "Slave Runaways in North Carolina," 89; Hudson, *Fugitive Slaves and the Underground Railroad,* 36; Genovese, *Roll, Jordan, Roll,* 648; Wood, "Some Aspects of Female Resistance," 607–8, 620; White, *Ar'n't I a Woman?* 70–76; Camp, *Closer to Freedom,* 28–34, 37; Schwalm, *Hard Fight for We,* 32–33.

66. *Life of Isaac Mason as a Slave,* 37. See also *Life and Adventures of James Williams,* 84.

67. William Parker, "The Freedman's Story in Two Parts," in Taylor, *I Was Born a Slave,* 750.

68. Hughes, *Thirty Years a Slave,* 100.

69. Pennington, *Fugitive Blacksmith,* 14.

70. *Narrative of Events in the Life of William Green,* 14–15.

71. *Life and Narrative of William J. Anderson,* 18.

72. *Narrative of the Life of Frederick Douglass,* 19.

73. *Narrative of the Life and Adventures of Henry Bibb,* 136.

74. *Life and Sufferings of Leonard Black,* 22–23.

75. Williams, *Sunshine and Shadow of Slave Life,* 15–16.

76. Ibid., 16.

77. Steward, *Twenty-Two Years a Slave,* 32; Drew, *North-Side View of Slavery,* 211.

78. Douglass, *My Bondage and My Freedom,* 297 (emphasis in original).

79. Drew, *North-Side View of Slavery,* 211.

80. *Narrative of Events in the Life of William Green,* 15. The gender of only one of these friends, a man, is revealed in Green's narrative.

81. Drew, *North-Side View of Slavery,* 53.

82. Parker, "Freedman's Story in Two Parts," 752. Although the gender of this friend is not specified, the friend was most likely male. As Jeff Forret's research has demonstrated, enslaved men conducted virtually all the trade in the underground economy. See Forret, "Slaves, Poor Whites," 795.

83. Campbell, *Autobiography,* 172.

84. William Summerson narrative, in Blassingame, *Slave Testimony,* 700.

85. Ibid., 699–702.

86. *Narrative of the Life of Frederick Douglass,* 106.

87. *Narrative of the Life and Adventures of Henry Bibb,* 47.

88. Hughes, *Thirty Years a Slave,* 103.

89. Franklin and Schweninger, *Runaway Slaves,* 229. Hudson's study of Kentucky concluded that before 1850, 21.6 percent of slaves escaped with company. After 1850, Hudson found that the phenomenon of group runaways had increased to 45.4 percent. Hudson, *Fugitive Slaves,* 33.

90. Johnson, "Runaway Slaves," 418.

91. Williams, *Sunshine and Shadow of Slave Life,* 10–12.

92. Ibid., 12.

93. Ibid., 16–17.

94. Jones, *Gullah Folktales,* 74.

95. "The Life of John Thompson, A Fugitive Slave," in Taylor, *I Was Born a Slave,* 450–51.

96. *Autobiography of James L. Smith,* 38, 42, 43–47.

97. *Narrative of Events in the Life of William Green,* 16.

98. *Life of Isaac Mason as a Slave,* 37–38.

99. Still, *Underground Railroad,* 196.

100. Drew, *North-Side View of Slavery,* 47.

101. Ibid., 53.

102. *Narrative of Henry Box Brown,* 34.

103. *Weekly Raleigh Register,* November 11, 1857, also reproduced in *Daily Cleveland Herald,* October 27, 1857; *North American and United States Gazette* (Philadelphia), October 28, 1857.

104. *Liberator,* September 10, 1858, also reproduced in the *Ripley (OH) Bee,* September 4, 1858.

105. *Reminiscences of Levi Coffin,* 209–10, 213.

106. *Narrative of Henry Box Brown,* 34 (emphasis in original).

5. Enslaved Men, the Grapevine Telegraph, and the Underground Railroad

1. See for example, George M. Fredrickson and Christopher Lasch, "Resistance to Slavery," in Bracey, Meier, and Rudwick, *American Slavery*, 182.

2. Costa, *Crowns of Glory, Tears of Blood*, 81.

3. Johnson, "On Agency," 118.

4. *Life and Sufferings of Leonard Black*, 50–51.

5. *Narrative of the Life of James Watkins*, 16; Petition of Richard Coke et al. to the Legislature of the State of Texas, ca. 1859, microfilm reel 15, fr. 474, RSFB, ser. 1.

6. See Camp, *Closer to Freedom*, 99–109.

7. Petition of Richard Coke et al. to the Legislature of the State of Texas, ca. 1859, microfilm reel 15, fr. 474, RSFB, ser. 1.

8. Petition of John B. Walker et al. to the Virginia Legislature, ca. December 1818, microfilm reel 18, fr. 162, microfilm reel 19, fr. 425, and microfilm reel 21, fr. 523, RSFB, ser. 1.

9. Petition of Citizens of Rutherford County to the Tennessee General Assembly, ca. 1825, in Schweninger, *Southern Debate over Slavery*, 1:93. See also petition of J. W. Jackson et al. to the Delaware Legislature, ca. February 1849, microfilm reel 2, fr. 665, RSFB, ser. 1.

10. Petition of Benjamin Olive et al. to the North Carolina Legislature, ca. December 1850, microfilm reel 7, fr. 327, RSFB, ser. 1. See also petition of Peter Tubble et al. to the Tennessee General Assembly, January 6, 1860, microfilm reel 14, fr. 599, RSFB, ser. 1.

11. Petition of Micah Jenkins et al. to the South Carolina Legislature, October 16, 1820, in Schweninger, *Southern Debate over Slavery*, 1:62–63.

12. Petition of the South Carolina Association to the Senate, ca. 1823, in Schweninger, *Southern Debate over Slavery*, 1:78–83 (emphasis in original).

13. Petition of Joseph Johnson to the South Carolina Legislature, ca. 1828, microfilm reel 10, fr. 475, RSFB, ser. 1.

14. Petition of A. E. Scudday et al. to the South Carolina Legislature, ca. 1835, microfilm reel 11, fr. 119, RSFB, ser. 1. See also petition of M. H. DeLeon to the South Carolina Legislature, ca. 1834, microfilm reel 11, fr. 124, RSFB, ser. 1.

15. Petition of William Galtin et al. to the North Carolina General Assembly, December 19, 1831, microfilm reel 6, fr. 338, RSFB, ser. 1. Also reproduced in Schweninger, *Southern Debate over Slavery*, 1:134–35. See also petition of John Utsey et al. to the South Carolina Legislature, ca. 1820, microfilm reel 9, fr. 604, RSFB, ser. 1.

16. Petition of Isaac Croom et al. to the North Carolina General Assembly, ca. November 1831, microfilm reel 6, fr. 323, RSFB, ser. 1; Petition of Elly Godbold to the South Carolina Legislature, ca. 1858, microfilm reel 11, fr. 653, RSFB, ser. 1.

17. Rawick, Hillegas, and Lawrence, *American Slave*, supp. ser. 1, vol. 3, pt. 1, p. 84; Rawick, *American Slave*, vol. 8, pt. 2, p. 17.

18. Rawick, *American Slave*, supp. ser. 2, vol. 8, pt. 2, p. 3336.

19. Rawick, Hillegas, and Lawrence, *American Slave*, supp. ser. 1, vol. 6, pt. 1, p. 323.

20. Rawick, *American Slave*, vol. 8, pt. 1, p. 349.

21. Camp, *Closer to Freedom*, 28–30; O'Donovan, *Becoming Free in the Cotton South*, 38–39.

22. Richard Eppes Diary, June 9, July 16, 1859, June 22, August 5, 30, 1860, M, pt. 3, reel 13, RASP.

23. Rawick, *American Slave*, vol. 13, pt. 3, pp. 95–96.

24. Rawick, *American Slave*, vol. 12, pt. 2, p. 214.

25. Rawick, *American Slave*, vol. 11, pt. 7, p. 67.

26. Pringle, *Chronicles of Chicora Wood*, 27–30.

27. *Narrative of the Life of Moses Grandy*, 7–39; Cecelski, *Waterman's Song*, 27, 34.

28. Ball, *Slavery in the United States*, 28–29.

29. *Narrative of Henry Watson*, 34.

30. Williams, *Sunshine and Shadow of Slave Life*, 8–9.

31. *Narrative of the Life of James Watkins*, 12.

32. William Pettigrew to John Williams, November 4, 1852, Pettigrew Family Papers, J, pt. 2, reel 10, RASP.

33. Barrow, *Plantation Life*, 408.

34. Robert Rives to Floyd L. Whitehead, May 5, 1838, Floyd L. Whitehead Papers, E, pt. 6, reel 40, RASP.

35. *Narrative of the Life of James Watkins*, 16.

36. Richard Eppes Diary, December 28, 1860, M, pt. 3, reel 13, RASP.

37. Marrinda Jane Singleton in Perdue, Barden, and Phillips, *Weevils in the Wheat*, 267.

38. Williams, *Sunshine and Shadow of Slave Life*, 50.

39. Ball, *Slavery in the United States*, 162–63.

40. Rawick, *American Slave*, vol. 8, pt. 2, p. 17; Johnson, *Twenty-Eight Years a Slave*, 18–19; *Autobiography of James L. Smith*, 30; *Narrative of Henry Box Brown*, 38; *Narrative of the Life of Moses Grandy*, 56.

41. Kenneth Greenberg, "The Confessions of Nat Turner: Text and Context," in Greenberg, *Confessions of Nat Turner*, 22–23; Oates, *Fires of Jubilee*, 142.

42. Guha, *Elementary Aspects of Peasant Insurgency*, 251.

43. Rawick, Hillegas, and Lawrence, *American Slave*, supp. ser. 1, vol. 6, pt. 1, p. 11.

44. Rawick, Hillegas, and Lawrence, *American Slave*, supp. ser. 1, vol. 8, pt. 3, p. 1084.

45. Washington, *Up from Slavery* 8–9.

46. Enclosed in a letter from Coleman Smith to Col. Carter, October 31, 1857, Carter Papers, L, pt. 1, reel 7, RASP.

47. Bruce, *New Man*, 86; Robinson, *From Log Cabin to the Pulpit*, 92.

48. Rawick, *American Slave,* supp. ser. 2, vol. 3, pt. 2, p. 607; Rawick, *American Slave,* supp. ser. 2, vol. 10, pt. 9, p. 4128.

49. Rawick, Hillegas, and Lawrence, *American Slave,* supp. ser. 1, vol. 7, pt. 2, p. 581; Rawick, *American Slave,* vol. 13, pt. 4, p. 79.

50. Rawick, Hillegas, and Lawrence, *American Slave,* supp. ser. 1, vol. 7, pt. 2, p. 694.

51. Rawick, *American Slave,* vol. 7 (OK), 146; Rawick, *American Slave,* vol. 4, pt. 1, p. 52.

52. Rawick, Hillegas, and Lawrence, *American Slave,* supp. ser. 1, vol. 10, pt. 5, p. 1938; Rawick, *American Slave,* vol. 4, pt. 1, p. 52; Rawick, Hillegas, and Lawrence, *American Slave,* supp. ser. 1, vol. 9, pt. 4, p. 1667.

53. Rawick, Hillegas, and Lawrence, *American Slave,* supp. ser. 1, vol. 6, pt. 1, p. 323; Rawick, *American Slave,* vol. 14, pt. 1, p. 331; Rawick, *American Slave,* vol. 4, pt. 1, p. 52; Rawick, Hillegas, and Lawrence, *American Slave,* supp. ser. 1, vol. 9, pt. 4, pp. 1667–69; Washington, *Up from Slavery,* 19.

54. Bruce, *New Man,* 86.

55. Narrative of James Curry, in Blassingame, *Slave Testimony,* 136.

56. Scott, *Domination and the Arts of Resistance,* 137 (emphasis in original).

57. Hahn, *Nation under Our Feet,* 59.

58. *History of William Webb,* 13.

59. Ibid., 18–30.

60. Ibid., 29–30.

61. Ibid., 26.

62. Sidbury, *Ploughshares into Swords,* 221.

63. Ibid.; Egerton, *Gabriel's Rebellion;* Pearson, *Designs against Charleston;* Egerton, *He Shall Go Out Free;* Mary Kemp Davis, "'What Happened in This Place?': In Search of the Female Slave in the Nat Turner Slave Insurrection," in Greenberg, *Nat Turner,* 162–76; Greenberg, "Confessions of Nat Turner," 12–13. See also Winthrop Jordan's discussion of gender and slave revolts: Jordan, *Tumult and Silence,* 172–75.

64. Sidbury, *Ploughshares into Swords,* 87, 90–91 (emphasis in original).

65. Egerton, *Gabriel's Rebellion,* 53, 55.

66. Sidbury, *Ploughshares into Swords,* 91–92.

67. Edward A. Pearson, "Introduction: Culture and Conspiracy in Denmark Vesey's Charleston," in Pearson, *Designs against Charleston,* 129, 65, 113–14, 63. Across Upper Guinea, the *poro* was a fraternal council that boys joined upon reaching puberty. It governed local affairs, made laws, tried criminals, and settled village disputes. For more on the *poro* and slave culture in the Lowcountry, see Creel, *"Peculiar People."*

68. Egerton, *He Shall Go Out Free,* 134–35.

69. *Narrative and Writings of Andrew Jackson,* 15.

70. Siebert, *Underground Railroad.*

71. Gara, *Liberty Line,* 42.

72. Griffler, *Front Line of Freedom;* Hagedorn, *Beyond the River;* Horton and Horton, *In Hope of Liberty;* Quarles, *Black Abolitionists.*

73. See Gara, *Liberty Line,* 54–55.

74. See Franklin and Schweninger, *Runaway Slaves,* 68–71, 130–31, 292–93.

75. Williams, *Sunshine and Shadow of Slave Life,* 15.

76. *Life and Narrative of William J. Anderson,* 20.

77. *Narrative and Writings of Andrew Jackson,* 15.

78. *Life of William Grimes,* 51.

79. "Life of John Thompson," 452–53.

80. Williams, *Sunshine and Shadow of Slave Life,* 29, 34, 31–32.

81. Ibid., 25–26. See also *Narrative of Some Remarkable Incidents in the Life of Solomon Bayley,* 4.

82. *Liberator,* November 17, December 1, 1843.

83. Jackson, *Experience of a Slave in South Carolina,* 26.

84. *Narrative of William W. Brown,* 95–96; "Life of John Thompson," 451.

85. *Life of William Grimes,* 11.

86. *Narrative of the Life and Adventures of Henry Bibb,* 136–38.

87. Kaye, "Neighbourhoods and Solidarity," 12, 13. See also Kaye, *Joining Places.*

88. See the following newspapers for example: *New England Weekly Review,* August 27, 1842; *Liberator,* January 31, 1845, September 13, 1850. See also the following court cases from upcountry South Carolina: Anderson District, Court of Magistrates and Freeholders, Trial Papers, microfilm reel C2916, case 101; microfilm reel C2917, cases 128, 136, 139, 151, 161; microfilm reel C2918, cases 208, 250, 257, 271, 276; microfilm reel C2919, cases 329, 373; microfilm reel C2775, case 405, SCDAH; Fairfield District, Court of Magistrates and Freeholders, Trial Papers, 1839–1865, fols. 9, 17, 53, box 1, SCDAH; Laurens District, Court of Magistrates and Freeholders, Trial Papers, 1808–1865, fols. 14, 57, 58, box 1, SCDAH; Pickens District, Court of Magistrates and Freeholders, Trial Papers, 1829–1862, fols. 23, 25, SCDAH; Kershaw District, Court of Magistrates and Freeholders, Trial Papers, 1800–1861, fols. 11, 64, 65, 66, box 1, fols. 92, 100, box 2, SCDAH.

89. Narrative of James Curry, in Blassingame, *Slave Testimony,* 142.

90. Roper, *Narrative of the Adventures and Escape,* 65.

91. "Life of John Thompson," 455.

92. *Narratives of the Suffering of Lewis and Milton Clarke,* 31.

93. *Life and Times of Frederick Douglass,* 159.

94. Pennington, *Fugitive Blacksmith,* 13, 15 (emphasis in original).

95. Brown, *Slave Life in Georgia,* 98, 103.

96. Pennington, *Narrative of Events of the Life of J. H. Banks,* 74.

97. Johnson, *Sword of Honor,* 27–28, 31.

98. Ibid., 25–42. See also Marshall, "Enslaved Women Runaways," 67–68.

99. Rawick, *American Slave,* vol. 17, pp. 146–54.

100. *Reminiscences of Levi Coffin,* 166–67.

101. Parker, *His Promised Land.* See for example, 73, 91–96, 100–104, 105–17, 121.

102. Ibid., 71.

103. Ibid., 100, 100–104.

104. Oakes, "Political Significance of Slave Resistance," 93–95.

105. Ibid., 98. McCurry, *Confederate Reckoning,* 218–62; Ira Berlin, "Who Freed the Slaves? Emancipation and Its Meaning," in Perman, *Major Problems,* 288–97; Williams, *I Freed Myself.*

Epilogue

1. *Life and Times of Frederick Douglass,* 168–73.

2. Sidbury, *Ploughshares into Swords,* 252.

3. Costa, *Crowns of Glory, Tears of Blood,* 81.

4. *Narrative of the Life of Frederick Douglass,* 106–8.

Bibliography

Primary Sources

Manuscripts and Microfilm Collections

Dew, Charles B., ed. Slavery in Ante-Bellum Southern Industries. *Bethesda, MD: University Publication of America, 1991. Microfilm.*

Series A: Selections from the Duke University Library, Durham, NC
Dismal Swamp Land Company Records, 1688, 1763–1871, 1879, A, reels 14–22.
Jones, Jeremiah T. Papers, 1841–1878, A, reel 4.
Redding, James Grist. Business Records, 1791–1920, A, reels 5–13.
Tillingshast Family Papers (Slave Task Book), 1849–1851, A, reel 4.

Series B: Selections from the Southern Historical Collection, University of North Carolina, Chapel Hill
Furnace, Louisa. Account Books, 1831–1860, B, reels 21–22.
Hawkins Family Papers, 1738–1865, B, reels 8–21.

Series D: Selections from the University of Virginia Library, Charlottesville
Weaver-Brady Papers, 1824–1891, D, pt. 1, reels 24–37.

Schweninger, Loren, ed. Race, Slavery, and Free Blacks. Ser. 1, Petitions to Southern Legislatures, 1777–1867. *Bethesda, MD: University Publications of America, 1999. Microfilm.*

Schweninger, Loren, ed. Race, Slavery, and Free Blacks. Ser. 2, Petitions to Southern County Courts, 1775–1867. *Bethesda, MD: University Publications of America, 2005. Microfilm.*

Stampp, Kenneth, ed. Records of Ante-bellum Southern Plantations from the Revolution through the Civil War, Ser. A–N. *Bethesda, MD: University Publications of America, 1985–2001. Microfilm.*

Series E: Selections from the University of Virginia Library
Cocke Family Papers, 1725–1939, E, pt. 4, reels 1–71.
Whitehead, Floyd L. Papers, 1837–1845, E, pt. 6, reel 40.

Series F: Selections from the Manuscript Department, Duke University Library
Cornhill Plantation Book of John Blount Miller and John F. Furman, 1827–1873,
McDonald Furman Papers, F, pt. 2, reel 9.
"Rockingham" Plantation Journal, 1828–1829, F, pt. 2, reel 8.

Series I: Selections from Louisiana State University
King, Roswell Jr., Diary, 1838–1845, I, pt. 2, reel 20.

A. Ledoux & Co. Plantation Journal, 1856–1857, I, pt. 1, reel 9.

Series J: Selections from the Southern Historical Collection, Manuscripts Department, Library of the University of North Carolina at Chapel Hill

Barrow, Robert Ruffin. Plantation Journal, 1857–1858, Robert Ruffin Barrow Papers, J, pt. 5, reel 2.

Bayside Plantation Records, 1846–1866, J, pt. 5, reel 6.

Ervin, William Ethelbert. Diaries, 1839–1856, J, pt. 6, reel 17.

Fripp, John Edwin. Diary, John Edwin Fripp Papers, 1817–1905, J, pt. 3, reel 25.

Gavin, David. Diary, 1855–1874, J, pt. 3, reels 10–11.

Greenlee, James Hervey. Diary, 1837–1902, J, pt. 14, reels 1–4.

Hudson, Franklin A. Diaries, 1852–1859, J, pt. 5, reels 12–13.

Nevitt, John. Diary, 1826–1854, J, pt. 6, reel 3.

Pettigrew Family Papers, J, pt. 2, reels 1–29.

Steel, Frank F. Letters, 1859–1861, J, pt. 6, reel 29.

Walker, John. Plantation Journal, John Walker Papers, 1824–1844, J, pt. 9, reels 32–33.

Series L: Selections from the Earl Gregg Swem Library, College of William and Mary

Austin-Twyman Papers, 1765–1865, L, pt. 4, reels 1–35.

Carter Papers, 1667–1862, L, pt. 1, reels 1–18.

Series M: Selections from the Virginia Historical Society

Eppes, Richard. Diary, M, pt. 3, reels 12–16.

Friend, Charles. Diary, Friend Family Papers, M, pt. 3, reel 18.

Henry Family Papers, 1763–1920, M, pt. 5, reel 34.

Series N: Selections from the Mississippi Department of Archives and History

Elley Plantation Book, 1855–1856, N, reel 10.

North Carolina Department of Archives and History, Raleigh

Blount, John Gray. Papers.

Chowan County Slave Records Criminal Actions Concerning Slaves.

Gates County Criminal Actions Concerning Slaves.

Registration of Slaves to Work in the Great Dismal Swamp, 1847–1861.

South Carolina Department of Archives and History, Columbia

Anderson District, Court of Magistrates and Freeholders, Trial Papers, 1819–1865.

Fairfield District, Court of Magistrates and Freeholders, Trial Papers, 1839–1865.

Kershaw District, Court of Magistrates and Freeholders, Trial Papers, 1800–1865.

Laurens District, Court of Magistrates and Freeholders, Trial Papers, 1808–1865.

Pickens District, Court of Magistrates and Freeholders, Trial Papers, 1829–1862.

Spartanburg District, Court of Magistrates and Freeholders, Trial Papers, 1824–1865.

Southern Historical Collection, University of North Carolina, Chapel Hill

Pilsbury, Rebecca S. C. Diary, 1848–1851.

Plantation Journal, Hugenin and Johnston Family Papers.

Newspapers

Daily National Intelligencer (Washington, DC).
Fayetteville Observer (Fayetteville, NC).
Liberator (Boston, MA).
New England Weekly Review (Hartford, CT).
Raleigh Register, and North-Carolina Gazette (Raleigh, NC).

Published Primary Sources

Abrahams, Roger D., ed. *African American Folktales: Stories from Black Traditions in the New World.* New York: Pantheon, 1985.

Adams, Edward C. L. *Congaree Sketches, Scenes from Negro Life in the Swamps of the Congaree and Tales by Tad and Scip of Heaven and Hell with Other Miscellany.* Chapel Hill: University of North Carolina Press, 1927.

Aime, Valcour. *Plantation Diary of the Late Valcour Aime, Formerly Proprietor of the Plantation Known as The St. James Sugar Refinery, Situated in the Parish of St. James and Now Owned by Mr. John Burnside.* New Orleans: Clark & Hofeline Printers and Publishers, 1878.

Allston, Robert F. W. *The South Carolina Rice Plantation as Revealed in the Papers of Robert F. W. Allston.* Edited by J. H. Easterby. Chicago: University of Chicago Press, 1945.

Anderson, William J. *Life and Narrative of William J. Anderson, Twenty-four Years a Slave; Sold Eight Times! In Jail Sixty Times!! Whipped Three Hundred Times!!! or The Dark Deeds of American Slavery Revealed. Containing Scriptural Views of the Origin of the Black and of the White Man. Also, a Simple and Easy Plan to Abolish Slavery in the United States. Together with an Account of the Services of Colored Men in the Revolutionary War—Day and Date, and Interesting Facts.* Chicago: Daily Tribune Book and Job Printing Office, 1857.

Armstrong, Orlando Kay. *Old Massa's People: The Old Slaves Tell Their Story.* Indianapolis: Bobbs-Merrill, 1931.

Bacon, A. M., and Elsie C. Parsons. "Folk-Lore from Elizabeth City County, Virginia." *Journal of American Folklore* 35, no. 137 (July–September 1922): 250–327.

Ball, Charles. *Fifty Years in Chains; or, The Life of an American Slave.* New York: H. Dayton, 1859.

———. *Slavery in the United States: A Narrative of the Life and Adventures of Charles Ball, a Black Man, Who Lived Forty Years in Maryland, South Carolina and Georgia, as a Slave Under Various Masters, and was One Year in the Navy with Commodore Barney, during the Late War.* New York: John S. Taylor, 1837.

Barrow, Bennet H. *Plantation Life in the Florida Parishes of Louisiana, 1836–1846.* Edited by Edwin Adam Davis. New York: AMS Press, 1967.

Bayley, Solomon. *A Narrative of Some Remarkable Incidents in the Life of Solomon Bayley, Formerly a Slave in the State of Delaware, North America.* London: Harvey & Darton, 1825.

Berlin, Ira, Marc Favreau, and Steven F. Miller, eds. *Remembering Slavery: African Americans Talk about Their Personal Experiences of Slavery and Emancipation.* New York: New Press, 1996.

Bibb, Henry. *Narrative of the Life and Adventures of Henry Bibb, an American Slave, Written by Himself.* New York: Author, 1849.

Black, Leonard. *The Life and Sufferings of Leonard Black, a Fugitive from Slavery.* New Bedford, MA: Benjamin Lindsey, 1847.

Blassingame, John W. ed. *Slave Testimony: Two Centuries of Letters, Speeches, Interviews and Autobiographies.* Baton Rouge: Louisiana State University Press, 1977.

Blight, David W., ed. *A Slave No More: Two Men Who Escaped to Freedom: Including Their Own Narratives of Emancipation* New York: Harcourt, 2007.

Bratton, Mary Jo Jackson, ed. "Fields's Observations: The Slave Narrative of a Nineteenth-Century Virginian." *Virginia Magazine of History and Biography* 88, no. 1 (1980): 78–80.

Breeden, James O., ed. *Advice among Masters: The Ideal in Slave Management in the Old South.* Westport, CT: Greenwood, 1980.

Brown, Henry Box. *Narrative of Henry Box Brown, Who Escaped from Slavery, Enclosed in a Box Three Feet Long and Two Wide. Written from a Statement of Facts Made by Himself. With Remarks upon the Remedy for Slavery.* Boston: Brown & Stearns, 1849.

Brown, John. *Slave Life in Georgia: A Narrative of the Life, Sufferings, and Escape of John Brown, a Fugitive Slave, Now in England.* London: W. M. Watts, 1855.

Brown, William Wells. *Narrative of William W. Brown, a Fugitive Slave.* Boston: The Anti-Slavery Office, 1847.

Bruce, Henry Clay. *The New Man: Twenty-Nine Years a Slave, Twenty-Nine Years a Free Man.* York, PA: P. Anstadt & Sons, 1895.

Campbell, Israel. *An Autobiography. Bond and Free; or, Yearnings for Freedom, from My Green Brier House. Being the Story of My Life in Bondage, and My Life in Freedom.* Philadelphia: Author, 1861.

Clarke, Lewis Garrard, and Milton Clarke. *Narratives of the Sufferings of Lewis and Milton Clarke, Sons of a Soldier of the Revolution, During a Captivity of More than Twenty Years Among the Slaveholders of Kentucky, One of the So-Called Christian States of North America.* Boston: Bela Marsh, 1846.

Clifton, James, ed. *Life and Labor on Argyle Island: Letters and Documents of a Savannah River Plantation, 1833–1867.* Savannah: Beehive Press, 1978.

Coffin, Levi. *Reminiscences of Levi Coffin, The Reputed President of the Underground Railroad; Being a Brief History of the Labors of a Lifetime in Behalf of the Slave, with the Stories of Numerous Fugitives, Who Gained Their Freedom through His Instrumentality, and Many Other Incidents Reminiscences of Levi Coffin.* Cincinnati: Robert Clark & Co., 1880.

Crayon, Porte. "The Dismal Swamp." *Harper's Monthly Magazine* 13, no. 76 (September 1856): 441–55.

Devereux, Margaret. *Plantation Sketches.* Cambridge, MA: Riverside, 1906.

Douglass, Frederick. *Life and Times of Frederick Douglass: His Early Life as a Slave, His Escape from Bondage, and His Complete History to the Present Time.* Hartford, CT: Park Publishing Co., 1881.

———. *My Bondage and My Freedom.* Part 1, *Life as a Slave.* Part 2, *Life as a Freeman.* New York: Miller, Orton & Mulligan, 1855.

———. *Narrative of the Life of Frederick Douglass, an American Slave.* Boston: Anti-Slavery Office, 1845.

Drew, Benjamin, ed. *A North-Side View of Slavery. The Refugee; or, The Narratives of Fugitive Slaves in Canada. Related by Themselves, with an Account of the History and Condition of the Colored Population of Upper Canada.* Boston: J. P. Jewett & Company, 1856.

Grandy, Moses. *Narrative of the Life of Moses Grandy, Late a Slave in the United States of America.* London: Gilpin, 1843.

Grant, Hugh Fraser. *Planter Management and Capitalism in Ante-bellum Georgia: The Journal of Hugh Fraser Grant.* Edited by Albert V. House. New York: Columbia University Press, 1954.

Green, William. *Narrative of Events in the Life of William Green, (Formerly a Slave.) Written by Himself.* Springfield, MA: L. M. Guernsey, 1853.

Grimes, William. *Life of William Grimes, the Runaway Slave.* New York: Author, 1825.

Harris, Joel Chandler. *The Complete Tales of Uncle Remus.* Boston: Houghton Mifflin, 1955.

———. *Daddy Jake the Runaway and Short Stories Told after Dark by Uncle Remus.* New York: Century, 1889.

———. *Nights with Uncle Remus: Myths and Legends of the Old Plantation.* Boston: Houghton Mifflin, 1883.

———. *Uncle Remus: His Songs and Sayings: The Folklore of the Old Plantation.* New York: D. Appleton, 1880.

———. *Uncle Remus and His Friends: Old Plantation Stories, Songs and Ballads with Sketches of Negro Character.* Boston: Houghton Mifflin, 1892.

Hayden, William. *Narrative of William Hayden, Containing a Faithful Account of His Travels for a Number of Years, Whilst a Slave, in the South.* Cincinnati: Author, 1846.

Henson, Josiah. *The Life of Josiah Henson, Formerly a Slave, Now an Inhabitant of Canada, as Narrated by Himself.* Boston: A. D. Phelps, 1849.

Heyward, Duncan Clinch. *Seed from Madagascar.* Chapel Hill: University of North Carolina Press, 1937.

Huger, Alice Ravenel, ed. *A Carolina Rice Plantation of the Fifties.* New York: William Morrow & Co., 1936.

Hughes, Louis. *Thirty Years a Slave: From Bondage to Freedom: The Institution of Slavery as Seen on the Plantation and in the Home of the Planter.* Milwaukee: South Side Printing Company, 1897.

Hurston, Zora Neale. *Mules and Men*. New York: Harper Perennial, 1990.

Jackson, Andrew. *Narrative and Writings of Andrew Jackson, of Kentucky; Containing an Account of His Birth, and Twenty-Six Years of His Life While a Slave; His Escape; Five Years of Freedom, Together with Anecdotes Relating to Slavery; Journal of One Year's Travels; Sketches, etc. Narrated by Himself; Written by a Friend*. Syracuse: Daily and Weekly Star Office, 1847.

Jackson, John Andrew. *The Experience of a Slave in South Carolina*. London: Passmore & Alabaster, 1862.

Jacobs, Harriet A. *Incidents in the Life of a Slave Girl. Written by Herself*. Boston: Author, 1861.

Johnson, Hannibal A. *The Sword of Honor: A Story of the Civil War*. Hallowell, ME: Register Printing House, 1906.

Johnson, Thomas L. *Twenty-Eight Years a Slave, or The Story of My Life in Three Continents*. Bournemouth, UK: W. Mate & Sons, 1909.

Jones, Charles Colcock. *The Religious Instruction of the Negroes in the United States*. Savannah: Thomas Purse, 1842.

Jones, Charles Colcock, Jr. *Gullah Folktales from the Georgia Coast*. Athens: University of Georgia Press, 2000.

Kemble, Anne. *Journal of a Residence on a Georgian Plantation in 1838–1839*. Athens: University of Georgia Press, 1984.

Lane, Lunsford. *The Narrative of Lunsford Lane, Formerly of Raleigh, N.C. Embracing an Account of His Early Life, the Redemption by Purchase of Himself and Family from Slavery, and His Banishment from the Place of His Birth for the Crime of Wearing a Colored Skin. Published by Himself*. Boston: J. G. Torrey, Printer, 1842.

Laws of the State of North Carolina, Passed by the General Assembly at the Session of 1846–47. Raleigh: Thomas J. Lemay, 1847.

Long, John Dixon. *Pictures of Slavery in Church and State; Including Personal Reminiscences, Biographical Sketches, Anecdotes, etc. etc. with an Appendix, Containing the Views of John Wesley and Richard Watson on Slavery*. Philadelphia: Author, 1857.

Mason, Isaac. *Life of Isaac Mason as a Slave*. Worcester, MA: Author, 1893.

Northup, Solomon. *Twelve Years a Slave: Narrative of Solomon Northup, a Citizen of New-York, Kidnapped in Washington City in 1841, and Rescued in 1853*. Auburn, NY: Derby & Miller, 1853.

Offley, Greensbury W. *A Narrative of the Life and Labors of the Rev. G. W. Offley, a Colored Man, Local Preacher and Missionary*. Hartford, CT: Author, 1859.

Olmsted, Frederick Law. *Cotton Kingdom: A Traveller's Observations on Cotton and Slavery in the American Slave States*. New York: Mason Brothers, 1862.

———. *A Journey in the Backcountry*. New York: Mason Brothers, 1861.

———. *A Journey in the Seaboard Slave States: With Remarks on Their Economy*. London: Dix & Edwards, 1856.

Osofsky, Gilbert, ed. *Puttin' On Ole Massa: The Slave Narratives of Henry Bibb, William Wells Brown, and Solomon Northup.* New York: Harper & Row, 1969.

Parker, Allen. *Recollections of Slavery Times.* Worchester, MA: Chas. W. Burbank & Co., 1895.

Parker, John. *His Promised Land: The Autobiography of John P. Parker, Former Slave and Conductor on the Underground Railroad.* Edited by Stuart Seely Sprague. New York: Norton, 1996.

Parsons, Elsie Clews. *Folk-Lore from the Cape Verde Islands.* Cambridge, MA: American Folk-lore Society, 1923.

———. *Folk-Lore of the Antilles, French and English.* New York: American Folk-lore Society, 1933.

———. *Folk-Lore of the Sea Islands, South Carolina.* New York: American Folk-lore Society, 1923.

———. *Folk-Tales of Andros Island, Bahamas.* Lancaster, PA: American Folk-lore Society, 1918.

———. "Tales from Guilford County, North Carolina." *Journal of American Folk-lore* 30, no. 116 (April–June 1917): 168–200.

Pearson, Edward A., ed. *Designs against Charleston the Trial Record of the Denmark Vesey Slave Conspiracy of 1822.* Chapel Hill: University of North Carolina Press, 1999.

Pennington, James W. C. *The Fugitive Blacksmith; or, Events in the History of James W. C. Pennington, Pastor of a Presbyterian Church, New York, Formerly a Slave in the State of Maryland, United States.* London: Charles Gilpin, 1849.

———. *A Narrative of Events of the Life of J. H. Banks, an Escaped Slave, from the Cotton State, Alabama, in America.* Liverpool: M. Rourke, Printer, 1861.

Perdue, Charles L., Thomas E. Barden, and Robert K. Phillips, eds. *Weevils in the Wheat: Interviews with Virginia Ex-Slaves.* Charlottesville: University Press of Virginia, 1976.

Phillips, Ulrich, ed. *A Documentary History of American Industrial Society.* Vol. 1 of 10, *Plantation and Frontier Documents, 1649–1863: Illustrative of Industrial History in the Colonial & Ante-bellum South.* New York: Burt Franklin, 1969.

Pringle, Elizabeth W. Allston. *Chronicles of Chicora Wood.* New York: Charles Scribner, 1922.

———. *A Woman Rice Planter.* New York: Macmillan, 1914.

Rawick, George P., ed. *The American Slave: A Composite Autobiography,* 19 vols. Westport, CT: Greenwood, 1972.

———. *The American Slave.* Supplement ser. 2, 10 vols. Westport, CT: Greenwood, 1979.

Rawick, George P., Jan Hillegas, and Ken Lawrence, eds. *The American Slave.* Supplement ser. 1, 12 vols. Westport, CT: Greenwood, 1977.

Redpath, James, ed. *The Roving Editor; or, Talks with Slaves in the Southern States.* University Park: Pennsylvania State University Press, 1996.

Robinson, William H. *From Log Cabin to the Pulpit, or, Fifteen Years in Slavery.* Eau Clair, WI: James H. Tifft, 1913.

Roper, Moses. *A Narrative of the Adventures and Escape of Moses Roper, from American Slavery.* Philadelphia: Merrihew & Gunn, 1838.

Rose, Willie Lee, ed. *A Documentary History of Slavery in North America.* New York: Oxford University Press, 1976.

Ruffin, Edmund. "Observations Made during an Excursion to the Dismal Swamp." *Farmer's Register* 4, no. 9 (January 1837): 513–21.

Russell, William Howard. *My Diary North and South.* Boston: T. O. H. P. Burnham, 1863.

Schweninger, Loren, ed. *The Southern Debate over Slavery.* Vol. 1, *Petitions to Southern Legislatures, 1778–1864.* Urbana: University of Illinois Press, 2001.

———. *The Southern Debate over Slavery.* Vol. 2, *Petitions to Southern County Courts, 1775–1867.* Urbana: University of Illinois Press, 2007.

Smiley, Portia. "Folk-Lore from Virginia, South Carolina, Georgia, Alabama, and Florida." *Journal of American Folklore* 32, no. 125 (July–September 1919): 357–83.

Smith, Harry. *Fifty Years of Slavery in the United States of America.* Grand Rapids: West Michigan Printing, 1891.

Smith, James Lindsay. *Autobiography of James L. Smith, Including, Also, Reminiscences of Slave Life, Recollections of the War, Education of Freedmen, Causes of the Exodus, etc.* Norwich, CT: Bulletin, 1881.

Sterling, Dorothy, ed. *We Are Your Sisters: Black Women in the Nineteenth Century.* New York: Norton, 1984.

Steward, Austin. *Twenty-Two Years a Slave, and Forty Years a Freeman; Embracing a Correspondence of Several Years, While President of Wilberforce Colony, London, Canada West.* Rochester, NY: William Alling, 1857.

Taylor, Yuval, ed. *I Was Born a Slave: An Anthology of Classic Slave Narratives,* 2 vols. Edinburgh: Payback Press, 1999.

Thompson, John. *The Life of John Thompson, a Fugitive Slave; Containing His History of Twenty-five Years in Bondage, and His Providential Escape. Written by Himself.* Worcester: Author, 1856.

Thorpe, T. B. "Cotton and Its Cultivation." *Harper's New Monthly Magazine* 8, no. 46 (March 1854): 447–63.

———. "Sugar and the Sugar Region of Louisiana." *Harper's New Monthly Magazine* 7, no. 42 (November 1853): 746–68.

Tragle, Henry I., ed. *The Southampton Slave Revolt of 1831: A Compilation of Source Material.* Amherst: University of Massachusetts Press, 1971.

Turner, Nat. *The Confessions of Nat Turner and Related Documents.* Edited by Kenneth S. Greenberg. Boston: Bedford, 1996.

———. *The Confessions of Nat Turner, the Leader of the Late Insurrection in Southampton, Va.* Baltimore: T. R. Gray, 1831.

Twelvetrees, Harper, ed. *The Story of the Life of John Anderson, the Fugitive Slave.* London: W. Tweedie, 1863.

Walker, David. *Walker's Appeal, in Four Articles; Together with a Preamble, to the Coloured Citizens of the World, but in Particular, and Very Expressly, to Those of the United States of America, Written in Boston, State of Massachusetts, September 28, 1829.* Boston: David Walker, 1830.

Washington, Booker T. *Up from Slavery: An Autobiography.* Garden City, NY: Doubleday & Co., 1901.

Watkins, James. *Narrative of the Life of James Watkins, Formerly a "Chattel" in Maryland, U.S.* Bolton, UK: Kenyon and Abbatt, 1852.

Watson, Henry. *Narrative of Henry Watson, a Fugitive Slave.* Boston: Bela Marsh, 1848.

Webb, William. *The History of William Webb, Composed by Himself.* Detroit: Egbert Hoekstra, 1873.

Williams, Isaac D. *Sunshine and Shadow of Slave Life. Reminiscences as Told by Isaac D. Williams to "Tege."* East Saginaw, MI: Evening News Printing and Binding House, 1885.

Williams, James. *Life and Adventures of James Williams, a Fugitive Slave, with a Full Description of the Underground Railroad.* San Francisco: Women's Union Print, 1873.

Secondary Sources

Akyeampong, Emmanuel Kwaku. *Drink, Power, and Cultural Change: A Social History of Alcohol in Ghana, c. 1800 to Recent Times.* Portsmouth, NH: James Currey, 1996.

Andrews, William L., ed. *African American Autobiography: A Collection of Critical Essays, New Century Views.* Englewood Cliffs, NJ: Prentice Hall, 1993.

Ayers, Edward L. *Vengeance and Justice: Crime and Punishment in the Nineteenth Century American South.* New York: Oxford University Press, 1984.

Ayers, Edward L., and John C. Willis, eds. *The Edge of the South: Life in Nineteenth-Century Virginia.* Charlottesville: University Press of Virginia, 1991.

Baer, Florence E. *Sources and Analogues of the Uncle Remus Tales.* Folklore Fellows Communications, No. 228. Helsinki: Academia Scientiarum Fennica, 1980.

Baker, William J., and J. A. Mangan, eds. *Sport in Africa: Essays in Social History.* New York: Africana, 1987.

Baptist, Edward E., and Stephanie M. H. Camp, eds. *New Studies in the History of American Slavery.* Athens: University of Georgia Press, 2006.

Barnes, L. Diane. *Artisan Workers in the Upper South Petersburg, Virginia, 1820–1865.* Baton Rouge: Louisiana State University Press, 2008.

Bascom, William R. *African Folktales in the New World.* Bloomington: Indiana University Press, 1992.

———. "Four Functions of Folklore." *Journal of American Folklore* 67, no. 266 (October–December 1954): 333–49.

Benda-Beckmann, Keebet von, and Fernanda Pirie, eds. *Order and Disorder: Anthropological Perspectives.* New York: Berghahn, 2007.

Berlin, Ira, and Philip D. Morgan, eds. *Cultivation and Culture: Labor and the Shaping of Slave Life in the Americas.* Charlottesville: University Press of Virginia, 1993.

Berry, Daina Ramey. *"Swing the Sickle for the Harvest Is Ripe": Gender and Slavery in Antebellum Georgia.* Urbana: University of Illinois Press, 2007.

Black, Daniel P. *Dismantling Black Manhood: An Historical and Literary Analysis of the Legacy of Slavery.* New York: Garland, 1997.

Blassingame, John W. *The Slave Community: Plantation Life in the Antebellum South.* New York: Oxford University Press, 1979.

Blight, David W., ed. *Passages to Freedom: The Underground Railroad in History and Memory.* Washington, DC: Smithsonian Books, 2004.

Bracey, John H., August Meier, and Elliott M. Rudwick, eds. *American Slavery: The Question of Resistance.* Belmont, CA: Wadsworth, 1971.

Brain, Robert. *Friends and Lovers.* St. Albans, UK: Paladin, 1977.

Brown, David, and Clive Webb. *Race in the American South: From Slavery to Civil Rights.* Gainesville: University Press of Florida, 2007.

Buckley, Karen Lynne. *Danger, Death, and Disaster in the Crowsnest Pass Mines, 1902–1928.* Calgary: University of Calgary Press, 2004.

Burke, Diane Mutti. *On Slavery's Border: Missouri's Small-Slaveholding Households, 1815–1865.* Athens: University of Georgia Press, 2010.

Callahan, Richard J. *Work and Faith in the Kentucky Coal Fields: Subject to Dust.* Bloomington: Indiana University Press, 2009.

Camp, Stephanie M. H. *Closer to Freedom: Enslaved Women and Everyday Resistance in the Plantation South.* Chapel Hill: University of North Carolina Press, 2004.

———. "The Pleasures of Resistance: Enslaved Women and Body Politics in the Plantation South, 1830–1861." *Journal of Southern History* 68, no. 3 (August 2002): 533–72.

Carnes, Mark C., and Clyde Griffen, eds. *Meanings for Manhood: Constructions of Masculinity in Victorian America.* Chicago: University of Chicago Press, 1990.

Carney, Judith Ann. *Black Rice: The African Origins of Rice Cultivation in the Americas.* Cambridge, MA: Harvard University Press, 2001.

Cashin, Joan E. *Our Common Affairs: Texts from Women in the Old South.* Baltimore: Johns Hopkins University Press, 1996.

Cecelski, David S. *The Waterman's Song: Slavery and Freedom in Maritime North Carolina.* Chapel Hill: University of North Carolina Press, 2001.

Chambers, Keith S. "Indefatigable Elsie Clews Parsons, Folklorist." *Western Folklore* 32, no. 3 (July 1973): 180–98.

Christmon, Kenneth. "Historical Overview of Alcohol in the African American Community." *Journal of Black Studies* 25, no. 3 (January 1995): 318–30.

Clayton, Bruce, and John A. Salmond, eds. *"Lives Full of Struggle and Triumph": Southern Women, Their Institutions, and Their Communities.* Gainesville: University Press of Florida, 2003.

Cooper, William J., and Thomas E. Terrill. *The American South: A History*. 2 vols. Lanham, MD: Rowman & Littlefield, 2009.

Costa, Emilia Viotti da. *Crowns of Glory, Tears of Blood: The Demerara Slave Rebellion of 1823*. New York: Oxford University Press, 1994.

Cott, Nancy F. "Passionlessness: An Interpretation of Victorian Sexual Ideology, 1790–1850." *Signs* 4, no. 2 (Winter 1978): 219–36.

Counihan, Carole. *The Anthropology of Food and Body: Gender, Meaning, and Power*. New York: Routledge, 1999.

Creel, Margaret Washington. *"A Peculiar People": Slave Religion and Community-Culture among the Gullahs*. New York: New York University Press, 1988.

Crowley, Daniel J. *African Folklore in the New World*. Austin: University of Texas Press, 1977.

Cunard, Nancy, ed. *Negro Anthology Made by Nancy Cunard, 1931–1933*. London: Wishart & Co., 1934.

Davis, Charles T., and Henry Louis Gates Jr., eds. *The Slave's Narrative*. Oxford; New York: Oxford University Press, 1985.

D'Emilio, John, and Estelle B. Freedman. *Intimate Matters: A History of Sexuality in America*. Chicago: University of Chicago Press, 1997.

Desch-Obi, T. J. *Fighting for Honor: The History of African Martial Art Traditions in the Atlantic World*. Columbia: University of South Carolina Press, 2008.

Dew, Charles B. *Bond of Iron: Master and Slave at Buffalo Forge*. New York: Norton, 1994.

———. "David Ross and the Oxford Iron Works: A Study of Industrial Slavery in the Early Nineteenth-Century South." *William and Mary Quarterly: A Magazine of Early American History* 31, no. 2 (April 1974): 189–224.

———. "Disciplining Slave Ironworkers in the Antebellum South: Coercion, Conciliation, and Accommodation." *American Historical Review* 79, no. 2 (April 1974): 393–418.

Dickson, Bruce D. "The 'John and Old Master' Stories and the World of Slavery: A Study in Folktales and History." *Phylon* 35, no. 4 (4th Qtr. 1974): 418–29.

Douglas, Mary, ed. *Constructive Drinking: Perspectives on Drink from Anthropology*. Cambridge: Cambridge University Press, 1987.

Douglas, Mary, and Phyllis M. Kaberry, eds. *Man in Africa*. Garden City, NY: Anchor, 1971.

Duberman, Martin B., Martha Vicinus, and George Chauncey, eds. *Hidden from History: Reclaiming the Gay and Lesbian Past*. New York: Penguin, 1990.

Dunaway, Wilma A. *The African-American Family in Slavery and Emancipation*. Cambridge: Cambridge University Press, 2003.

———. *Slavery in the American Mountain South*. Cambridge: Cambridge University Press, 2003.

Durant, Thomas J., and J. David Knottnerus, eds. *Plantation Society and Race Relations: The Origins of Inequality*. Westport, CT: Praeger, 1999.

Dusinberre, William. *Them Dark Days: Slavery in the American Rice Swamps.* New York: Oxford University Press, 1996.

Egerton, Douglas R. "Gabriel's Conspiracy and the Election of 1800." *Journal of Southern History* 56, no. 2 (May 1990): 191–214.

———. *Gabriel's Rebellion: The Virginia Slave Conspiracies of 1800 and 1802.* Chapel Hill: University of North Carolina Press, 1993.

———. *He Shall Go Out Free: The Lives of Denmark Vesey.* Lanham, MD: Rowman & Littlefield, 2004.

Elkins, Stanley M. *Slavery: A Problem in American Institutional and Intellectual Life.* Chicago: University of Chicago Press, 1959.

Escott, Paul D. *Slavery Remembered: A Record of Twentieth-Century Slave Narratives.* Chapel Hill: University of North Carolina Press, 1979.

Evans-Pritchard, Edward E. *Social Anthropology and Other Essays.* New York: Free Press, 1962.

Everett, Michael W., Jack O. Waddell, and Dwight B. Heath, eds. *Cross-Cultural Approaches to the Study of Alcohol: An Interdisciplinary Perspective.* The Hague: Mouton, 1976.

Faderman, Lillian. *Surpassing the Love of Men: Romantic Friendship and Love between Women from the Renaissance to the Present.* New York: Morrow, 1981.

Fanon, Frantz. *Black Skin, White Masks.* London: Pluto, 1986.

Farnham, Christie. *The Education of the Southern Belle: Higher Education and Student Socialization in the Antebellum South.* New York: New York University Press, 1994.

Fogel, Robert William, and Stanley L. Engerman. *Time on the Cross: The Economics of American Negro Slavery.* Boston: Little, Brown, 1974.

Follett, Richard J. *The Sugar Masters: Planters and Slaves in Louisiana's Cane World, 1820–1860.* Baton Rouge: Louisiana State University Press, 2005.

Forret, Jeff. "Conflict and The 'Slave Community': Violence among Slaves in Upcountry South Carolina." *Journal of Southern History* 74, no. 3 (August 2008): 551–88.

———. *Race Relations at the Margins: Slaves and Poor Whites in the Antebellum Southern Countryside.* Baton Rouge: Louisiana State University Press, 2006.

———. "Slaves, Poor Whites, and the Underground Economy of the Rural Carolinas." *Journal of Southern History* 70, no. 4 (November 2004): 783–824.

Foster, Thomas A. "The Sexual Abuse of Black Men under American Slavery." *Journal of the History of Sexuality* 20, no. 3 (September 2011): 445–64.

Foucault, Michel. *The History of Sexuality.* New York: Pantheon, 1978.

Fox-Genovese, Elizabeth. *Within the Plantation Household: Black and White Women of the Old South.* Chapel Hill: University of North Carolina Press, 1988.

Franklin, John Hope, and Alfred A. Moss. *From Slavery to Freedom: A History of African Americans.* New York: McGraw-Hill, 1994.

Franklin, John Hope, and Loren Schweninger. *Runaway Slaves: Rebels on the Plantation.* New York: Oxford University Press, 1999.

Fraser, Rebecca J. *Courtship and Love among the Enslaved in North Carolina.* Jackson: University Press of Mississippi, 2007.

―――. "Courtship Contests and the Meaning of Conflict in the Folklore of Slaves." *Journal of Southern History* 71, no. 4 (November 2005): 769–802.

Frazier, Edward Franklin. *The Negro Family in the United States.* Chicago: Chicago University Press, 1939.

Friend, Craig Thompson, and Lorri Glover, eds. *Southern Manhood: Perspectives on Masculinity in the Old South.* Athens: University of Georgia Press, 2004.

Friend, Craig Thompson, and Anya Jabour, eds. *Family Values in the Old South.* Gainesville: University Press of Florida, 2009.

Fry, Gladys-Marie. *Night Riders in Black Folk History.* Knoxville: University of Tennessee Press, 1975.

Gara, Larry. *The Liberty Line: The Legend of the Underground Railroad.* Lexington: University Press of Kentucky, 1999.

Garner, Thurman. "Black Ethos in Folktales." *Journal of Black Studies* 15, no. 1 (September 1984): 53–66.

Gaspar, David Barry, and Darlene Clark Hine, eds. *More Than Chattel: Black Women and Slavery in the Americas, Blacks in the Diaspora.* Bloomington: Indiana University Press, 1996.

Genovese, Eugene D. *Roll, Jordan, Roll: The World the Slaves Made.* New York: Pantheon, 1974.

Gilmore, David D. *Manhood in the Making: Cultural Concepts of Masculinity.* New Haven, CT: Yale University Press, 1990.

Glass, Brent D. "The Miner's World: Life and Labor at Gold Hill." *North Carolina Historical Review* 62, no. 4 (October 1985): 420–47.

Glave, Dianne D., and Mark Stoll, eds. *"To Love the Wind and the Rain": African Americans and Environmental History.* Pittsburgh: University of Pittsburgh Press, 2006.

Glover, Lorri. *Southern Sons: Becoming Men in the New Nation.* Baltimore: Johns Hopkins University Press, 2007.

Gomez, Michael A. *Exchanging Our Country Marks: The Transformation of African Identities in the Colonial and Antebellum South.* Chapel Hill: University of North Carolina Press, 1998.

Gorn, Elliott J. "'Gouge and Bite, Pull Hair and Scratch': The Social Significance of Fighting in the Southern Backcountry." *American Historical Review* 90, no. 1 (February 1985): 18–43.

Green, Fletcher M. "Gold Mining: A Forgotten Industry in Antebellum North Carolina." *North Carolina Historical Review* 14, no. 1 (January 1937): 1–19.

Greenberg, Kenneth S. *Honor and Slavery: Lies, Duels, Noses, Masks, Dressing as a Woman, Gifts, Strangers, Humanitarianism, Death, Slave Rebellions, the Proslavery Argument, Baseball, Hunting, and Gambling in the Old South.* Princeton, NJ: Princeton University Press, 1996.

―――. *Nat Turner: A Slave Rebellion in History and Memory.* Oxford: Oxford University Press, 2003.

————. "The Nose, the Lie, and the Duel in the Antebellum South." *American Historical Review* 95, no. 1 (February 1990): 57–74.

Griffin, Rebecca J. "'Goin' Back Over There to See That Girl': Competing Social Spaces in the Lives of the Enslaved in Antebellum North Carolina." *Slavery and Abolition* 25, no. 1 (April 2004): 94–113.

Griffler, Keith P. *Front Line of Freedom: African Americans and the Forging of the Underground Railroad in the Ohio Valley.* Lexington: University Press of Kentucky, 2004.

Gross, Ariela Julie. *Double Character: Slavery and Mastery in the Antebellum Southern Courtroom.* Princeton: Princeton University Press, 2000.

Guha, Ranajit. *Elementary Aspects of Peasant Insurgency in Colonial India.* Durham, NC: Duke University Press, 1999.

Gustav-Wrathall, John Donald. *Take the Young Stranger by the Hand: Same-Sex Relations and the YMCA.* Chicago: University of Chicago Press, 1998.

Gutman, Herbert George. *The Black Family in Slavery and Freedom, 1750–1925.* New York: Pantheon, 1976.

————. *Slavery and the Numbers Game: A Critique of Time on the Cross.* Urbana: University of Illinois Press, 1975.

Hadden, Sally E. *Slave Patrols: Law and Violence in Virginia and the Carolinas.* Cambridge, MA: Harvard University Press, 2001.

Hagedorn, Ann. *Beyond the River: The Untold Story of the Heroes of the Underground Railroad.* New York: Simon & Schuster, 2002.

Hahn, Steven. *A Nation under Our Feet: Black Political Struggles in the Rural South, from Slavery to the Great Migration.* Cambridge, MA: Belknap Press of Harvard University Press, 2003.

Hall, Gwendolyn Midlo. *Slavery and African Ethnicities in the Americas: Restoring the Links.* Chapel Hill: University of North Carolina Press, 2005.

Hansen, Karen V. *A Very Social Time: Crafting Community in Antebellum New England.* Berkeley: University of California Press, 1994.

Heath, Dwight B., ed. *International Handbook on Alcohol and Culture.* Westport, CT: Greenwood, 1995.

Henderson, William. "The Slave Court System in Spartanburg County." *Proceedings of the South Carolina Historical Association* (1976): 31–37.

Herman, Robert D., ed. *Gambling.* New York: Harper & Row, 1967.

Herskovits, Melville J. *Dahomey: An Ancient West African Kingdom.* New York: J. J. Augustin, 1938.

————. *The Myth of the Negro Past.* Boston: Beacon, 1941.

————. "Some Next Steps in the Study of Negro Folklore." *Journal of American Folklore* 56, no. 219 (January–March 1943): 1–7.

Heywood, Linda M. *Central Africans and Cultural Transformations in the American Diaspora.* Cambridge: Cambridge University Press, 2002.

Hine, Darlene Clark, and Earnestine Jenkins. *A Question of Manhood: A Reader in U.S. Black Men's History and Masculinity.* Vol. 1, *"Manhood Rights": The Con-*

struction of Black Male History and Manhood, 1750–1870. Bloomington: Indiana University Press, 1999.

Hoffman, Ronald, and Peter J. Albert, eds. Women in the Age of the American Revolution. Charlottesville: University of Virginia Press, 1989.

Hopkins, James F. A History of the Hemp Industry in Kentucky. Lexington: University Press of Kentucky, 1951.

Horton, James Oliver, and Lois E. Horton. In Hope of Liberty: Culture, Community, and Protest among Northern Free Blacks, 1700–1860. New York: Oxford University Press, 1997.

Howard, John. Men Like That: A Southern Queer History. Chicago: University of Chicago Press, 2001.

Hudson, J. Blaine. Fugitive Slaves and the Underground Railroad in the Kentucky Borderland. Jefferson, NC: McFarland, 2002.

Hudson, Larry E. To Have and to Hold: Slave Work and Family Life in Antebellum South Carolina. Athens: University of Georgia Press, 1997.

———. Working toward Freedom: Slave Society and Domestic Economy in the American South. Rochester, NY: University of Rochester Press, 1994.

Iliffe, John. Honour in African History. Cambridge: Cambridge University Press, 2004.

Innes, Stephen, ed. Work and Labor in Early America. Chapel Hill: University of North Carolina Press, 1988.

Jabour, Anya. "Male Friendship and Masculinity in the Early National South: William Wirt and His Friends." Journal of the Early Republic 20, no. 1 (Spring 2000): 83–111.

———. Scarlett's Sisters: Young Women in the Old South. Chapel Hill: University of North Carolina Press, 2007.

Jeffrey, Thomas E. "'Our Remarkable Friendship': The Secret Collaboration of Calvin H. Wiley and John W. Cuningham." North Carolina Historical Review 67, no. 1 (1990): 28–58.

Johnson, Michael P. "Runaway Slaves and the Slave Communities in South Carolina, 1799 to 1830." William and Mary Quarterly 38, no. 3 (July 1981): 418–41.

Johnson, Patrick E. Sweet Tea: Black Gay Men of the South. Chapel Hill: University of North Carolina Press, 2008.

Johnson, Walter. "On Agency." Journal of Social History 37, no. 1 (Fall 2003): 113–24.

Jones, Jacqueline. Labor of Love, Labor of Sorrow: Black Women, Work, and the Family from Slavery to the Present. New York: Basic Books, 1985.

Jordan, Winthrop D. Tumult and Silence at Second Creek: An Inquiry into a Civil War Slave Conspiracy. Baton Rouge: Louisiana State University Press, 1993.

Joyner, Charles W. Down by the Riverside: A South Carolina Slave Community. Urbana: University of Illinois Press, 1984.

Kaye, Anthony E. Joining Places: Slave Neighborhoods in the Old South. Chapel Hill: University of North Carolina Press, 2007.

————. "Neighbourhoods and Solidarity in the Natchez District of Mississippi: Rethinking the Antebellum Slave Community." *Slavery and Abolition* 23, no. 1 (April 2002): 1–24.

Kimmel, Michael S. *The History of Men: Essays in the History of American and British Masculinities.* Albany: State University of New York Press, 2005.

————. *Manhood in America: A Cultural History.* New York: Free Press, 1996.

Kolchin, Peter. *American Slavery, 1619–1877.* New York: Hill & Wang, 1993.

————. "Reevaluating the Antebellum Slave Community: A Comparative Perspective." *Journal of American History* 70, no. 3 (December 1983): 579–601.

Kulikoff, Allan. *Tobacco and Slaves: The Development of Southern Cultures in the Chesapeake, 1680–1800.* Chapel Hill: University of North Carolina Press, 1986.

Ladner, Joyce A. *Tomorrow's Tomorrow: The Black Woman in Perspective.* New York: Anchor, 1972.

Lander, E. M. "Slave Labor in South Carolina Cotton Mills." *Journal of Negro History* 38, no. 2 (April 1953): 161–73.

Lantz, Herman R. "Family and Kin as Revealed in the Narratives of Ex-Slaves." *Social Science Quarterly* 60, no. 4 (March 1980): 667–75.

Lemle, Russell, and Marc E. Mishkind. "Alcohol and Masculinity." *Journal of Substance Abuse Treatment* 6, no. 4 (1989): 213.

Levine, Lawrence W. *Black Culture and Black Consciousness: Afro-American Folk Thought from Slavery to Freedom.* New York: Oxford University Press, 1977.

Lewis, Ronald L. *Black Coal Miners in America: Race, Class, and Community Conflict, 1780–1980.* Lexington: University Press of Kentucky, 1987.

————. *Coal, Iron, and Slaves: Industrial Slavery in Maryland and Virginia, 1715–1865.* Westport, CT: Greenwood, 1979.

Libby, David J. *Slavery and Frontier Mississippi, 1720–1835.* Jackson: University Press of Mississippi, 2004.

Lichtenstein, Alex. "'That Disposition to Theft, with Which They Have Been Branded': Moral Economy, Slave Management, and the Law." *Journal of Social History* 21, no. 3 (Spring 1988): 413–40.

Lindman, Janet Moore. "Acting the Manly Christian: White Evangelical Masculinity in Revolutionary Virginia." *William and Mary Quarterly* 57, no. 2 (April 2000): 393–416.

Lipscomb, Terry W., and Theresa Jacobs. "The Magistrates and Freeholders Court." *South Carolina Historical Magazine* 77 (January 1976): 62–65.

Lockley, Timothy J. *Lines in the Sand: Race and Class in Lowcountry Georgia, 1750–1860.* Athens: Georgia University Press, 2004.

————. "Trading Encounters between Non-Elite Whites and African Americans in Savannah, 1790–1860." *Journal of Southern History* 66, no. 1 (February 2000): 25–48.

Lussana, Sergio. "'No Band of Brothers Could Be More Loving': Enslaved Male

Homosociality, Friendship, and Resistance in the Antebellum American South." *Journal of Social History* 46, no. 4 (Summer 2013): 872–95.

———. "To See Who Was Best on the Plantation: Enslaved Fighting Contests and Masculinity in the Antebellum South." *Journal of Southern History* 76, no. 4 (November 2010): 901–22.

Malone, Ann Patton. *Sweet Chariot: Slave Family and Household Structure in Nineteenth-Century Louisiana*. Chapel Hill: University of North Carolina Press, 1992.

Maranda, Pierre, and Elli Köngäs Maranda, eds. *Structural Analysis of Oral Tradition*. Philadelphia: University of Pennsylvania Press, 1971.

Marcus, Sharon. *Between Women: Friendship, Desire, and Marriage in Victorian England*. Princeton: Princeton University Press, 2007.

Marrs, Aaron W. *Railroads in the Old South: Pursuing Progress in a Slave Society*. Baltimore: Johns Hopkins University Press, 2009.

Marshall, Amani M. "Enslaved Women Runaways in South Carolina, 1820–1865." PhD diss., Indiana University, 2007.

Martin, Jonathan D. *Divided Mastery: Slave Hiring in the American South*. Cambridge, MA: Harvard University Press, 2004.

Mavor, Elizabeth. *The Ladies of Llangollen: A Study in Romantic Friendship*. London: Joseph, 1971.

McCurry, Stephanie. *Confederate Reckoning: Power and Politics in the Civil War South*. Cambridge, MA: Harvard University Press, 2010.

McKay, Jim, Michael A. Messner, and Donald F. Sabo, eds. *Masculinities, Gender Relations, and Sport*. Thousand Oaks, CA: Sage, 2000.

McMillen, Sally Gregory. *Motherhood in the Old South: Pregnancy, Childbirth, and Infant Rearing*. Baton Rouge: Louisiana State University Press, 1990.

———. *Southern Women: Black and White in the Old South*. Arlington Heights, IL: Harlan Davidson, 1992.

Megginson, William J. *African American Life in South Carolina's Upper Piedmont, 1780–1900*. Columbia: University of South Carolina Press, 2006.

Meisenhelder, Susan. "Conflict and Resistance in Zora Neale Hurston's Mules and Men." *Journal of American Folklore* 109, no. 433 (Summer 1996): 267–88.

Messerschmidt, James W. *Masculinities and Crime: Critique and Reconceptualization of Theory*. Lanham, MD: Rowman & Littlefield, 1993.

Miller, Neil. *Out of the Past: Gay and Lesbian History from 1869 to the Present*. London: Vintage, 1995.

Miller, Randall M. "The Fabric of Control: Slavery in Antebellum Southern Textile Mills." *Business History Review* 55, no. 4 (Winter 1981): 471–90.

Moody, Vernie A. *Slavery on Louisiana Sugar Plantations*. New York: AMS Press, 1976.

Moore, Lisa. "'Something More Tender Still Than Friendship': Romantic Friendship in Early-Nineteenth-Century England." *Feminist Studies* 18, no. 3 (Autumn 1992): 499–520.

Morgan, Jennifer L. *Laboring Women: Reproduction and Gender in New World Slavery.* Philadelphia: University of Pennsylvania Press, 2004.

Morgan, Philip D. "The Ownership of Property by Slaves in the Mid-Nineteenth-Century Low Country." *Journal of Southern History* 49, no. 3 (August 1983): 399–420.

———. *Slave Counterpoint: Black Culture in the Eighteenth-Century Chesapeake and Lowcountry.* Chapel Hill: University of North Carolina Press, 1998.

———. "Work and Culture: The Task System and the World of Lowcountry Blacks, 1700 to 1880." *William and Mary Quarterly* 39, no. 4 (October 1982): 563–99.

Morton, Patricia, ed. *Discovering the Women in Slavery: Emancipating Perspectives on the American Past.* Athens: University of Georgia Press, 1996.

Moynihan, Daniel P. *The Negro Family: The Case for National Action.* Washington, DC: Office of Policy Planning and Research, U.S. Department of Labor, 1965.

Musher, Sharon Ann. "Contesting 'The Way the Almighty Wants It': Crafting Memories of Ex-Slaves in the Slave Narrative Collection." *American Quarterly* 53, no. 1 (March 2001): 1–31.

Nardi, Peter M. *Men's Friendships.* Newbury Park, CA: Sage, 1992.

Netting, Robert McC. "Beer as a Locus of Value among the West African Kofyar." *American Anthropologist* 66, no. 2 (April 1964): 375–84.

Oakes, James. "The Political Significance of Slave Resistance." *History Workshop* 22, no. 1 (Autumn 1986): 89–107.

Oates, Stephen B. *The Fires of Jubilee: Nat Turner's Fierce Rebellion.* New York: Harper Perennial, 2009.

O'Donovan, Susan E. *Becoming Free in the Cotton South.* Cambridge, MA: Harvard University Press, 2007.

Outland, Robert B. "Slavery, Work, and the Geography of the North Carolina Naval Stores Industry, 1835–1860." *Journal of Southern History* 62, no. 1 (February 1996): 27–56.

Owens, Harry P., ed. *Perspectives and Irony in American Slavery.* Jackson: University Press of Mississippi, 1976.

Ownby, Ted. *Subduing Satan: Religion, Recreation, and Manhood in the Rural South, 1865–1920.* Chapel Hill: University of North Carolina Press, 1990.

Parish, Peter J. *Slavery: The Many Faces of a Southern Institution.* Preston, UK: Bookcraft, 1979.

Park, Robert. "The Conflict of Fusion of Cultures with Special References to the Negro." *Journal of Negro History* 4, no. 2 (April 1919): 111–33.

Parker, Freddie L. "Slave Runaways in North Carolina, 1775–1835." PhD diss., University of North Carolina at Chapel Hill, 1987.

Partanen, Juha. *Sociability and Intoxication: Alcohol and Drinking in Kenya, Africa, and the Modern World.* Helsinki: Nordic Council for Alcohol and Drug Research, 1991.

Patterson, Orlando. *Rituals of Blood: Consequences of Slavery in Two American Centuries.* Washington, DC: Civitas/CounterPoint, 1998.

Penningroth, Dylan C. *The Claims of Kinfolk: African American Property and Community in the Nineteenth-Century South.* Chapel Hill: University of North Carolina Press, 2003.

Perman, Michael. *Major Problems in the Civil War and Reconstruction,* 2nd ed. Boston: Houghton Mifflin, 1998.

Pflugrad-Jackisch, Ami. *Brothers of a Vow: Secret Fraternal Orders and the Transformation of White Male Culture in Antebellum Virginia.* Athens: University of Georgia Press, 2010.

Phillips, Ulrich B. *American Negro Slavery: A Survey of the Supply, Employment and Control of Negro Labor as Determined by the Plantation Regime.* New York: D. Appleton, 1918.

———. *Life and Labor in the Old South.* Boston: Little, Brown, 1929.

Pittman, David J., and Charles R. Snyder. *Society, Culture, and Drinking Patterns.* New York: Wiley, 1962.

Plath, Lydia, and Sergio Lussana, eds. *Black and White Masculinity in the American South, 1800–2000.* Newcastle upon Tyne: Cambridge Scholars Publishing, 2009.

Pollitzer, William S. *The Gullah People and Their African Heritage.* Athens: University of Georgia Press, 1999.

Proctor, Nicolas W. *Bathed in Blood: Hunting and Mastery in the Old South.* Charlottesville: University Press of Virginia, 2002.

Quarles, Benjamin. *Black Abolitionists.* New York: Oxford University Press, 1969.

Raboteau, Albert J. *Slave Religion: The "Invisible Institution" in the Antebellum South.* New York: Oxford University Press, 1978.

Rainwater, Lee, and William L. Yancey, eds. *The Moynihan Report and the Politics of Controversy.* Cambridge, MA: MIT Press, 1967.

Robert, Joseph Clarke. *The Tobacco Kingdom: Plantation, Market, and Factory in Virginia and North Carolina, 1800–1860.* Durham, NC: Duke University Press, 1965.

Rorabaugh, William J. *The Alcoholic Republic: An American Tradition.* New York: Oxford University Press, 1979.

Rosaldo, Michelle Zimbalist, and Louise Lamphere, eds. *Woman, Culture, and Society.* Stanford, CA: Stanford University Press, 1974.

Rotundo, E. Anthony. *American Manhood: Transformations in Masculinity from the Revolution to the Modern Era.* New York: Basic Books, 1993.

———. "Romantic Friendship: Male Intimacy and Middle-Class Youth in the Northern United States, 1800–1900." *Journal of Social History* 23, no. 1 (Autumn 1989): 1–25.

Rucker, Walter C. *The River Flows On: Black Resistance, Culture, and Identity Formation in Early America.* Baton Rouge: Louisiana State University Press, 2007.

Schipper, Mineke. *Imagining Insiders: Africa and the Question of Belonging.* London: Cassell, 1999.

Schwalm, Leslie A. *A Hard Fight for We: Women's Transition from Slavery to Freedom in South Carolina.* Urbana: University of Illinois Press, 1997.

Schwarz, Philip J. *Twice Condemned: Slaves and the Criminal Laws of Virginia, 1705–1865.* Baton Rouge: Louisiana State University Press, 1988.

Schweninger, Loren. *Black Property Owners in the South, 1790–1915.* Urbana: University of Illinois Press, 1990.

Scott, James C. *Domination and the Arts of Resistance: Hidden Transcripts.* New Haven: Yale University Press, 1990.

———. *Weapons of the Weak: Everyday Forms of Peasant Resistance.* New Haven: Yale University Press, 1985.

Scott, Joan Wallach. *Gender and the Politics of History.* New York: Columbia University Press, 1988.

Scott, Julius S. "The Common Wind: Currents of Afro-American Communication in the Era of the Haitian Revolution." PhD diss., Duke University, 1986.

Sidbury, James. *Ploughshares into Swords: Race, Rebellion, and Identity in Gabriel's Virginia, 1730–1810.* New York: Cambridge University Press, 1997.

Siebert, Wilbur Henry. *The Underground Railroad from Slavery to Freedom: The American Negro, His History and Literature.* New York: Arno, 1968.

Smith, Mark M. *Mastered by the Clock: Time, Slavery, and Freedom in the American South.* Chapel Hill: University of North Carolina Press, 1997.

Smith-Rosenberg, Carroll. "The Female World of Love and Ritual: Relations between Women in Nineteenth-Century America." *Signs* 1, no. 1 (Autumn 1975): 1–29.

Sofola, J. A. "The Onyenualagu (Godparent) in Traditional and Modern African Communities: Implications for Juvenile Delinquency." *Journal of Black Studies* 14, no. 1 (September 1983): 21–30.

Spindel, Donna J. "Assessing Memory: Twentieth-Century Slave Narratives Reconsidered." *Journal of Interdisciplinary History* 27, no. 2 (Autumn 1996): 247–61.

Stampp, Kenneth M. *The Peculiar Institution: Slavery in the Ante-Bellum South.* New York: Knopf, 1956.

———. "Rebels and Sambos: The Search for the Negro's Personality in Slavery." *Journal of Southern History* 37, no. 3 (August 1971): 367–92.

Starobin, Robert S. *Industrial Slavery in the Old South.* New York: Oxford University Press, 1970.

Stealey, John Edmund. "Slavery and the Western Virginia Salt Industry." *Journal of Negro History* 59, no. 2 (April 1974): 105–31.

Stevenson, Brenda E. *Life in Black and White: Family and Community in the Slave South.* New York: Oxford University Press, 1996.

Still, William. *The Underground Railroad.* New York: Arno, 1968.

Stouffer, Samuel Andrew. *The American Soldier: Combat and Its Aftermath.* Vol. 2. Princeton: Princeton University Press, 1949.

Stuckey, Sterling. *Slave Culture: Nationalist Theory and the Foundations of Black America.* New York: Oxford University Press, 1987.

————. "Through the Prism of Folklore: The Black Ethos in Slavery." *Massachusetts Review* 9, no. 3 (Summer 1968): 417–37.

Sugden, John Peter. *Boxing and Society: An International Analysis.* Manchester: Manchester University Press, 1996.

Sydnor, Charles Sackett. *Slavery in Mississippi.* Gloucester, MA: P. Smith, 1965.

Tadman, Michael. "The Demographic Cost of Sugar: Debates on Slave Societies and Natural Increase in the Americas." *American Historical Review* 105, no. 5 (December 2000): 1534–75.

Tallichet, Suzanne E. *Daughters of the Mountain: Women Coal Miners in Central Appalachia.* University Park: Pennsylvania State University Press, 2006.

Tegnaeus, Harry. *Blood-Brothers: An Ethno-Sociological Study of the Institutions of Blood-Brotherhood with Special Reference to Africa.* Stockholm: Ethnographical Museum, 1952.

Thornton, John K. *Africa and Africans in the Making of the Atlantic World, 1400–1800.* Cambridge: Cambridge University Press, 1998.

Toledano, Roulhac B. "Louisiana's Golden Age: Valcour Aime in St. James Parish." *Louisiana History: The Journal of the Louisiana Historical Association* 10, no. 3 (Summer 1969): 211–24.

Tosh, John. "What Should Historians Do with Masculinity? Reflections on Nineteenth-Century Britain." *History Workshop* 38, no. 1 (Autumn 1994): 179–202.

Trelease, Allen W. *The North Carolina Railroad, 1849–1871, and the Modernization of North Carolina.* Chapel Hill: University of North Carolina Press, 1991.

Turner, Lorenzo Dow. *Africanisms in the Gullah Dialect.* Chicago: University of Chicago Press, 1949.

Valsecchi, Pierluigi. "The 'True Nzema': A Layered Identity." *Africa* 71, no. 3 (August 2001): 391–425.

Vicinus, Martha. *Intimate Friends: Women Who Loved Women, 1778–1928.* Chicago: University of Chicago Press, 2004.

Wade, Richard Clement. *Slavery in the Cities: The South 1820–1860.* New York: Oxford University Press, 1964.

Walsh, Lorena S. *Motives of Honor, Pleasure and Profit: Plantation Management in the Colonial Chesapeake, 1607–1763.* Chapel Hill: University of North Carolina Press, 2010.

Walvin, James. "Slaves, Free Time and the Question of Leisure." *Slavery and Abolition* 16, no. 1 (April 1995): 1–13.

Washburne, Chandler. *Primitive Drinking: A Study of the Uses and Functions of Alcohol in Preliterate Societies.* New York: College and University Press, 1961.

Weeks, Jeffrey. "'Sins and Diseases': Some Notes on Homosexuality in the Nineteenth Century." *History Workshop* 1, no. 1 (Spring 1976): 211–19.

Weiner, Marli Frances. *Mistresses and Slaves: Plantation Women in South Carolina, 1830–80.* Urbana: University of Illinois Press, 1997.

West, Emily. *Chains of Love: Slave Couples in Antebellum South Carolina.* Urbana: University of Illinois Press, 2004.

White, Deborah Gray. *Ar'n't I a Woman? Female Slaves in the Plantation South.* New York: Norton, 1985.

———. "Female Slaves: Sex Roles and Status in the Antebellum Plantation South." *Journal of Family History* 8, no. 3 (Fall 1983): 248–61.

White, Luise. "Blood Brotherhood Revisited: Kinship, Relationship, and the Body in East and Central Africa." *Africa* 64, no. 3 (August 1994): 359–72.

Wiggins David K. "The Play of Slave Children in the Plantation Communities of the Old South." *Journal of Sport History* 7 (Summer 1980): 21–39.

Wiggins, David K., and Patrick B. Miller, eds. *The Unlevel Playing Field: A Documentary History of the African American Experience in Sport.* Urbana: University of Illinois Press, 2003.

Williams, David. *I Freed Myself: African American Self-Emancipation in the Civil War Era.* Cambridge: Cambridge University Press, 2014.

Wood, Betty. "Some Aspects of Female Resistance to Chattel Slavery in Low Country Georgia, 1763–1815." *Historical Journal* 30, no. 3 (September 1987): 603–22.

———. *Women's Work, Men's Work: The Informal Slave Economies of Lowcountry Georgia.* Athens: University of Georgia Press, 1995.

Wood, Peter H. *Black Majority: Negroes in Colonial South Carolina from 1670 through the Stono Rebellion.* New York: Knopf, 1974.

Woodward, C. Vann, and George P. Rawick. "History from Slave Sources." *American Historical Review* 79, no. 2 (April 1974): 470–81.

Woodward, Kath. "Rumbles in the Jungle: Boxing, Racialization and the Performance of Masculinity." *Leisure Studies* 23, no. 1 (January 2004): 5–17.

Wyatt-Brown, Bertram. *The Shaping of Southern Culture: Honor, Grace, and War, 1760s-1890s.* Chapel Hill: University of North Carolina Press, 2001.

———. *Southern Honor: Ethics and Behavior in the Old South.* New York: Oxford University Press, 1982.

Young, Jason R. *Rituals of Resistance: African Atlantic Religion in Kongo and the Lowcountry South in the Era of Slavery.* Baton Rouge: Louisiana State University Press, 2007.

Index

Page references given in *italics* indicate illustrations or material contained in their captions.

New Directions in Southern History

Series Editors
Michele Gillespie, Wake Forest University
William A. Link, University of Florida

The Lost State of Franklin: America's First Secession
Kevin T. Barksdale

The Civil War Guerrilla: Unfolding the Black Flag in History, Memory, and Myth
edited by Joseph M. Beilein Jr. and Matthew C. Hulbert

Bluecoats and Tar Heels: Soldiers and Civilians in Reconstruction North Carolina
Mark L. Bradley

Becoming Bourgeois: Merchant Culture in the South, 1820–1865
Frank J. Byrne

Cowboy Conservatism: Texas and the Rise of the Modern Right
Sean P. Cunningham

A Tour of Reconstruction: Travel Letters of 1875
Anna Dickinson (J. Matthew Gallman, ed.)

Raising Racists: The Socialization of White Children in the Jim Crow South
Kristina DuRocher

Lum and Abner: Rural America and the Golden Age of Radio
Randal L. Hall

Mountains on the Market: Industry, the Environment, and the South
Randal L. Hall

The New Southern University: Academic Freedom and Liberalism at UNC
Charles J. Holden

Entangled by White Supremacy: Reform in World War I–era South Carolina
Janet G. Hudson

Bloody Breathitt: Politics and Violence in the Appalachian South
T. R. C. Hutton

Cultivating Race: The Expansion of Slavery in Georgia, 1750–1860
Watson W. Jennison

De Bow's Review: The Antebellum Vision of a New South
John F. Kvach

Remembering The Battle of the Crater: War as Murder
Kevin M. Levin

My Brother Slaves: Friendship, Masculinity, and Resistance in the Antebellum South
Sergio A. Lussana

The Political Career of W. Kerr Scott: The Squire from Haw River
Julian Pleasants

The View from the Ground: Experiences of Civil War Soldiers
edited by Aaron Sheehan-Dean

Reconstructing Appalachia: The Civil War's Aftermath
edited by Andrew L. Slap

Blood in the Hills: A History of Violence in Appalachia
edited by Bruce E. Stewart

Moonshiners and Prohibitionists: The Battle over Alcohol in Southern Appalachia
Bruce E. Stewart

The U.S. South and Europe: Transatlantic Relations in the Nineteenth and Twentieth Centuries
edited by Cornelis A. van Minnen and Manfred Berg

Southern Farmers and Their Stories: Memory and Meaning in Oral History
Melissa Walker

Law and Society in the South: A History of North Carolina Court Cases
John W. Wertheimer

Family or Freedom: People of Color in the Antebellum South
Emily West

www.ingramcontent.com/pod-product-compliance
Lightning Source LLC
Chambersburg PA
CBHW030304100426
42812CB00002B/554